Thinking Through Digital Media

Thinking Through Digital Media

Transnational Environments and Locative Places

Dale Hudson and Patricia R. Zimmermann

First published in 2015 by
PALGRAVE MACMILLAN®
in the United States—a division of St. Martin's Press LLC,
175 Fifth Avenue, New York, NY 10010.

Where this book is distributed in the UK, Europe and the rest of the world,
this is by Palgrave Macmillan, a division of Macmillan Publishers Limited,
registered in England, company number 785998, of Houndmills,
Basingstoke, Hampshire RG21 6XS.

Palgrave Macmillan is the global academic imprint of the above companies
and has companies and representatives throughout the world.

Palgrave® and Macmillan® are registered trademarks in the United States,
the United Kingdom, Europe and other countries.

ISBN: 978–1–137–43361–9 (hc)
ISBN: 978–1–137–43362–6 (pbk)

Library of Congress Cataloging-in-Publication Data is available from the
Library of Congress.

A catalogue record of the book is available from the British Library.

Design by Newgen Knowledge Works (P) Ltd., Chennai, India.

First edition: April 2015

10 9 8 7 6 5 4 3 2 1

Contents

Figures

Acknowledgments

Oceans, not landmasses, should open our thinking, asserted postcolonial scholar (and partner of Dale Hudson) Sheetal Majithia, as we fantasized the possibility of mounting a book on digital media several years ago.

As a project analyzing how digital media asks us to think through migrations, movements, and flows, as well as checkpoints, borders, and stoppages, this book aligns itself more with oceans than with territories controlled by nation-states or transnational corporations. Oceans not only suggest the environmental issues of water, ecologies, pollution, and commodity shipping, but also provide a rich source of metaphors to unpack thinking about the forms and functions of the transnational: flows, drifts, tsunamis, gales, layers, winds, routes, navigation, maps, cartographies, sextants, journeys, voyages, wars, battles, ports, docks, floods, piracies, seas, and explorations. Oceans intersect in straits, gulfs, and passages.

This book emerges out of many different flows and histories, oceans not of water, but of valued colleagues and collaborative projects. We first worked together ten years ago at Ithaca College (New York), mounting the Roy H. Park School of Communications large lecture course, Introduction to Film Aesthetics and Analysis. Refuting the construct of teaching a different country or decade each week, we mixed national and transnational cinemas, genres and modes, forms and styles in each screening to generate collisions that produced new ways of seeing. Although that course focused on animation, documentary, experimental, and narrative film, it honed our thinking and our collaborations about the power of alliances and collisions.

Through our team teaching, we transitioned to working together on the Finger Lakes Environmental Film Festival (FLEFF), which moved to Ithaca College in 2005. Patricia Zimmermann and Tom Shevory codirect the festival, with Assistant Provost Tanya Saunders serving

as executive producer. As part of the rebranding of FLEFF from a festival considering the environment as nature with analogue film to reimaging the environment as a series of dynamic intersecting layers of social, political, technological, natural, and aesthetic formations, we launched two initiatives that ended up rerouting our thinking about digital media and its possibilities. The first was developing remix projects with archival film and live music—whether classical, jazz, or electronic—to locate the festival within the vibrant music ecologies of Ithaca, New York, especially Ithaca College's renowned School of Music and Ithaca's well-recognized independent music scene. The second was the institution of an annual new media exhibition to explore how digital artists and collectives engaged this wider definition of the environment. The first FLEFF new media exhibition was curated by Tim Murray, Tom Shevory, and Patricia Zimmermann, and all subsequent exhibitions curated by Dale Hudson with Sharon Lin Tay and then, in 2014, with Claudia Pederson.

Our work with FLEFF over the last decade has been like navigating an ocean on a small boat without a sextant and map or GPS. As the festival was redesigned to engage a variety of communities from an international and interdisciplinary perspective and to adopt a more inclusive, if complex, notion of the environment beyond pastoralism, we found the projects that we curated and programmed dislodged our previous conceptions about animation, documentary, experimental, interactive, and narrative media. We could feel and see these were new turbulent oceans. Some of our ideas in this book first appeared in *Afterimage, Screen, Studies in Documentary Film*, and FLEFF's website and in its blogs.

The ideas, the writing, and the thinking in this book would not have materialized without the collegiality of our FLEFF team. We thank Tanya Saunders for her continued support, vision, inspiration, and leadership with the festival. She pushed it from a traditional film festival toward a more dynamic interdisciplinary event. We also thank Tom Shevory, the codirector of the festival, whose shining brilliance and laser-insights are only matched by his warm collegiality and good humor. FLEFF is mounted with a very large team, all of whom have contributed to our thinking and to this ocean of collegiality, so rare in the academy: Traevena Byrd, Marlon Byrd, Jairo Geronymo, Warren Schlesinger, Deborah Martin, Brad Hougham, Peter Bardaglio, Todd Schack, Kati Lustyik, Cynthia Henderson, Phil Wilde, Ann Michel, Diane Gayeski, Fe Nunn, Brett Bossard, Andrew Utterson, Bryan Roberts, Virginia Mansfield Richardson, Steve Tropiano, Steve

Ginsberg, Claudia Pederson, Nicholas Knouf, Tom Torello, Heather Hedges, and Jenny Stockdale.

FLEFF's global partners opened us to oceans of ideas and media forms we had never considered. For these important conversations across oceans, we thank Voices from the Waters Film Festival in India; Promedios/Chiapas Media Project in México and the United States; Engage Media in Indonesia; Cinema Tropical, Outcast Films, Kino International, Microcinema International, Black Maria Film and Video Festival, Scribe Video Center, Geovision, Northeast Historic Film, Smithsonian Institution, and UCLA Film and Television Archive in the United States; Dérive in Uganda and Belgium; dGenerate Films in the United States and China; Flahertiana Film Festival in Russia; Insights International in Canada; Global Alliance against the Traffic of Women in Thailand; and Short Shorts Film Festival in Japan.

The projects that we write about in this book came to our attention through our work with FLEFF and its various partners. Through our programming of some of these artists/makers/collectives, we had the honor of immersing in their projects and ideas with live audiences. But mounting exhibitions, festivals, workshops, and master classes is not possible without economic resources. For this important support, we thank the following funders for supporting FLEFF, and by extension, our research, writing, and this book: Ithaca College Office of the Provost, the Park Foundation, the Experimental Television Center re-grant of New York State Council on the Arts, and the Arts Council of the Southern Finger Lakes through the New York State Council on the Arts. We also thank Adelaide Park Gomer for her support of the festival and for new media that interrogates environmental questions.

As a result of FLEFF, we have lived in another, new ocean of global media artists whose work has taught us new ways to think about animation, documentary, experimental, interactive, and narrative media—and the world. This book features more than 130 digital media projects. Most of these projects were collaborative efforts. We estimate—crudely, to be sure, and probably too low—that these projects represent over 250 people from around the globe, showing that digital media swims in oceans beyond the North Atlantic. These 250 artists, coders, activists, students, and intellectuals deserve our thanks for the oceans that they set us afloat in, the intellectual storms that they provoke, and for the navigation they provided to bring us to new ideas and cartographies. As our colleague and friend Scott MacDonald has often commented, artists/makers are the true theorists, we scholars are simply journalists tracing and collecting their vision.

Beyond FLEFF, other institutions and initiatives have functioned as necessary ports for refueling and reprovisioning. We thank the Robert Flaherty Film Seminars, now in their sixtieth year, for providing continued inspiration to think and act with its annual intensive retreat seminars. We especially thank programmers who have influenced our thinking: Kathy Geritz, Irina Leimbacher, Chi-hui Yang, Carlos A. Gutiérrez, Mahen Bonetti, Amalia Córdova, Ruth Bradley, Kathy High, and Sally Berger. We also thank a longtime ally of the seminar and also of documentary films, Erik Barnouw, whose book *Documentary: A History of Non-fiction Film* (1974) provided a model for how to discuss works from a more international perspective, with a grace and clarity we can only hope to approach. We also thank the Society for the Humanities at Cornell University, especially its visionary director, Tim Murray, for hosting intensive small symposia on digitality that have in themselves proved that tempestuous seas are the most productive sites for new ideas.

We have been involved in documentary and experimental communities, both scholarly and artistic, for many decades. We want to name the colleagues from these communities who have provided sustenance, friendship, ethics, and empathy for us: Brian Winston, Bill Nichols, Jan Christopher Horak, Helen De Michiel, Alexandra Juhasz, B. Ruby Rich, Robin Blaetz, Sharon Lin Tay, Sam Gregory, Liz Miller, Mandy Rose, Irina Aristarkhova, Brenda Longfellow, John Greyson, Tom Waugh, Chuck Kleinhans, Julia Lesage, John Hess, Gina Marchetti, Anna Siomopoulos, Grace An, Lisa Patti, Roger Hallas, Matthew Fee, and Leshu Torchin. We thank the Visible Evidence conferences on documentary, International Symposium on Electronic Art, Documentary Now in London, American Comparative Literature Association, Society for Film and Media Studies, Sundance Film Festival, and Morelia International Film Festival. We especially thank Richard Herskowitz, curator and programmer of three key festivals—the Houston Cinema Arts Film Festival, the Virginia Film Festival, and the Cinema Pacific Film Festival—that have not only featured our scholarly work in public presentations, but have also stirred us. We also thank the National Alliance of Media Arts and Culture, especially its former executive directors, Jack Walsh and Helen De Michiel, for their leadership to reposition the field of public media into a full exploration of the democratic possibilities of new media.

Our transnational orientation derives in part from our own multiple and migratory locations in upstate New York, western Massachusetts, and the urban metropolises of New York, Singapore, and Abu Dhabi. We thank Ithaca College, where we both worked together, for providing the institutional space of FLEFF, which pushed us to consider the vibrant upstate new media arts community and its long hundred-year-plus history of arts and technology innovation. Dale thanks the Five College Consortium of Amherst, Hampshire, Mount Holyoke, and Smith Colleges and the University of Massachusetts, particularly Amherst College where he first taught courses on new media. He also thanks New York University Abu Dhabi (NYUAD), where he works with extraordinary students from around the world and incredible colleagues at NYUAD and NYU's other campuses in New York and Shanghai. Patricia thanks the city of Houston, for deepening her thinking about borders and their multiplicities. She thanks Nanyang Technological University in Singapore, especially the Wee Kim Wee School of Communications, where she taught in 2004. She returned in 2010 as the Shaw Foundation Professor of New Media, mounting a new media exhibition of 25 people and works titled Open Space/Singapore/Southeast Asia, a project spurring much of the writing in this book. She thanks the Shaw Foundation in Singapore, as well as cocurators Nikki Draper and Sharon Lin Tay. At NTU, she thanks in particular Ben Detenber, Stephen Teo, Allan Chan, Mark Cenite, and Cherian George. In the upstate New York new media community, we thank Tim Murray, Renate Ferro, Stephanie Rothenberg, Andrew Utterson, Claudia Pederson, Nicholas Knouf, and Roger Hallas for conversations rich in insight. In the lower Canada media and scholarly communities, we especially thank John Greyson, Brenda Longfellow, and Tom Waugh for their intellectual ferocity.

Many of the ideas developed in this book first found their way out of the swirling oceans of our minds onto the calmer shores of community at various conferences and speaking engagements. We thank Brian Winston for inviting us to deliver a plenary session on locative media at the Visible Evidence XV conference that he mounted at Lincoln University. Patricia thanks York University (Canada), Yale University, Dartmouth College, Brown University, Cornell University, University of Oregon, the Nigerian Film Institute (Nigeria), University of St. Andrews (Scotland), National University of Singapore, University of Hong Kong, Sun Yat Sen University (China), Middlesex University (United Kingdom) for invitations to present her research. She also thanks the American Film Showcase program of the US State Department, as well as the US Embassy in Conakry, Guinea, and the US Consulate in Guangzhou, China, for invitations to speak at universities and to civil society activists about new media and collaboration.

Several grants supported the research and writing of this project. From Ithaca College, Patricia received funding from the James Pendleton Fund in the Roy H. Park School of Communications, the Office of the Provost, multiple Reassigned Time Awards, and a summer research grant. Dale thanks NYUAD's Vice Chancellor Al Bloom, Provost Fabio Piano, Dean of Social Science Hervé Crès and Dean of Arts and Humanities Judith Miller for supporting his research, as well as helping him to bring Eduardo Cachucho and Babak Fakhamzadeh to Abu Dhabi for the inaugural Dérive.app workshop and to bring Stewart Auyash and Patrica Zimmermann for a talk/workshop on Conflict Zones. He also thanks Associate Vice-Chancellor Carol Brandt and the Office of Global Education and Outreach for supporting research and teaching trips to Doha and Mumbai, whose benefits are clearly visible in this book, and Deputy Vice Chancellor Hilary Ballon, whose vision for NYUAD's core curriculum provided an ideal location for integrating interdisciplinary and transnational thinking exemplified in digital media projects into a globally inflected undergraduate education. He thanks Pat Cahill, Erin Cassese, Soko Starobin, and coach Maurice Stevens in his writing group through the National Center for Faculty Development and Diversity.

Dale thanks Enrico Aditjondro, Eduardo Cachucho, Sharon Daniel, Babak Fakhamzadeh, Ismail Farouk, Christina McPhee, and Carlos Motta, who have served on the juries for FLEFF exhibitions; the Global Alliance against the Traffic of Women (GAATW) in Bangkok for sponsoring the prize for the Trafficking Identities exhibition; Sharon Lin Tay for her collaboration as a co-curator on six exhibitions; Claudia Costa Pederson for her contributions as assistant curator on Viral Dissonance exhibition; Lamia Alami, Awam Amkpa, Jonny Farrow, Khulood Kittaneh, and Anna Schrade for recommending projects, both for this book and for FLEFF exhibitions. He also thanks Virginia Danielson, Renji Jacob and Nicholas Martin at the NYUAD Library for their collaboration on the special digital collection of films from the Gulf film festivals, as well as Reindert Falkenburg, Philip Kennedy, and Nils Lewis for supporting his programming of MENASA films at the NYUAD Institute. He thanks his extraordinary research assistant Rend Beiruti for her self-motivation and attention to detail in securing images and permissions for this book and her contribution to the special collection.

Dale thanks his friends and colleagues who have supported this project in various ways and for many productive conversations and collaborations: Tarek Al-Ghoussein, Nezar Andary, Robin Blaetz, Özge Calafato, Una Chaudhuri, Anne Ciecko Scandar Copti, Catherine Coray, Omima El Araby, Radha Hegde, Leonard Retel Helmrich, Seung-hoon Jeong, Alex Keller, Doreen Lee, Jill Magi Jennifer and Kevin McCoy, Monika Mehta, Pascal Menoret, Jenny Perlin, Catherine Portuges, Goffredo Puccetti, Sana Odeh, Rajeswari Sunder Rajan, Ron Robin, Qiuxia Shao, Robert J. C. Young, and Alia Yunis, everyone at the Abu Dhabi Film Festival and the various arts institutions in Doha, Dubai, and Sharjah. He thanks Awam Amkpa for being an intellectual and institutional role model and championing new conceptualizations of art. None of Dale's thinking about film would have been possible without the groundbreaking scholarship of Ella Shohat and Robert Stam, who reinvigorated our field with new paradigms, vocabularies, and objects of study. Not only does their work continue to provoke and push debates further, but they also continue to open the field to previously marginalized or ignored voices. He is also incredibly grateful for their warmth and friendship. He thanks Patty Zimmermann for her brilliance and indomitable energy in confronting the intellectual challenges and opportunities of the moment. Teaching with Patty at Ithaca College was a transformative experience, and he is grateful to have learned so much from her over the years from late-night conversations in the projection booth, at conferences, or in seminars. He thanks her for inviting him to curate digital media for FLEFF and later to coauthor conference papers, which became articles, which became the basis for this book. He is grateful to have her as a friend. He thanks his family—both human and feline—for support, interest, and encouragement from as nearby as Maharashtra and as far away as California. Finally, he thanks Sheetal Majithia for her loving patience, critical insights, and indefatigable optimism, particularly over the course of this book's realization—and for encouraging him to leap into new oceans. She makes the world a better place.

Patricia thanks Zillah Eisenstein, Carla Golden, Andrew Utterson, Steve Tropiano, Steve Ginsberg, Tim Murray, Renate Ferro, Mary Zebell, Vincent Grenier, Phil Wilde, Ann Michel, and Jairo Geronymo for sustaining community through intensely creative friendship. She thanks Tom Shevory for over a decade of energizing collaboration as codirectors of FLEFF, and for two decades of friendship. Without the collegiality, comradeship, intellectual moxie, and rigorous timelines of Dale Hudson, this book would not exist. Patricia gives Dale a loud shout-out for his ferocity, his fearlessness, and his ability to dig deep into the unknown. His friendship has taught her that with passion, verve, and daring, insight flows almost constantly. Dale's energizing collaborative style smashes the forced isolations of academic work, and regrounds thinking and writing in conversation with a larger world. She acknowledges her mother, Alice Rodden Zimmermann, and her brother, Byron Zimmermann, for their generosity from Houston, Texas. She also deeply thanks Stewart Auyash for his loving support on every and all levels, including much-needed sailing trips for solace and solitude, and travels across many continents for pleasure and work. He brings joyous big love to any and all bodies of water. And she thanks Sean Zimmermann Auyash for his endless embrace of a transnational criticality—and his endless provocations and interrogations about this project.

We thank the anonymous readers for their valuable and insightful feedback on the book's proposal and sample chapters, as well as Darrell Varga for being the first to post a comment on the open-peer review process. We thank Joan Harkness Hantz for designing the artwork that appears on the cover, which originally served as the art for Microtopias, the FLEFF 2012 theme, as well as Jenny Stockdale and the FLEFF marketing team for commissioning it and clearing it for this book cover. Finally, we thank Palgrave MacMillan for taking on this project with such gusto and professionalism. We would not have a book for you to read without the acute vision of Robyn Curtis and Shaun Vigil, and the sharp assist of Mark Rinaldi and escpecially Erica Buchman. We thank them for this extraordinary opportunity to move through, within, against, and between a multiplicity of ideas, projects, landmasses, and oceans.

Introduction

Thinking Through Digital Media: Transnational Environments and Locative Places charts media practices developed from analogue technologies as they migrate to the ones for digital media and digital networks. Conventional definitions of film, photography, television, and video no longer make sense as distinct media, given accelerated developments in digital technology and radically different ways of harnessing these technologies around the world. Comparably, the terms multimedia, interactive, and screen no longer make sense in ways that they once might have, nor do other terms from analogue media ecologies, such as animation, documentary, experimental, narrative, or so-called hybrid forms. Digital media ecologies are increasingly based on explorations of code and user interface; interrogations of archives, databases, and networks; production via automated scraping, filtering, cloning, and recombinatory techniques; applications of user-generated content (UGC) layers; crowdsourcing ideas on social-media platforms; narrowcasting digital selves on "free" websites that claim copyright; and provocative performances that implicate audiences as participants.

This book, thus, examines a range of digital media projects from online projects that almost everyone can access to offline projects that include site-specific gallery installations or live performances and thus only a privileged few can access. We analyze individual and collaborative projects developing at the intersections of imbedded technologies, micropublics, human-machine performances, migratory histories, affective geographies, and critical cartographies to forward a set of *speculations* rather than arguments with conclusions. The book embraces thinking between code and celluloid, streaming and projection, modular and linear structures, causalities by random access and chronology. Above all, this book engages multiple iterations across multiple platforms rather than a singular "master cut" for theatrical exhibition or "limited edition" for the art market. The animation, documentary, experimental, narrative, and interactive projects discussed in this book are less concerned with what things look like than with taking things apart to explore what they do or can do. The projects probe *how* things work together rather than *what* they represent.

Our goal is to offer a means of thinking *about* digital media by looking at projects that think *through* digital media. Our book contends that digital media practice becomes more artistically creative with deepened knowledge from digital media studies—and that digital media studies become more intellectually informed through hands-on experience of digital media practice, whether as a viewer, user, or participant; thus, digital media studies and digital media practice converge—and are never mutually exclusive. The book focuses on artistic practice informed by critical studies and intellectual histories. Projects unfold across different platforms (e.g., computer screens, mobile screens, gallery spaces, open streets, public squares, private malls, social media, narrowcasting) and in different iterations (e.g., websites, downloads, videos, images, video games, performances) to convene critically engaged media users. Since there is no universal way to convey a story, render an image, evoke an affect, or pose a question, we examine digital media through comparative frameworks that integrate intellectual and artistic experience—whether curating existing work or producing new work, generating original content or reworking found footage, researching in archives or directing live action and animation. We seek to understand the significance of these projects within larger social and artistic dialogues and debates.

We analyze contemporary digital media practices within three intersecting matrixes: comparative film, media, and cultural studies; cyberculture, Internet, and digital studies; and postcolonial, transnational, and globalization studies. We look to ecocritical, posthumanist, and object-oriented methods to elaborate ways to think about and through digital media. We focus on media produced over the last two decades to generate an argument about digital media from different cultures and histories and to frame ongoing debates on topics such as participation/surveillance, climate change, mass migration, structural inequality, and perpetual war. Many projects we examine were exhibited at the Finger Lakes Environmental Film Festival (FLEFF) and its global network of partners in the Open Cinema Project. FLEFF explores environmentalism as a broad category not limited to nature and conservation but expansive to culture and sustainability. It includes topics such as the rights of workers, women, and nonhuman animals; access to clean water, safe food, and digital networks; migrations driven by military and economic interventions; proliferation of flexible labor, free zones, informal economies, and e-waste; and freedom of movement for people and ideas. Sustainability becomes the nodal point for intersections of nature and culture. "An ecological way of thinking, then, demands tracing these complex intersections in order to understand them—and then act on them," explain FLEFF codirectors. "Ecology means understanding how things, people, and ideas are interconnected."[1]

Digital Encounters and Global Perspectives

The linguistic turn emphasized the role of language in mediating and producing reality. Recently, thinking has moved to consider objects through an iconic or pictorial turn, shifting analysis from *interpretations of representation* toward *encounters with presentation*.[2] Objects are understood to have their own ontologies. This interest in the encounter highlights key differences between digital and analogue media. Our encounters with digital media are often tactile because we tap on keys and screens and click buttons on mouses or controllers to make software process data and metadata. Celluloid prints of films have a materiality, but they are not designed to be touched by everyone. All gauges—70mm, 35mm, 16mm, 8mm, Super8, and so forth—require particular projectors and trained projectionists. In contrast, digital media is designed to be touched by almost anyone. DVDs and VCDs can run on a specifically designed playback machine (e.g., a DVD player), a computer, or a gaming console. Unlike a VHS or Beta tape, DVDs and VCDs possess random access memory (RAM), which allows for a temporality of "always-present": no rewind or fast-forward required. Digital images are always potentially present. As Lev Manovich notes, digital media abandons anthropocentric representations of linear time for immediate access anywhere.[3]

Holly Willis argues that digital technologies prompt a reinvention of the moving image that alters media practices. "Filmmaking," she argues, is "less about creating pristine images of perfectly orchestrated and highly composed events and more about collecting a body of materials that will then be manipulated extensively, pixel by pixel if necessary," so that digital media follows a more general shift from a culture of representation (indexical registration of images on celluloid or analogue video) to one of capturing, processing, manipulating, and repurposing images.[4] She suggests that *practice* displaces the indexical relationship of signification.[5] Practice changes the relationship between animation, documentary, experimental, narrative, and interactive media and the photorealism of indexicality as it shifts from chemical-based celluloid and magnetic-grounded analogue video to digitally coded and rendered images. Digital technologies challenge us to redefine media and conventions based on analogue technologies. In contrast to theorizations of cinematic realism as endemic of human imagination (André Bazin), psychoanalytical structures of desire (Laura Mulvey, Rosalind Krauss, Mary Ann Doane), material structures (Jean-Louis Comolli), or industrial conventions (David Bordwell and Janet Staiger), Manovich emphasizes the role of algorithms and databases in digital media.[6] Information is organized and structured in databases. Algorithms render information into sequences of simple operations without manipulation by human users. Digital media foregrounds encounters with presentations of the globally diverse perspectives of machines and animals, both human and nonhuman.

We use the term "digital media" rather than earlier terms such as "multimedia" to be inclusive of a wide variety of projects, involving everything from automated machine acts to live performance by human and nonhuman actors, and to avoid historical confusion. Over the past few decades, related terms have been proposed in particular contexts: *expanded cinema* looked to John Whitney's computer animation experiments in the 1960s; *electronic media* emphasized physical computing; *new media* is sometimes used reductively for web-based journalism, blogging, and social media—and the adjective "new" sometimes even confuses in the way that the same adjective in "new wave cinema" does not; *interactive media* tended to describe applications of web and mobile technologies. This last term is confusing since it is used both by corporations, seeking to amass data on customers for marketing, and by artists, seeking to enhance engagement. For many, interaction refers only to technologies and excludes the applications of these technologies. The term "interactive media" has been criticized for its inaccuracy: the media is *reactive to* user input from a defined subset of possibilities rather than *interactive with* users.[7] It differs from performers interacting with audiences during plays or concerts that are open to the unexpected. Despite its imprecision, we include it as a dominant mode of commercial and noncommercial media, along with animation, documentary, experimental, and narrative.

The term "digital media" highlights the role of code—metaphorically, digits as *numbers*—that can manipulate and initiate—metaphorically, digits as *fingers*—automated processes, which now include voice recognition and eye tracking. Digital media engages the production of content and context through processes of mediation involving code (algorithms, bits, codecs, databases), suggesting digital media ecologies for animation, documentary, experimental, interactive, and narrative practice. A major distinguishing characteristic of digital media from analogue media is that the digital is not fixed or confined to one form (like a film or video) nor does it need to be "run" in a necessarily linear mode like a single-channel documentary. Instead, digital objects are fluid, malleable, responsive, and changing. They recalibrate the relationship between maker/designer, audience, and content/context into a more open system. Once associated with cinemas and televisions, screens are now more linked with computers, phones, tablets, watches, and glasses. Unlike the public display at cinemas or the collective experience of television, these smaller "smart" screens are often used by one person at a time. Moreover, they invite or even require input from users. "Film" becomes a term of convenience, one that persists despite its reference to outmoded technologies, pedagogies, and epistemologies. The convenience of film's persistence, however, comes with the often-limiting perspectives of conventions based on analogue media paradigms.

Within the field of film studies, documentaries and experimental films have historically been modes where minoritized perspectives emerge to dislodge assumptions about media, particularly the ones disseminated by movies and video games as "entertainment" or by news and documentaries as "objective." Digital media extends this unsettling of assumptions, displacing analogue assumptions (e.g., indexicality, objectivity) along with their universalist (eurocentric) and humanist (anthropocentric) underpinnings. Our book contributes to ongoing debates prompted by accelerated digitalization and globalization since the 1990s. More than a decade ago, Tara McPherson described the "unbearable whiteness of much of digital theory." She argued against importing the naturalized whiteness of the universal subject from film theory.[8] Lisa Nakamura examined textual and visual representations of race and racism on distributed networks from chatroom avatars to social networks.[9] Working from indigenous media rather than commercial narrative features (the focus of early film theorists), Faye Ginsburg developed the notion of the "parallax effect" in relation to mediation and subject position that calls into question theorizations based on audiovisual representation and communication.[10]

Nonetheless, many studies of digital media reproduce the same biases of analogue media, focusing on projects from the North Atlantic and Asia Pacific regions as universizable and scalable. They ignore the diversity of applications of digital media. "Because of its close connection to the Internet however, from its inception New Media art was a worldwide movement," write Mark Tribe and Reena Jana; "the Internet facilitated the formation of communities without regard for geography."[11] Although they mention biennales in Johannesburg and Gwangju alongside projects from India and México during the 1990s, they avoid the question of digital divides—a major concern during that decade. Although distributed very differently among their populations, cities in both South Africa and South Korea had access to the Internet. In part, this book decenters focus on what was called the "wired world"—parts of Australia, Canada, Europe, Japan, South Korea, New Zealand, and United States. It loosens definitions to consider what was once called the unwired side of a digital divide, figuring it as an active agent in thinking through digital media over the past two decades. This book examines a number of collectives and organizations that think through digital media in divergent ways. Some of the most dynamic, innovative sites for digital media include the global art world "hot spots," such as China (PRC), India, Indonesia, Iran, Nigeria, Saudi Arabia (KSA), Singapore, South Africa, Qatar, Turkey, and the United Arab Emirates (UAE).

Outside the North Atlantic world, distinctions between modern and postmodern have rarely made sense. Filmmaking in India, for example, has seldom been concerned exclusively with such issues since its dominant narrative structure draws on an array of transhistorical conventions. These richly textured films demand complex multifocal interpretations. By North Atlantic standards, even the most traditional A-grade *masala* or C-grade "quickie" might appear avant-garde. Such films make the ways that multiple modernities differ from (a singular) "the modern" apparent. "Feeling modern" becomes a means to express modernity's uneven and unequal globalization. Scholars have proposed "transmodernity," "alternative modernities," "incomplete modernities," "pirate modernities," "street-level modernities," and "overlapping modernities" to contest spatial and temporal frameworks imposed by a singular, linear European modernity in the contexts of South Asia, China, Latin America, eastern Europe, and Africa.[12] The term "competing modernities" makes micro-comparison within Japanese culture and between European ones, such as German and US forms.[13] Modernities are no longer contained to the early twentieth century but continue in the present. Moreover, modern artists are not concerned with official timelines that render particular styles or approaches antiquated or impure. With the popularization of the Internet across digital divides, access to an ever-expanding informal archive of digitized (often pirated) media suggests that terms inherited from an analogue era need revision. Laura Marks traces seven parallels between Islamic thought and new media art, thereby recovering the place of early modern mathematics and spirituality within theorizations of digitality.[14] The rejection of a strict distinction between modern and postmodern operates within the postcolonial condition in which digital media ecologies emerge.

The term "postcolonial" does not define a moment following the end of colonialism and the triumph of decolonization. Instead, it defines a moment after the effects of western European, East Asian, and settler (Australian, Canadian, Israeli, New Zealander, and US) colonialism have connected the world in ways that cannot be undone. Since colonialism implies complete domination of one group by another, terms such as "neocolonial," "paracolonial," and "transcolonial" have been proposed for colonial relations that do not obliterate sovereignty or follow official decolonization. Such distinctions, however, divert attention from what could be called alternative, overlapping, or competing colonialisms. They reify colonialism as an officially state-sanctioned enterprise, thereby disassociating it from its private manifestations in the chartered companies since the fifteenth century. Some scholars, for example, argue that the Dutch East India Company represents a precursor to contemporary multinational and transnational corporations like Apple, Google, Microsoft, Samsung, and Sony. The postcolonial condition suggests all of these conditions, as most people have been touched by colonialism.[15] It persists—and, as Robert Young argues, the need for postcolonial studies remains—in globalization's transnational interconnections, integrations, and inequalities through the World Wide Web (WWW) and under the World Trade Organization (WTO).[16] Global perspectives on digital media require the historical and theoretical rigor of postcolonial studies to make sense of our transnational environments.

Transnational Environments and Locative Places

Everyday, digital technologies affect our lives and constitute us within transnational environments. We often think *through* digital media without much awareness about how it affects us. Digitality constructs everyday life through distributed networks such as the Internet, particularly hypertext files on the WWW and message exchange via e-mail, wireless local area network (WLAN) technologies, short message service (SMS) communication, cellular and digital (broadband) telephone networks, personalized news and information aggregators, graphical user interface (GUI) where software processes our commands through point-and-click user acts, radio-frequency identification (RFID) tags, optical machine-readable representation of data in bar codes like universal product code (UPC-A) and matrix codes like quick response (QR), global positioning system (GPS) satellites and receivers, web applications (apps) such as Google Maps or Google Earth, narrowcasting platforms such as YouTube and Twitter for distributing UGC to wide audiences, digital fingerprints and identities created on social networking sites like Facebook, data harvesting of data that we "gift" to corporations via such sites, video cameras on phones and tablets, peer-to-peer (P2P) file sharing and BitTorrents, crowdsourcing platforms, and biometric interfaces such as voice-, iris-, gesture-, and facial-recognition software. Digitality changes us.

As consumer-grade web browsers like Netscape Navigator popularized the Internet in the 1990s, Nicholas Negroponte proposed the digital marks a movement from atoms to bits.[17] For him, "being digital" was largely about interface, specifically ways that digital media is distributed from producers to users with distinctions between the two sides of the circuit sometimes indistinguishable. Information is customized based on Internet Protocol (IP) address or GPS location, or personalized based on the browser fingerprint of past reading habits, in a post-information era where broadcasting and even narrowcasting are less dominant as modes of distribution. Henry Jenkins extended this premise into historical and theoretical analyses of amateur media, particularly in relation to media fandom, arguing that digital media is defined by "spreadability" (*potential* dispersal, including unauthorized) rather than "stickiness" (*centralized* aggregation) in an era when corporations no longer tightly control media.[18] Although such understandings of digital media across networks are compelling, they sometimes occlude structural inequalities. With the advent of globalized neoliberal economic policies since the 1990s, both material and cultural inequalities have become more pronounced. Digital divides continue to affect digital media production, distribution, exhibition, and reception. Media conveying feminist, queer, postcolonial, indigenous, ecocritical, and posthuman perspectives are often sidelined when historicizing and theorizing digitality, as are media that reject or ignore the "rules" of commercial film, television, and video games. Negroponte imagined a digital divide might develop according to generational difference, rather than racial, national, or classed difference, thereby avoiding "a social divide between the information-rich and the information-poor, the haves and the have-nots, the First and the Third Worlds."[19] His techno-utopianism about an emerging transnational cyberspace has been widely critiqued with examples from places as seemingly disparate as rural communities in Africa and urban ones in the United States during the late 1990s.[20] Since 2005, Negroponte's nonprofit One Laptop per Child Association (OLPCA) has worked to narrow the divide through inexpensive, energy-conserving, durable, and Internet-ready computers like the XO-1 designed for "developing countries." Over two and a half million computers have been shipped to Latin America (Argentina, Colombia, México, Paraguay, Perú, Uruguay), Africa (Ghana, Rwanda, Sierra Leone), and the United States (Alabama). Although the importance of access cannot be underestimated, the ongoing digital-divide question is not confined to Internet access. Digital divides raise questions about the ability to produce and distribute information. Webpages with content in local languages about local topics from local perspectives or applications that function according to cultural considerations (modesty, indirect conventions of expression, measures to sidestep official censorship) cannot be universalized. Shortcomings exist on *all sides* of the digital divides. One side is limited by access, another challenged by overconfidence in its own interpretations of access, another truncated by short-sidedness to corporate appropriations of hacks, and still another reduced by uncritical acceptance of intellectual property regulations. Shortsighted, universalizing assumptions short-circuit most theorizations of digitality. We look to digital media that destabilizes analogue assumptions.

The interfaces between physical computing and the "virtual world" complicate our sense of space and place. Digital media is often accessed via digital networks, presenting opportunities as well as limitations in conceiving new or alternative forms of collaborative knowledge production. Ulises Mejias argues that the digital network is both "a *model* or template for organizing society" and "an *episteme*, a system for organizing knowledge about the world," that "allows us to understand the 'networked' world, to see everything in terms of networks, and to apply network logic even to things that are not networks."[21] Like many scholars, he draws upon Manuel Castells's concept of

"network society."[22] For Mejias, digital networks function according to "nodocentrism" that "renders illegible everything that is not a
node." Networks privilege nodes and discriminate against non-nodes;
the digital network may be understood as a system that "constructs a
social reality in which nodes can only see other nodes."[23] Alexander
Galloway's insights into protocol are insightful in this regard.[24]
Protocol allows nodes within a distributed network to communicate
with one another. The nodes must "speak the same language," he suggests, sustaining the illusions of connectivity, collectivity, participation, and even democratization.[25] Protocol "most forcefully displays
its political character at moments of disconnectivity."[26]

Since "no responsible person can afford to be a Luddite," Mejias
explains, we should aspire for the disruption of "fighting networks
with networks" in order to apprehend what lies beyond the limits
of nodes. This strategy requires "changing the way we understand
others and ourselves," particularly "the way we imagine and engage
difference."[27] Timothy Murray describes "a deeply archaeological
shift from *projection* to *fold* that is emphasized, if not wholly embodied, by the digital condition." The fold enables elastic and multidirec-
tional (rather than single-point perspectives of Euclidean systems of
individual subjectivity) knowledge found within "the *in-between* of
seemingly opposed technologies, cultures, and philosophies with the
possession of affect and material."[28] Digital technologies can structurally challenge the residues of anthropocentrism and eurocentrism
in analogue media.

New media ecologies produce transnational environments, where
physical and bodily location simultaneously matters and does not
matter. Geographical Information Systems (GIS) and GPS locate us
on a grid. But IP addresses can be routed through different proxies
and domains, such as virtual local area networks (VLAN), so that
a place is not always contingent on geographic coordinates. Gerard
Goggin predicts next-generation networks will move from WLAN or
WiFi to mobile broadband (often using Worldwide Interoperability
for Microwave Access or WiMAX), highlighting a "centrality of the
internet" in a likely transition from circuit-switched telecommunications to packet-switched networks based on IP addresses.[29] Digital
media and digital networks operations are not immediately accessible or even comprehensible to anyone. More than operating software or hacking apps, digital literacy requires specialized knowledge.
Although interactivity and participation are heavily promoted as
potentially democratic, it is a form of monitoring and surveillance.[30]

The Tor Project, an anonymity software, conceals the user's identity. It reroutes Internet activity through a volunteer system of thousands of relays that resemble the nested layers of an onion, as in the term "onion routing." In the United States, the National Security Agency (NSA) targets Tor users in its surveillance. The Electronic Frontier Foundation (EFF; www.eff.org) and other civil rights organizations work to defend privacy and expression within the highly controlled space of the Internet.

Within media practice, Christiane Paul notes "a pronounced shift from the use of 'static' computers to a growing reliance on mobile, locative media," which collapses "the boundaries between the translocal (connections between different sites) and the locative or site specific."[31] One of the complexities of web-based projects, she explains, is that "the WWW itself quickly became a mirror for the 'real' world, with corporations and e-commerce, colonizing the landscape."[32] Industry journalists promote "contextual technologies," operating according to "five forces"—mobile, social media, big data, sensors, and location-based applications—that will thrive economically as long as users trust corporate privacy policies.[33] Paul, however, notes that context can be physical, social, organizational, and economic, so that "from a global perspective, context is about location, enriching the specifies of a particular place," and "from a local perspective, context is about activity and agency, the ability to engage with location."[34] Location, however, is no longer an obvious designation—something locatable in space.

Space suggests abstraction, something unknowable but embodied through place. Space can be defined by longitude and latitude of geographic coordinate systems that often use the Cartesian grid of mathematical calculations along x-, y-, and z-axes. Space also can be defined in terms of time and space as in GIS or GPS. Cyberspace suggests virtual realities. In contrast, places are material, embodied, and experienced. During the 1970s, Henri Lefebvre, Yi-Fu Tuan, and others argued for understandings of geography that considered not only physical coordinates but also aesthetic and ethical locations.[35] Despite the limitations of humanist groundings, which include universalism and anthropocentrism, their ideas continue to inspire across academic disciplines and artistic media. They ask us to think through space rather than merely think about space as something that is already given. "Place, at its basic level, is space invested with meaning in the context of power," writes Tim Cresswell. Place is "a way of seeing, knowing, and understanding the world" that can be "an act of resistance against a rationalization of the world" or one that "leads to reactionary and exclusionary xenophobia, racism, and bigotry."[36] Extending Lefebvre and Tuan, Cresswell includes insights from Doreen Massey's work on a "global sense of place" (*routes* rather than *roots*) and his own work on "people without a place" (e.g., the homeless, refugees, and LBGT groups made to feel "out of place").[37] For Massey, accelerated movement of people, images, and information reconfigures place for relationality, multiplicity, and openness. Place is always heterogeneous and unfinished.[38] Globalization's "time-space compression needs differentiating socially" in terms of understanding mobility and communication, she explains, looking to "progressive" and "outward-looking" places rather than "self-enclosing and defensive" ones.[39] Cresswell brings to this discussion Auturo Escobar's writing on "subaltern strategies for localization" that advocate for place-based identities amid globalization's "delocalizing effects."[40]

Digital networks are experienced as what we might call *cyberplaces* rather than a universalized cyberspace. The Internet might be promoted as a virtual space, but it is experienced as a virtual place. We draw upon Massey and Cresswell to localize and politicize place within transnational movements and neoliberal transformations of space.[41] Étienne Balibar characterizes borders as polysemic, having different meaning for "a rich person from a rich country" and "a poor person from a poor country." This model suggests Marc Augé's non-places be likewise differentiated.[42] Airport terminals, train stations, and bus terminals are experienced and remembered differently by minoritized (e.g., women, children, the elderly) and criminalized (e.g., racialized) groups. If place is the production of social relationships between objects, then locative places suggest contestation and dissent are bound to locations that might be physical, geopolitical, emotional, or nomadic. We look to projects that call attention to the possibilities as well as the limitations of digital media within the closed commercial network spaces.

Locative places often emerge where the laws of transnational environments are reinterpreted. Hollywood and Silicon Valley might criminalize hacking and piracy—a position reiterated in its advertising evoking public-service announcements. But hacking is often associated with social good. "Hacktivism techniques include denial-of-service (DoS) attacks, website defacement, information theft, and virtual sabotage. Famous examples of hacktivism include the recent knocking out of the PlayStation Network, various assistances to activists participating in the Arab Spring, such as attacks on Tunisian and Egyptian government websites, and attacks on Mastercard and Visa after they ceased to process payments to WikiLeaks."[43] "Informational control technologies (computerized land records, GIS city maps, biometric IDs) were initiated to make pirate modernity legible to property," writes Ravi Sundaram. "In turn informational protocols were periodically broken, counterfeited and bypassed by pirate modernity."[44] "Where cinema screens were once filled with outdated films from the United States or India, pirate media means that Nigerian audiences can watch films contemporaneously with audiences in New York or Bombay," points out Brian Larkin. "Instead of being marginalized by official distribution networks, Nigerian consumers can now participate in the immediacy of an international consumer culture—but only through the mediating capacity of piracy."[45] Tilman Baumgärtel has studied the role of piracy in the Philippines, where like in 31 other states there is larger market for "illegal software" than for "commercial software."[46] University-level teaching in film studies is sometimes possible only due to pirated DVDs or online sites such as YouTube and UbuWeb. "Piracy thrives around the world, not only because technology and failures in enforcement of existing laws enable it to thrive, but because consumers are willing to pay lower prices for much lower quality product," explains Moradewun Adejunmobi. "In a context of infrastructural deficits and weak regulation, therefore, piracy does not completely disable opportunities for profit; rather it depresses the levels of investment in production beyond a certain point, and little would be gained by investing more in production than the consumer is willing to pay for the end product."[47] Locative practices require contextualization within postcolonial political economies. Contestation cannot ethically be dismissed as incivility.

Often operating as contestations and speculations, digital media objects can enter into physical reality through locative media, new media art, and video games, particularly "mods" (modifications) and "hacks," that require spectators to become users or even actors in the performance. A hacker ethos of "taking things apart" emerges when digital media transcends the limitations of screens to engage audiences as participants. These real-time acts dismantle assumptions about how the digital is embedded in everyday life, from the seemingly innocuous to the overtly controlling. Digital media can help reverse engineer both the technologies that connect and disconnect us, such as e-mail and social networking, and the concepts that we use to think about media, such as analogue animation, documentary, experimental, and narrative.

Thinking through (and with) Digital Media

Our book speculates on how we think through digital media about an increasing digital world. We focus on conceptual changes beyond the techno-utopianism associated with *Wired* magazine during the reconfiguration of the world by the WWW and under the WTO. We look at digital media that extends but sometime unsettles analogue media practices contingent upon modernist faith in indexicality between reality and representation. Digital media is somewhat unconcerned with modernist divisions based on mode or genre (animation, documentary, experimental, interactive, or narrative media) or on media (graphic design, high art, photography, film, television, video, internet art). Rather than the postmodern, we look to the postcolonial and the posthuman as theoretical frameworks for thinking *about* digital media that itself thinks *through* digital paradigms. We bring together digital media that is both politically and artistically engaged with a world reconfigured by digital media and digital networks. Applications such as the WWW and networks such as WLANs often alter our impressions of the time-space compressions and structural inequalities of contemporary globalization. The world does not divide neatly into East and West, First, Second, and Third Worlds, or Global North and Global South. At the same time, the structural inequalities inaugurated and formalized under both colonialism and decolonization continue to determine access. If a wired world was controlled by territory, then a wireless world is controlled by nodes. It is fractal, fractured, and fragmented. We look to digital media projects that claim locative places within these transnational environments, where micro-publics convene in improvisational, transitory, and tactical ways.

Katherine Hayles suggests that we might need to rethink curricula to respond to new ways of thinking used by our students for whom "faster communication, more intense and varied information streams, more integration of humans and intelligent machines, and more interactions of language with code" are not new but have always existed.[48] She uses the example of the "traditional English [literature and language, sometimes also culture] department," organized by "outmoded" periodization, nationalities, and genres that "fail to account for much of contemporary scholarship." These categories focus on "content rather than problems," failing to provide students with "essential preparation" for "entering the information-intensive and media-rich environments in which their careers will be forged and their lives lived."[49] We make a similar argument about film studies, which inherits antiquated models ("history, theory, criticism," "production and craft") that segregate studies and practice, particularly in hierarchal and evaluative ways (filmmakers as artistically or intellectually superior to film scholars, or the inverse) and fail to recognize that media and the world have changed in substantive ways since the pre-digital era.

It is no longer useful to introduce students to film studies, for example, by studying only examples from Hollywood, Europe, and East Asia. The advent of relatively inexpensive digital cameras, editing software, and networked capacity for streaming and file sharing allows for a much more accurate impression of the world and its varied perspectives. Our curricula need to reflect this shift. Applied to the arts, collaboration between humans and nonhumans with an openness to postcolonial and posthuman difference would operate differently from the compartmentalized specialization in conventional film production departments where students learn technical skills based on the needs of decades-outdated, Hollywood-style, Taylorist or post-Taylorist production. Moreover, as Hayles observes in research in history and literature, *display* often displaces *narrative*: complexity is more significant than causality. She suggests the need to recognize potential ways that digital technologies change how we think in a "technogenesis," that is genetic mutations affected on the human body and brain as a consequence of interactions with intelligent machines.[50] We need to engage in close reading (deep attention, single information stream, single objects for long periods of time), hyper reading (skimming, scanning, fragmenting, and juxtaposing of multiple objects), as well as machine reading (automated functions often not possible by humans due to the sheer quantity of information).[51]

Jay David Bolter and Richard Grusin distinguish digital media's capacity for *remediation*—the processes by which a medium represents another medium. They differentiate remediation from Jean Baudrillard's concepts of simulation and simulacra insofar as remediation refashions and rehabilitates other media in "a process of reforming reality as well."[52] Digital media projects are governed by what Galloway calls "the interface effect" in ways that "software takes command," as Manovich argues.[53] Many digital media projects examined in this book exist through software partly on screens as interfaces. Scholars argue that screens no longer serve merely as *surfaces* onto which to project images, desires, and fears but instead function increasingly as *interfaces* that produce images, desires, and fears. Thus, screens function as contact zones between physical and virtual worlds where we enter into the digital enclosures of networked societies. They acquire some of what Mary Louise Pratt describes in relation to the contact zones of colonial encounters: "social spaces where disparate cultures meet, clash, and grapple with each other, often in highly asymmetrical relations of domination and subordination" and "the space where peoples geographically and historically separated come into contact with each other."[54] Digital media, then, requires a new elaboration to theories based on analogue media.

Conceptions of a cinematic apparatus, for example, are contingent on an idealized and universalized subject—something that scholars attentive to difference, such as sex and race, as well as antagonisms to European continental philosophy, have argued.[55] Apparatus theory, however, was also contingent on particular projection and sound technologies that animated particular editing patterns and sound designs according to particular cultural conventions of a film experience that do not necessarily apply to digital media, including the simple playback of a DVD on screen. Rachel Greene notes that early web browsers and search engines were not designed for art, suggesting the belated academic recognition of web-based projects and efforts to theorize them.[56] Narrow definitions of cinema as feature-length narrative film persist despite evidence that they are increasingly not only outdated but also counterproductive. Apart from the United States and Canada, P2P download has become the global cinematic mode. The tipping point for commercial cinemas to transition from 35mm projectors to Digital Cinema Packages (DCP) has begun—the cinematic experience of projected celluloid is increasingly rare.

Digitalization has also changed the way that commercial film industries operate. In addition to video games, television has become the dominant media of Hollywood, whose "major studies have stopped making films for grown-ups," in the words of the British Film Institute's *Sight and Sound* magazine, thereby earning television the title of "home cinema"—or, in the words of Hollywood élite David Lynch, "art-house has gone to cable."[57] Selling ringtones is as significant to Bollywood as televising music videos. For many kinds of digital media, the screen continues to serve as *a* surface (though not necessarily *the* surface) while simultaneously functioning as a contact zone between material and immaterial worlds. Users are not lulled, seduced, or terrorized into dream-like states in darkened theaters. Instead, they are folded into a digital enclosure where multiple forms of interaction and participation with media and multiple forms of reading coexist, compete, and comingle. Users activate software. They play a role in video games. They construct—and give away—identities via social media. Or they simply click play and screen a video clip. What users encounter might be professionally produced but recontextualized, such as song-and-dance sequences from the latest Bollywood hits ripped from a DVD, or it might be nonprofessionally produced, as in an amateur music video (AMV), such as a local dance club lip-synching and dancing to the same song. Sometimes it is difficult to discern professional from nonprofessional media. Web series have been "astroturfed" (made to look amateur, as in *fake* grassroots) on YouTube as an amateur series, including *lonelygirl15 (LG15)* (United States 2006–2008), whose creators now own a media company, EQAL, that develops web content for CBS Broadcasting, one of the commercial networks in the United States, or Weibo in China. At the same time, nonprofessional artists narrowcast themselves on YouTube, securing loyal followings and sometimes industry deals in places like Nigeria, Saudi Arabia, and the United States. We are connected and disconnected from one another in different ways. P2P downloads often precede theatrical premières. Whether the transnational media corporations (TMCs) that own the brand Hollywood can adapt their business practices to digital paradigms is less interesting than the myriad ways artists, activists, coders, designers, students, and intellectuals are working together and thinking through digital media and digital networks.

Mediation fades to the recesses of consciousness as television news adopts the representational strategies of the Internet, shifting from a single screen to multiple windows within a screen where reporters and newsreaders chat about events with immediacy and simultaneity, while graphic logos for special stories fade in and out and the text for "breaking news" scrolls across the screen's bottom edge. At the same time, as Anne Friedberg argues, the window—whether Alberti's *finestra aperta* ("open window") that devised the illusion of one-point perspective or the windows of a Microsoft operating system—is constitutive of the meaning of what it frames.[58] This desktop aesthetic gives the illusion of Marsha Kinder's concept of "databases narratives," in which a surplus of information emphasizes a "duel process of selection and combination."[59] Although many digital media scholars dismiss the notion of interactivity as anything new or as anything possible beyond user "reactivity within a vast network of choices," David Hogarth argues that "interactive technologies could extend and deepen modes of engagement to provide a range of extra-textual and ancillary spaces." The Internet could serve as an archive for material, as well as facilitate less corporate filtering of content. "Digital documentaries promise to make sense of the world in less restrictive ways," such as DVD productions with "a graphic nonlinear view of the world, richer and more layered than traditional 'discourses of sobriety'" or online productions that "may allow new forms of dialogue with documentary form, undermining authoritative (and authoritarian) modes of communication along the way."[60]

The implications of a paradigm shift do not end there. As Hayles argues, the arts and humanities have joined the sciences and social sciences in thinking differently through digital technologies. She mentions new attention to properties of *design* and *navigation* that determine the kinds of meaning that users make from digital media. Designs utilizing massive databases point to increased recognition of the limitations of individuals and the need for collaboration from conception to implementation.[61] Our book itself engages with digital media paradigms for research, including our publisher's open peer-review trial, which allowed proposal comments with the aim of integrating collaborative feedback into the manuscript. Thinking through digital media, we feel, extends this openness to consider collaboration between nonhumans, including machines—that is, with the artificial intelligence (AI) of computers and other things.

Jussi Parikka has argued that "new AI" sometimes resembles or models itself after the distributed intelligence of insects.[62] Like bees, objects (servers, monitors, hard drives) may seem "individually dumb" but function ways that are "highly efficient when coupled with their environment."[63] Objects become "smart." He also looks at computer viruses and parasite computing that modify their hosts and themselves take on forms of life according to new materialist perspectives. From a different orientation, Jane Bennett considers vitality by which she means "the capacity of things—edibles, commodities, storms, metals—not only to impede or block the will and designs of humans but also to act as quasi agents of forces with trajectories, propensities, or tendencies of their own."[64] She looks to "thing-power" in the form of assemblages within "a human-nonhuman working group" with an aim of thinking about vibrant matter in relation to key political terms such as "public," "political participation," and "the political," speculating on "whether a polity might be a kind of ecosystem."[65]

Comparably, Ian Bogost imagines what it might be like to be a thing from a perspective that accepts that things themselves speculate, so that "one *speculates about how things speculate*."[66] He argues that the non-coherence of "the mess" might be more useful than organization of "the network" since "a mess is what is not graspable by *human* actors, unable to be ordered into a network."[67] Finally, Tim Morton has argued that mesh better describes interconnections of living and nonliving things than nature.[68] The mesh of living/nonliving evokes the web of the WWW and the web of spiders. As Parikka notes, since the nineteenth century spiders have been addressed as "the original inventors of telegraphy" because their webs "do not merely signal according to a binary setting (something has hit the web or has not hit the web) but transmit information regarding the 'general character and weight of any object touching it'."[69]

Such approaches suggest that thinking through digital media is also thinking *with* digital media. Digital media and digital networks require a sustained, collaborative process of thinking that includes some rethinking—and also some unthinking—of our assumptions. Thinking through digital media is necessarily incomplete and speculative. The human is displaced from its position of privilege, and the machine is recognized as intelligent. Moreover, machine acts are automated functions with a materiality and life of their own. As early as 1970, the rules for John Conway's "Life" or "Game of Life"—an auto-generative program—appeared in *Scientific American*'s "Mathematical Games" column, which hackers applied to their computers to watch a simulation of cells either die in isolated or overcrowded conditions or thrive and reproduce. Scott Draves's *Electric Sheep* (United States, 1999–present; www.electricsheep.org/) is a popular open-source screen-saver that can be downloaded on most computers. Flame algorithms can be data-clustering and fractal algorithms that produce two-dimensional images according to non-linear functions, log-density display, and structural coloring.[70] Moreover, the very materials that make physical computing possible are vibrant matter that potentially alters not only our brain but also our bodily chemistry. They affect chemical and physical aspects of humans who activate these automated processes in their interactions with AI.

By analyzing more than 130 projects, this book looks at collaborative projects between artists, activists, coders, designers, students, and intellectuals—in some cases working remotely—as well as ones by people who migrate from place to place for both voluntary and involuntary reasons. We need to engage an approach to thinking through digital media and digital networks that acknowledges our precarious position as formerly privileged coders and decoders—anthropocentric codecs, so to speak—of meaning precisely because digital media and digital networks themselves think and produce meaning. At the same time, we need to consider the effects on the planet by modern progress initiated by humans to assume responsibility for climate change and species extinction. We examine media that engages with digitality and networks as forms, subjects, structures, and modes of media practice. Rather than a comprehensive survey that purports to include everything or a general introduction that purports to include a representational sample of everything, we focus on projects that are deeply embedded in their historical moment of structural integration and inequality exasperated by globalization and an unwillingness to acknowledge the Anthropocene. The projects are overtly political, working from the assumption that non-political projects are often undeclared conservative ones since one seldom has to advocate for the political position of the status quo.[71] These projects prompt critical dialogues on militarized borders, interactivity as surveillance, rapidly accelerating disparity among populations in terms of wealth, power, and basic human rights such as food, lodging, water, and access to technology.

Each of our book's five chapters offers a different conceptual lens through which to locate and analyze digital media. The book situates digital media within the context of media history and theory to demonstrate how these projects actually continue traditions of documentary to document the real and create expository argumentation. It engages traditions of experimental film to experiment with the material and discursive realities of media. It imbricates traditions of narrative to narrate stories that might guide us toward more nuanced understandings of the worlds of experience that are not necessarily our own. And it mobilizes traditions of interactive media to interact with us by eliciting responses through play and provocation. At the same time, the book also expands thinking about analogue media practices in significant ways by speculating and improvising provisional solutions to questions of representation, audience, engagement, ethics, and collaboration.

Taking Things Apart to Convene Micropublics

Thinking through digital media highlights collaborative and participatory aspects of media practice to convene critical micropublics, yet
it also highlights the potential for control and surveillance. One of the
primary objectives of the hacker ethos of "taking things apart" is to
understand the invisible and inaudible aspects of digital media as well
as the larger networks that shape social interactions and productions
of knowledge along with state and corporate structures that seek to
contain them. Hacking and pirating draw upon Marxist theories
about the materiality of media as well as the political economies of its
production, circulation, and meaning. Walter Benjamin and Siegfried
Kracauer, for example, theorized photographic and cinematographic
possibilities like the close-up and slow motion that could reveal what
the human eye, trained by conventions of everyday life, overlooks.
Benjamin hoped that "the work of art" would counter the rise of fas-
cism; Kracauer believed film could bring about the "redemption of
physical reality."[1] Hacking and pirating offer comparable strategies
to make visible—in this case, propiatary locks on creativy and innovation. Transnational corporations, such as Apple, market and promote a discourse of do-it-yourself (DIY) that suggests that anyone and
everyone can control the means of both production and distribution.
These economies of desire have changed little since the era of classical
cinema when Benjamin and Kracauer wrote with the surplus meaning
of fan magazines that promised to reveal secrets behind Hollywood's
invisible style. At the same time, these corporations enforce copyright
in ways that can stifle creativity and innovation. Although maligned
in commercial media, especially Hollywood films, hacking and pirating engage democratic potentials of digital media and networks.
  Steven Levy defines a hacker ethic as (1) an unlimited and total
access to computers with a imperative of "taking things apart, seeing

how they work, and using this knowledge to create new and even more interesting things"; (2) a free exchange of information, particularly in the form of computer programs, for "overall greater creativity"; (3) a decentralized and open system that avoids bureaucracy since it "cannot accommodate the exploratory impulse of true hackers"; (4) an acceptance into a hacking community based on hacking rather than "superficial criteria" or "bogus criteria such as [academic] degrees, age, race, or position"; (5) a creation of things of art and beauty with the conviction that "the code of the program held a beauty of its own"; and (6) a belief that "computers can change your life for the better."[2] Applied to digital media, a hacker ethic strives toward social good through critical thinking. It takes apart the invisible technologies and seamless networks of power. It pirates software and mods hardware. In the context of transnational environments and locative places, hacking and pirating suggest a radical interdisciplinarity. As we inherit global crises from the limitations of disciplinary and disciplined thinking, hacking and pirating offer the possibility of interdisciplinary solutions. In part, the solution lies in recognizing our complicity. Much like hackers engage in taking things like software apart, artists, coders, activists, students, and intellectuals engage in taking things like ideas apart in locative media, video mashups, and computer games that implicate audiences as participants.

The hacker ethic of exploration and free sharing emerged across the Internet in bulletin board systems (BBSs), news groups, listservs, forums, multi-user dungeon/dimension (MUDs), multi-user object oriented environment (MOOs), and other virtual communities. Despite setbacks of the Digital Millennium Copyright Act in 1998, the dotcom bust in 2001, and the War on Terror in 2003 in the United States alone, digital media adopted different permutations of these forms from e-mail projects and websites that utilized primarily hypertext to networked installations and streamed audio or video from webcams. With the accelerated development of new technologies and concurrent accelerated antiquation of these technologies, web-based art refashions itself as browser art, software art, spam art, click environments, code poetry, generative art, and art hactivism, intersecting with mashups, machinima, and clip and GIF culture. In particular, increased bandwidth and data compression (source encoding) capacities have permitted artists and users greater options. Newer applications like graphical user interface (GUI), vector-graphics programs such as Flash, high-resolution animation, plug-ins, algorithmic "smart automation," and interactivity to websites offer a vast aesthetic improvement over hypertext and raster-graphics (bitmap) programs. The digital media projects analyzed in this chapter—locative media, video mashups, computer games—*take things apart*. They hack and pirate. Neither do they merely take images apart to excavate obscured meaning nor intervene into discourse. Instead, they are public actions into and around constructions and artifice.[3] In their practices, no object, machine, or concept is unified and unassailable. Artists, coders, intellectuals, students, and activists collaborate and implicate audiences. They unscrew backs of smartphones, modify chips and software, reroute and mashup apps, and interface with digital printers. These projects also migrate: they move relentlessly between analogue and digital, between the lived and the imagined. They migrate across and through different social spaces beyond theaters, and multiplexes, and the private spaces of television and game consoles. Also, they operate within and around micropublic zones such as kiosks, storefronts, community centers, galleries, festivals, fairs, clubs, and schools. These projects revise debates in animation, documentary, experimental, interactive, and narrative media concerning oppositional political practices.[4] These projects function as utopian and aspirational sites rather than as discourses of sobriety, operating in the hypothetical realms of "what if" rather than the more empirical documentary realm of "it was."[5]

As mashups and locative media combine with migratory archives, digital media projects open up zones for ongoing contestations and speculations about labor, the environment, and political histories. These projects move beyond images that attempt to fix meaning into much more fluid, mobile environments. Locative media practices, for example, use mobile digital technologies to map and interact with material spaces. They are iterative, mutating, provisional, and adaptive, functioning within quite a different mode than analogue media.[6] Their structuring of interactions and convening of micropublics is more salient than how they create images. Locative media practices shift the terms of animation, documentary, experimental, interactive, and narrative media production. They move from images to interfaces, from refined arguments to contestations and speculations.[7] Part of the new heterogeneous transnational media ecology, locative media expands on legacies of Fluxus and participatory art which foregrounded the assemblage of transitory publics.[8] However, locative media extends these practices by probing the interstitial zones between invisible, ubiquitous technologies, imbedded networks of control, the materiality of digital machines, and the necessity of embodied inter-action.[9] Locative media counters the immateriality of virtualization and the privatization of miniaturized handheld technologies. Mashups and locative media explore the production of social spaces beyond the image as a fixed text. They are not products or films, but nodal points for engagements, relationships, convivialities, conversations, mobilities, conjurings, and potentialities. They are unresolved, inconclusive, shape shifting, and adaptive. Some projects rework technologies that are widely available and controlled by corporations like GoogleMaps's fly-through function; others operate outside the locked-down system of corporate control through BitTorrent. By appropriating technologies, artists and collaborative groups create tactical media that elicit reflection upon the images and interfaces of everyday consumption and technologies. These projects share common structural and operational characteristics of this newly emerging digital media ecology.[10] They all foreground digitally networked technologies to remap temporal and spatial relationships. They mobilize experimentation as a critical engagement. They question location and mapping. They produce the archive and new conceptions of artifacts, rejecting the authority of previously established archives. They enact collaborative and participatory practices to generate micropublics, reconfiguring relationships between artists and audience.[11] They trouble the divide between analogue and digital, material and virtual. We do not suggest that these emerging animation, documentary, experimental, interactive, and narrative modalities replace their legacy analogue forms. Rather, we argue that they open up the legacy analogue modes to reappraisal and revision.

We offer examples that demonstrate some of the multitude of ways that digital media, particularly mashups and locative media, extends and challenges the politics of animation, documentary, experimental, interactive, and narrative media. Artists and collectives working with P2P file-sharing, mobile technologies, and migratory archives activate political engagements, microgeographies, and interventionist cartographies to probe the politics of terror and location of global sustainability.[12] Locative media and migratory archives conceive of their publics differently than analogue media. Rather than speaking about, to, with, or alongside their public, they deploy networked technologies to convene provisional and transitory micropublics. Their design imbeds collaborative processes. Some projects do not exist without enactment and engagement.

In live performances and real-time actions, locative media and migratory archives practices disturb, dislodge, and redesign digital technologies we use everyday, like bar codes on passports and chocolate bars, RFID tags used for antitheft devices in stores and for toll-collection on highways, GPS satellites and receivers, vector graphics in computer and video games, WLAN technologies, SMS communication, and cellular telephone networks. These various digital media practices reposition highly specialized technologies within the democratic discourse of amateurism, which refutes technology as inaccessible and too complicated. The emerging locative media and migratory archives movement has accelerated with legislations like the United States' Uniting and Strengthening America by Providing Appropriate Tools Required to Intercept and Obstruct Terrorism (USA PATRIOT) Act in 2001 and India's Prevention of Terrorism Act (PoTA) in 2002, which authorize unprecedented data mining, invasions of privacy, wiretapping, and Internet surveillance. Mashups and locative media focus on enactments rather than representations, conjuring provisional micropublics in public spaces. They invent new kinds of performative systems that open up liminal zones between digital and analogue, virtual and material, embodied and disembodied, game and reality, body and interface, history and mapping. Thinking through digital media provokes debate about the functions and power of technologies.[13] They *take apart* our assumptions and expectations.

Programming Video Mashups

Digital media is often interested in presenting—making anew through selection, recombination, and automation—more than it is interested in representing. It is simultaneously computational and representational. Computers "represent" in the playback based on various computations. In this sense, the video mashup might be called a quintessential digital form. Video mashups make apparent differences between analogue media's faith in *information* in contrast to digital media's manipulation of *data*. They remediate. They are disinterested in the direct (or indexical) relationships between mediation and the world in the pictorial (or iconic) possibilities through duplicating and manipulating information at the level of data. They take apart the binary structures of digital data and the ways that they operate and circulate. More than a structuring of visual meaning by disrupting conventions of linearity or causality, as in the work of the historical avant-garde or in Sergei Eisenstein's analytical montage, digital video mashups can access the automation of programming that restructures meaning as modular and multilayered. Video mashups weave new meaning between data and metadata, evoking Manovich's description of the computer as a combination of Joseph-Marie Jacquard's loom (c. 1801) that wove complex patterns mechanically via punched cards and Konrad Zuse's Z4 computer (c. 1945) that discarded iconic coding of cinema for the binary coding of numbers, as in Plankalkül (literally, "calculus plan") language.[14]

Torry Mendoza's *Kemosabe version 1.0* (United States, 2007; http://vimeo.com/474215) politicizes video mashups. It situates black-and-white images of the Lone Ranger and Tonto from the long-running television series, *The Lone Ranger* (United States, 1949–1957; cr. George W. Trendle and Fran Striker), to unpack the racial logic of classical television and cinema in the United States. The clarity of race and the linearity of racial distinctions disintegrate, as once-offensive images are appropriated and prepared for cultural critique. The short video disrupts the colonial racial logic of the so-called American Frontier by recalibrating the relationship between Tonto and the Lone Ranger. Through syncopated beats of dialogue and music, Mendoza reworks an offensive stereotype of Native Americans whose history in US cultural production begins with the dime novels of Zane Grey and continues through radio shows, comic books, serial movies, television series, sports mascots, and the branding of consumer products like Land O Lakes butter and Jeep Cherokee SUVs. Here, the ambiguous meaning of "kemosabe," Tonto's name for the Lone Ranger, foregrounds the productive possibilities for repurposing the toxins of colonialism's cultural artifacts.

The video begins with looped footage of Tonto (Jay Silverheels) who offers to help the Lone Ranger (Clayton Moore). Mendoza contrasts Tonto's stilted English-as-a-Second-Language ("me help you fight outlaw") with the Lone Ranger's oddly delivered line ("I...am...a lone ranger"). He flashes the black-and-white narrative with a color bar, signaling that attention is required to align representation with reality. Frequently captured in a high-angle shot, Tonto explains his existence to serve the Lone Ranger. Like other allegedly sympathetic racial stereotypes for minoritized groups in the United States, such as African American Mammies, Tonto has no family of his own—no obligations to anyone, even himself, apart for supporting the white-male hero. As the Lone Ranger explains he has "a plan," Mendoza interrupts him, the flashing black screens with words like "colonization," "manifest destiny," and "westward expansion," "forces assimilation," and "genocide." The Lone Ranger's plans are taken apart, hacked, pirated, and thus presented as menacing rather than heroic, as calculated rather than ordained. The video reassembles found footage, taking apart the normalized, treasured, and commemorated as classic racial stratifications on popular television. In contrast to Hollywood's proprietary practices, Mendoza makes the video available for free on Vimeo.

Other artists question the potential for digitization to alter our understanding of classical cinema and television in other ways, particularly the indexical evidence of reality left as a visible trace on celluloid. In Jean-Luc Godard's *Le Petit soldat* (France, 1960), the character Bruno Forestier (Michel Subor) asserts that photography is truth and that cinema is truth at 24 frames per second (24fps), that is, the standard speed of 35mm sound film. *Le Petit soldat* was banned in France for its truthfulness about French ambivalence over Algeria's War for Independence (1954–1962). The character of Forestier (again portrayed by Subor) appears again on screen in Claire Denis's *Beau travail* (France, 1999), a critique on ongoing French colonialism in Africa. Screening *Le Petit soldat* on DVD today, Bruno's truth becomes radically altered as digital compression replaces fully resolved photographic images with algorithms generating mostly unresolved frames. What really happens, then, when celluloid's 24fps is digitally rendered for 29.976fps? *Lossless* by Rebecca Baron and Doug Goodwin situates experimental and commercial films within digital media ecologies. They use custom software to control film's dematerialization as it is compressed for storage on DVDs and streaming online. Initially exhibited as an installation, Baron and Goodwin's experiments with digital performances of film consider faith in indexicality in a culture of mobile screens and P2P networks.[15]

Lossless emerged from Baron and Goodwin's interest in comparing celluloid images with digital renderings of them. Familiar with the loss of fidelity when 16mm experimental films are copied onto VHS, they assumed that MPEG-2s comparably impoverish images. This assumption was partially challenged when they downloaded high-quality digital renderings of 16mm films via file sharing and compared images from an ultra-resolution DVD of *The Wizard of Oz* (United States, 1939; dir. Victor Flemming) with a 35mm print. Fidelity between celluloid and MPEGs proved less interesting than differences. "Abandon the idea that one type of compression is better than another," they write in the exhibition's wiki, "and you may start to appreciate the qualities of this compression in its own right."[16] They developed the concept for *Lossless* by thinking through and with digital media. Programmers developed codecs (*compressor-dec*ompressors or *coder-dec*oders) to compress data onto compact discs and then decompress it as a video stream. Lossless codecs preserve entire audiovisual spectrum in files requiring as many as 400 discs. Lossy codecs discard data considered undetectable to human eyes and ears, including variations in luminance and chrominance, and variations in ranges within the audio spectrum, through color reduction and wavelength simplification. Run-length encoding (RLE) compresses information for individual pixels whose color signal does not change over time. Frames are reconstituted only during playback, a live performance of decoding of digital data into an analogue signal.

Lossless #1 (United States, 2007) reconsiders the materiality of film through the immateriality—or, more accurately, new materiality—of digital code. The only celluloid object in the series, the 16mm film loop, shows Dorothy Gale (Judy Garland) endlessly clicking her ruby slippers but going nowhere. Rendered by software that compares celluloid frames and digital renderings, the images appear to flicker on a pane of glass, roughly the size of a laptop screen. The flickering of ruby slippers mimics the flicker effect in early cinema before technicians developed multibladed rotating shutters to facilitate afterimages on the retina that generate illusions of continuous movement. The experiment encouraged Baron and Goodwin to understand film, whether celluloid or MPEG, as *performance*. Although we assume that DVDs playback video and audio without variation each time we hit play, Baron and Goodwin's experiments reveal ways in which micro-differences between each digital performance might be developed to take apart our expectations for a seamless, invisible relationship between data and metadata in playback.

Once rarified objects, digitized versions of experimental films are widely available for download, where they mingle with commercial blockbusters ripped from rented or pirated DVDs. The digitization of film, however, does not consign the avant-garde to the realm of clip culture and amateur mashups. Downloaded at controlled intervals, Maya Deren's anti-Hollywood experimental film *Meshes of the Afternoon* (United States, 1943) is rendered as a digital performance in *Lossless #2* (United States, 2008). Artifacts from the file-sharing protocol leave empty spaces within the frame that algorithms seek to complete, resulting in a digital mashing—or, to evoke the original film's themes, digital "meshing"—of images that dissolve and resolve on the screen of an iPod embedded into the gallery wall. *Lossless #2* reworks pirated digital copies of Deren's film, downloading MPEG-2 files through open-source P2P protocols of BitTorrent at controlled intervals. The algorithms and codecs fill in missing parts of the visual images. Visual images download randomly rather than sequentially, so that algorithms anticipate the color signals of pixels, resulting in new "meshes" in this digital performance.

Other videos in the series take apart assumptions about the seamless performance of metadata in lossy compression. In *Lossless #4* (United States, 2008), Baron and Goodwin remove the photographic image and substitute white arrows on a black background, which visually represent the digital instructions of where to move blocks of color. Their source material is Ernie Gehr's structuralist film *Serene Velocity* (United States, 1970), which rhythmically intercuts a long shot and a close-up, both taken down the same corridor, so that the image appears to zoom in and out. By removing fully resolved I-frames—digital equivalents to keyframes—from an MPEG-2 of *The Searchers* (United States, 1956; dir. John Ford), the algorithms for intermediate frames anticipate the color of pixels within each frame in an attempt to connect them into clean images. The film's iconic long shots of Ford's cowboys are rendered as a human and animal sludge, unfurling across the majestic landscape of Monument Valley, which, since it is rendered by RLE, is pulled apart in graphic blocks by the passing movement in *Lossless #3* (United States, 2008).

Figure 1.1   *Lossless #3.*

The video, thus, disrupts the absolute certainty of the film's colonial logic, embodied in Ethan Edwards (John Wayne), whose violent racism and misogyny erupts in an enraged search to murder his niece Debbie (Nathalie Wood), held "captive" by Native Americans. Ideological certainty collapses upon itself when the l-frames are removed, destabilizing the markers upon which much of the visual regime of colonial racism hinges. Horses, humans, and different races become indistinguishable. The searchers of the film's title are rendered as unresolved images in search of resolution within the next frame. The video also visualizes the environmental destruction of the US colonial discourse of Manifest Destiny to conquer and civilize "untamed" peoples and "wild" lands. The soundtrack reinforces this revolving uncertainty. *Lossless #5* (United States, 2008) intervenes into another of classical Hollywood's unsavory yet chaste moments by revealing the fetishism with Busby Berkeley's gendered choreography, generating serpentine images for new fetishisms.

These digital performances of classical Hollywood and experimental film become acts of reverse engineering upon sound cinema's truth at 24fps. If Benjamin theorized the work of art in the age of mechanical reproducibility, then digital technologies have made the concept of reproducibility—and its attendant questions of originality, fidelity, and authenticity—less relevant. Master negatives cannot be cloned, but they can be digitized. Lossless copies are theoretically perfect clones of master copies, bypassing the generational signal loss of mechanical reproductions in analogue formats. Reproducing art gives way to rendering media. The *Lossless* series make an important intervention that situates aphorisms such as Godard's within the materiality and immateriality of technologies.

Jeff Crouse, Stephanie Rothenberg, and Michael Schieben's *Laborers of Love* (LOL) (United States/Germany, 2013; http://laborersoflove.com/) invites audiences to become participants in directing video mashups of found sounds and images. The project hopes to encourage participants to recognize their own participation in structural inequalities through the convenience of online shopping. Offering users the ability to purchase videos customized for individual fantasies and desires, *LOL* examines how a crowdsourcing application can transform a diverse group of freelancers working from their home computers into producers of pornography. *LOL* extends Rothenberg and Crouse's previous collaboration in *Invisible Threads*, discussed below, which invited live audiences to become participants by ordering custom-made designer jeans that would partly be produced in a virtual sweatshop located in the social-networking environment of Second Life (SL). *Invisible Threads* disrupts assumptions about the seamlessness of online shopping and the invisibility of sweatshop labor by foregrounding the transmission and production of collaborative experiences. *LOL* makes a provocative critique of our potential complicity with the adult-entertainment industry. It uses the very technologies that the industry lobbied to have funded by state governments, such as an infrastructure with wider bandwidth to allow high-speed connection for streaming video in the United States. More significantly, *LOL* critiques our complicity with major online vendors such as Amazon, which now has portals in Australia, Brazil, Canada, China, India, France, Germany, Japan, México, Spain, the United Kingdom, and the United States.

Amazon's business model of growth through positive customer experience and efficiency is maintained by promoting productivity goals for its pickers, packers, movers, and unloaders, as they prepare products for shipping in warehouses. Due to uneven sales volumes, many are on-demand workers—temps paid less and fired at will, earning Amazon a reputation of fulfilling customer orders with "warehouse slaves."[17] *LOL* allows customers to purchase customized fantasies in the form of videos produced through crowdsourcing, that is, soliciting on-demand labor from a pool of anonymous workers. Specifically, *LOL* uses Amazon's Mechanical Turk (MTurk), a platform for "e-lance" (electronic freelance) for the micro-task market. Requesters (task creators) hire anonymous Workers (paid task completers) to complete "human intelligence tasks" (HITs) not presently possible through digital automation.[18] Requesters pay by credit card. Amazon keeps 10 percent. Workers are paid through Amazon gift certificates for simple tasks "still requiring human intelligence." Crowdsourcing tasks like translating texts or checking websites for duplicate pages become "artificial artificial intelligence." For Crouse, Rothenberg, and Schieben, the idea of customizing pornography is one such task. LOL. Laugh out loud.

Aaron Koblin's *The Sheep Market* (United States, 2006; www.thesheepmarket.com/) was one of the earliest digital media projects to consider MTurk by crowdsourcing the drawing "a sheep facing left." Users select individual drawings with their cursor from a collection of ten thousand drawn by MTurk workers. Koblin's project "makes no claims to participatory art." It sells "blocks of sheep drawings for [USD]20 as adhesive stamps with certificates of authenticity," as Christiane Paul observes.[19] With *LOL*, users choose on a continuum between speed and accuracy for their videos, adding description of three sources and selecting cut frequency and glitches. When the video is complete, an e-mail link and password is sent. Unlike the high-resolution video on for-profit pornography sites, *LOL* delivers low-resolution mashups whose metadata contains errors that cause glitches. The result is even more disruptive of expectations than Naomi Uman's *Removed* (México/United States, 1999), a feminist experimental film that bleached images of nude women from actual pornographic films. If pornography aimed at straight men convention-ally relies on the spectacle of an orgasmic female body, then Uman's milky-colored erasure of the female body rejects such codes of visual pleasure. *LOL*'s gallery includes examples more likely to amuse than arouse. By removing l-frames, the algorithms that generate interme-diate frames no longer can anticipate the intended colors for pixels, causing objects to morph in unexpected ways. Rather than clean con-nections, they produce dirty ones, degenerating conventional repre-sentations of sexual acts into abstracted, almost nonrepresentational, images. The movements of sexual acts are interrupted as bodies disin-tegrate into a colorful sludge. *LOL*'s satire is not directed at consumer entitlement to personalized high-quality adult entertainment at low price; rather, it satirizes crowdsourcing. Like the slacktivism of sign-ing online petitions or tweeting hastags, crowdsourcing micro-tasks hardly counters globalization's structural inequalities. With its satiri-cal tagline—"Stimulate yourself while stimulating the global econ-omy," *LOL* asks us to consider the everyday ways that we contribute to the exploitation of informal labor, using the mashup as a means of thinking through digital media.

Unplaying Competition unto Death

If hacking and piracy are ways to make software more useful to potential users from nondominant groups, then they can also offer a way for video games to convene micropublics through interactive and ludic means to consider nondominant points of view. Chapter 4 examines counter-gaming in more detail. In this section, we analyze a few projects that prompt critical reflection on the normalization of competition within transnational environments. Whether in trade or war, a discourse of winner and losers pervades dominant under-standings of our transnational connections. Analyzing the US Army's *America's Army* (United States, 2002) and Linden Lab's *Second Life* (United States, 2003), two "free" online games, Nick Dyer-Witheford and Greig de Peuter argue that video games recruit users into mili-tarism and capitalism through processes of "militainment" and "ludocapitalism."[20] Video games are generally premised on a logic of competition—often unto the death of the player's opponents, whether humans or bots. As a result, gameplay strategies and actions can become sites to take things apart. Hye Young Kim and Tohm Judson's *Bomberman 2014* (South Korea/United States, 2013; http://tohmjudson.com/gamedesigns/BOMBERMAN2014/BOMBERMAN2014.html) reworks a popular computer game from the 1980s by updating the implications of its gameplay for the 2010s around the place of urban bombings. The film *La Battaglia di Algeri/The Battle of Algiers* (Algeria/Italy, 1966; dir. Gillo Pontecorvo) serves as a benchmark for such representations. In the anticolonial struggle, three Algerian women place bombs in cafés and stores, where "innocent" *pieds noirs* (French "settlers") enjoy the fruits of colonialism. The film's ambivalence with regard to the murder of noncombatants offers a useful framework for understanding the role of violence in gameplay. More recent films such as *The Terrorist* (India, 1998; dir. Santosh Sivan) and *Paradise Now* (Palestine/France/Germany/Netherlands/Israel, 2005; dir. Hany Abu-Assad) shift bombing to suicide bombing among populations lacking access to drones, missiles, or shields. *Bomberman 2014* asks players to consider whether winning wars of terror are victories. Inspired by Hudson Soft's popular *Bomberman* (Japan, 1983), a strategic maze game where players kill their competitors and destroy obstacles with bombs to level-up and win, *Bomberman 2014* prompts players to reflect critically upon the act of bombing: in other words, it pushes the user to unthink the logic of killing people for points.

Whereas *Bomberman*'s original iteration was set in an anonymous maze of Planet Bomber, *Bomberman 2014* uses recognizable locations where bombers have destroyed property and injured and killed human and nonhuman life: Oklahoma City in 1995, Madrid in 2004, London in 2005, Mumbai in 2008, Boston in 2013. Like the original video game, players move their avatar using the arrow keys on their keyboard, evoking the pre–game-console era. The 2D bitmapped graphics are rendered in black, gray, white, blue, and green. By pressing the T-key, players can communicate with the other characters with statements ("goooodd aafftteerrnnooooonn") and questions ("have you seen my cat?") that appear in bitmap fonts inside pop-up bubbles. By pressing the space key, players detonate their bomb, causing the playing field to break into fragments, which turn yellow, white, and brown, to convey fire, and eventually fall away and disintegrate. A score then itemizes death and injury statistics. The report also includes the message: "You died." The simple contrast of cool-toned and warm-toned colors conveys the difference between civil society and civil war. It also points to the uncomfortable proximity of civil society's silence on covert wars during which drones and missiles often kill more civilians than suspected combatants in Afghanistan, Palestine, Pakistan, and Yemen. Unlike commercial video games, players have only one bomb and only one life, leaving them with the decision to injure and kill innocent bystanders or warn them of the impending explosion. Also, unlike the original *Bomberman*, the player's avatar is a civilian who blends into the other characters. Moreover, there is no danger of an opponent igniting a bomb first. Unsettling the typical convention of winning by amassing the largest number of points, *Bomberman 2014* proposes that winning might come through losing the game by conventional expectations, that is, by injuring and killing the fewest number of people by strategically situating one's icon. The video game takes apart assumptions.

Available in nine European languages, including Turkish, Molleindustria's *McDonald's Video Game* (Italy, 2006; www.mcvideogame. com/) invites players to "discover all the dirty secrets that made us one of the biggest companies of the world." The game is a satirical critique of corporate branding at the expense of sustainable business practices and global ethics. It requires players to negotiate between four sectors: an "agricultural section," where rainforests and villages are razed to make fields for growing soy and grazing cattle; a "feedlot," where cattle are both fed and slaughtered; "fast food," where employees serve customers; and "headquarters," where the board of directors, marketing department, and public relations office make decisions. The goal is to keep the corporation solvent despite everyday problems like news-making protests from antiglobalization groups over colonization of land, diseased cows resulting from industrial waste and hormones mixed into their fodder, public-health epidemics caused by genetically modified organisms (GMOs) and pesticides, and diseased animal carcasses being processed into food—all of which can affect public image of "the brand." The game's bright colors, simple graphics, and ambient sound effects evoke the childlike innocence of transnational corporations like McDonald's that use saturated promotional and advertising campaigns to addict children to their products. As the game's home screen makes clear: "Behind every sandwich there is a complex process you must learn to manage: from the creation of pastures to the slaughter, from the restaurant management to the branding." In most cases, users bankrupt the corporation within minutes.

If the satire has been missed through the tutorial or through game-play, the game includes a "why this game" page with a message from Ronald McDonald, the trademark red-haired clown and corporate mascot:

> For decades McDonald's corporation has been heavily criticized for his negative impact on society and environment.
> There are inevitably some glitches in our activity: rainforest destruction, livelihood losses in the third world, desertification, precarization [sic] of working conditions, food poisoning and so on...
> Denying all these well founded accusations would be impossible so we decided to create an online game to explain to young people that this is the price to pay in order to preserve our lifestyle.
> We'll continue on our way, with our well-known determination. Join us and have fun with us![21]

The satirical text draws upon the provincial chauvinisms fueling the wars on terror as means of defending against threats to a "way of life." Like culture jammer's educational pranks, such as the launch of gatt.org site by The Yes Men to critique the World Trade Organization (WTO)'s policies of structural inequality, discussed below, the page surprises by appearing to speak on behalf of the corporation in an uncharacteristically honest way. By claiming to indoctrinate children into corporate culture through a video game rather than deny such accusations, the page satirizes McDonald's actual marketing and promotional tactics aimed at children—specially designed Happy Meals with plastic toys, franchise restaurant playgrounds, and public school cafeteria kiosks. The page includes hyperlinked images of popular books that criticize the fast-food industry's complicity of the economic and environmental disaster, such as Jeremy Rifkin's *Beyond Beef* (1993), Naomi Klein's *No Logo: No Space, No Choice, No Jobs* (1999), and Eric Schlosser's *Fast Food Nation: The Dark Side of the All-American Meal* (2002). It also links to Morgan Spurlock's documentary on overeating McDonald's food, *Supersize Me* (United States, 2004). If video games can lure children into consuming fast food, then Molleindustria's game attempts to redirect them to healthier, more environmentally sustainable eating habits.

Performed at the artist collaborative C-Level Lab in Los Angeles' Chinatown on 19 May 2001, Eddo Stern and Mark Allen's *Tekken Torture Tournament* (United States, 2001) "converts virtual damage into bracing, but non-lethal electric shock" in a modified PlayStation, running Namco's martial-arts fighting game *TEKKEN*

3 (Japan, 1997).[22] The project prompts thinking about "untapped public aggression" and "painful electric shock." It also enhances the haptic-feedback experience of playing a console game and unsettles any immersion into gameplay through role-playing. *Tekken Torture Tournament* offers insights into the mental work of mediation. However, it rejects privileging mimetic realism in order to take apart the disembodied role-playing inherent in commercial video games. Receiving a nonlethal electric shock in the arm is a different kind of pain than receiving a roundhouse kick or side kick to the side or head. Stern is interested in simulation rather than realism, rerouting the kinetic visuals of fight games and films. The invocation of torture evokes the use of "enhanced interrogation" by the United States in its rendition centers across the globe, practices by which Israel encourages arrested Palestinians to become informants, and other human-rights violations by self-defined democracies in the name of security. The performance asks us to rethink the use of violence in the name of preventing violence. Like *Bomberman 2014* and *McDonald's Video Game*, the performance ask us to consider ways we are complicit with violence elsewhere, including dispossession and chronic malnutrition.

Pirating for Social Good

Piracy is criminalized in many parts of the world. However, it is prosecuted irregularly, in part due to ways that digital media lends itself to copying despite encryption layers. Since the 1980s, video and software pirates have flourished in postcolonial African, Asian, and Latin American global media cities. As Ravi Sundaram argues, these cities form informal and nonlinear networks that refuse "mandates of legal control."[23] He notes commercial distributors dump unsold CDs and DVDs into the pirated market in India in an effort to cash in on overproduction of unpopular or overpriced products. Brian Larkin observes an opposite direction in Nigeria, where video pirates become distributors of legal material.[24] Piracy includes immaterial goods, such as software, music, and films, and urban infrastructure of the electric grid and road system. Piracy becomes "a significant resource for subaltern populations unable to enter the legal world" in what he calls "creative 'corruption,'" "a giant difference engine."[25] For Sundaram, piracy is recycling, concerned with variation and recombination rather than duplication.[26] It thrives through easy replication and adaptation, innovation and proliferation. Neither alterity nor resistance, Sundaram posits "piracy disrupts capitalist control, but does so in a property regime that has little space for it."[27] Rather than the legible grid of the modernist city, he looks to the bazaar of the old city as the location for pirate modernity, unsettling assumptions of modernity's utopianism and augmenting its pragmatism.[28] Piracy, he notes, "does not seem to fit received models of creativity and innovation" but is part of "the favored language of global fear."[29] He situates piracy within the "endless imitative frenzy" of "media companies copying each other."[30] Piracy is a form of taking things apart: it recalibrates knowledge production in globally aware ways.

Produced through a collaboration between Jeebesh Bagchi, Monica Narula, and Shuddhabrata Sengupta of the Raqs Media Collective with Mrityunjay Chatterjee and Iram Ghufran at Sarai Media Lab in New Delhi, *Ectropy* (India, 2005) is a witty, topical hypertext work about surveillance, profiling, identity theft, biometrics, and violations of civil liberties within the paranoiac irrational space of ongoing global war. Ectropy suggests an increase in information or its organization in a system. In contrast, entropy describes a decrease. Ectropy also refers to a disease that manifests itself in eyelids that deteriorate, resulting in eyes that cannot close and often cannot see. *Ectrophy Index* (India, 2005; www.raqsmediacollective.net/ectropy. html) measures the tension between the entropic (systemic increases) and the ectropic (systemic decreases) within the current moment, particularly ways we inhabit virtual worlds of digital identities, biometrics, surveillance, identity theft, and data crashes. The project develops from the socially engaged artistic and intellectual practice of Raqs and Sarai. "We are keen to effect crossovers and transgressions that [...] give rise to a more layered and agile form of media practice that is more reflective of the contemporary in our spaces," explains Narula.[31] Sarai probes the epistemological ramifications of who has access to technologies, acknowledging that knowledge is produced online and off-line. Sarai contests power by facilitating a creative, informational commons.

Bagchi, Narula, and Sengupta formed Raqs in 1991/1992 after graduating from Jamia Milia Islamia University. Sometimes considered an acronym for "rarely asked questions" (a counterpart to frequently asked questions or FAQs on commercial websites), Raqs takes its name from the Hindi-Urdu, Arabic, and Persian word for dance that describes the state of a whirling dervish. Initially working in film and television, the collective began to create installations in collaboration with researchers at Sarai. These projects have been exhibited at prestigious international venues, such as *28°28' N / 77°15' E:: 2001–2002: An Installation on the Coordinates of Everyday Life in Delhi* (2002) at Documenta 11 in Kassel and *Five Pieces of Evidence* (2002) at the fifty-first Venice Biennale. Raqs cofounded Sarai Media Lab in 2000 with Ravi Vasudevan and Ravi Sundaram, launching it in 2001 at the Center for the Study of Developing Societies (CSDS). Sarai was conceived as a public meeting space where intellectuals could engage in creative interventions. Its name derives from *caravansarai*, a place where travelers could take shelter, find sustenance, and make companionships in Old Delhi, part of a wider network of sarais throughout medieval South Asia from Afghanistan, the Baluchistan desert, and the Tibetan plateau through Delhi to the Deccan peninsula in the south and the Irrawaddy basin in the east. They formed a vital communication network.[32] They are both "destinations and places of departure," Narula explains. The Sarai Media Lab becomes "a very public space where different intellectual, creative, and activist energies can intersect in an open and dynamic manner."[33] The word *sarai* is used in Hindi-Urdu, Punjabi, Bengali, Persian, and Turkish, suggesting a recovery of cultural commons.

Sarai is dedicated to imbedding new media practices within the longer histories of old media practices such as telegraphs, radio, and television through a project called Publics and Practices in the History of the Present (PPHP), which supports independent research and practice. The media lab published *Sarai Reader 01: The Public Domain* in 2001, with print and free download editions available.[34] It also awards micro-grants and manages several Reader-Lists as virtual communities for discussion. It distributes free and open-source software to dislodge "Microsoft's hegemony" and the arbitrary distinction between programmers and artists.[35] As Sengupta and Narula point out, Sarai postulates South Asian technoculture is not the exclusive domain of the cultural elite particularly native speakers of English. Instead, Sarai identifies "a creative, improvisational culture of 'making do,' adaptation, street-smart problem solving, creative mechanics and everyday inventiveness with recycling, and transformations of existing technologies to solve day-to-day urban problems."[36] With the ubiquity and low-cost access to the networks through cybercafés and mobile phones in both cities and villages, this technoculture includes e-mail, SMS, and instant messaging; informal P2P file sharing; and digital image processing and publishing. In particular, the use of shared computers informs the development of a different kind of technoculture than individual ownership of computers, suggesting how new media political economies have propelled a high degree of innovation from South Asia and Africa. A culture of "make do" (*jugadu*) solutions to real problems mobilize technoculture toward socially responsible and sustainable ends. Because this improvisation often transgresses laws, it can be considered part of Sundaram's "pirate modernity."

The Network of No_des (India, 2004) adopts the nodal structure of a rhizome that splits into fractal systems and is composed of memes. The project was conceived and realized by Raqs with Mrityunjay Chatterjee and Iram Ghufran at Sarai Media Lab, working with researchers at PPHP. The interpretive hypertext collage draws upon the researchers' field notes along with found media material, that is, "driftwood from web searches, messages in data bottles, re-mixed fragments of Hindi and Bengali film scenes and research notes from Sarai's ongoing exploration of new media street culture in Delhi to present an array of associational possibilities."[37] Nodes are produced to connect this flotsam of data, weaving threads of information to make connections that might not otherwise seem apparent—"basements in Delhi to depots for migrants in Ellis Island, philosophers to comic book superheroes, lost and found notices to the drying up of a sea, food to forgery and death sentences to internet matrimonials."[38] The project reveals surprising detours: remixing, reediting, and repurposing become a kind of foraging "in the undergrowth of the information economy."[39] The title also makes references to "desi," a colloquial expression for South Asians, exploring the media practices of young South Asians in urban New Delhi, whose ecological and economical utilization of knowledge resources might be called piracy. Youth edit, copy, paste, and share lost-cost versions of high-value information, using backstreet CD burners and basement hard drives.

The significance of the project emerges from its challenge to the then-dominant North Atlantic discourses that saw digital technologies as a simple convergence of computing and communications, as Sengupta and Narula have argued in an article republished in *Isis International*, the online journal published by the feminist advocacy organization in Quezon City, Philippines, suggesting a South-to-South (S2S) flows of a pirate modernity.[40] This convergence culture, they point out, obscures the diverse knowledge-producing processes of computing and information-sharing processes of communication that diverge from "a global value-added cultural commodity that is transferable from one place to another." In other words, they are interested in locatizations of media practice that produce different kinds of knowledge than might have been intended by the inventors of particular proprietary digital technologies and systems. They work around the origins of India's antipiracy laws in the colonial Copyright Act of 1847, which "was partly motivated by the colonial government's need to monitor local print culture and to anticipate local dissent."[41] They take things apart, hack, and pirate—not only technologies but also networks of social bias sometimes naturalized in discourses of intellectual property. Assuming knowledge is created through the cultural practices of repurposing and reutilizing fragments from popular cinema, music, and posters, Sarai distributes free Hindi-language software to tech-savvy populations who lacked the English-language skills required during the early years of the Internet.

Working in collaboration with the Delhi-based NGO, Ankur: Society for Alternatives in Education, Sarai's Cybermohalla ("cyber-neighborhood" or "cyber-locality") Project is a space where underserved populations such as factory workers and school dropouts create digital and analogue media: animations, blogs, installations, performances, graphic novels, and bilingual books and magazines. Pramod Nayar has argued that Cybermohalla allows for "a move towards a postcolonial appropriation of cyberspace" that engages rather than represses heterogeneity, contestability and contingency "in the postcolonial context where the public space is not truly 'public' because disempowerment and processes" marginalize particular groups in what he terms "postcolonial subalternization"[42] He offers the example of a community-building project in which "practitioners" (participants) record everyday conversations in the streets, combining "the familiar and the banal" from tea shops and street barbers to local videowallas (gray-market video sellers) and public call offices/cybercafés to constitute what Sarai calls the "matrix of cultural and intellectual life of a neighborhood." In other words, Cybermohalla instructs underserved communities in thinking through digital media: making media becomes a means of conceiving identity and claiming a right to agency. It also serves as archive for the community, including a collection of mobile textual forms, such as stickers, postcards, and calendars.

As a project about digital storytelling, Cybermohalla's practitioners shape media narratives on the everyday heterogeneities that emerge through conversations and protests in Hindi, Hinglish, and English. It encourages openness to innovation and excitement, refuting the enclosures of technical training with its rules and regulations.

It differs not only from professional training at film schools like Marwah Studios in Noida Film City (near Delhi) and Whistling Woods International Institute of Film, Fashion, and Media in Mumbai, but also from typical programs for underserved populations that tend to emphasize practical skills such as word processing. In addition to low-end cameras and audio-recorders, practitioners enter the streets with notebooks to record ("scavenge") narratives, reflections, and descriptions of events that they will later share with others in ongoing conversation. The project trains in critical and technical skills. "It's not just the mainstream understanding of a link between technology and development, or between education and employment," explains Shveta, a former social worker, "but also the notion, a class-based bias of looking at certain peoples as culture deficits, waiting for a delivery system of ideas, words, concepts and skills, that invariably gets articulated under the garb of the language of 'lack' and 'empowerment.'"[43] The project reconfigures expectations based on imported models from India or elsewhere. "The processes are not determined by their ultimate purposes. Skills, forms and materials are not introduced into the labs with a fixed, predetermined purpose or instrumentality," she adds. "We're not working with or within a curriculum, or 'evolving' one." Cybermohalla unsettles the digital divide: Linux, as Nayar notes, has been indigenized as IndLinux.[44]

While organizations like Sarai work to educate underserved populations so that they can become practitioners and write their own stories, artists such as Owen Mundy and Ben Grosser work to educate overserved populations. The education, however, differs. Rather than workshops, these artists design apps. The difference in part reflects uneven and unequal access to digital technologies and the Internet. Cybercafés are inexpensive in most parts of India, but they still remain out of reach for many populations. On the other side of the digital divides, populations live their lives online as part of what has been called the "digital generation." The battles between social-networking platforms, which saw the demise of early iterations of Friendster and MySpace, can seem cartoonish due to the frivolous assumptions about what the platforms offered—gifts of stickers in the early days, "likes" today. These battles demonstrate ways that social media developed into a means of outsourcing information-gathering to customers, whose digital profiles become a valuable commodity for marketing and advertising. Like online shopping, social networking is a means of giving personal data to corporations, which can tag and sort this data for resale. Every post, every comment, every "follow," every "share," and every "like" manifests a digital identity over which users have little control. By integrating communications apps, such as e-mail and SMS, into social networking, platforms like Facebook become places to store purportedly private information. Mundy's *Give Me My Data* (United States, 2010; http://www.give-memydata.com) is a Facebook app that allows users to export their data from the social-networking site into various text editors. The free app's logo reworks the design and style of the Facebook logo. Rather than a white lower-case *f* on the blue field, whose branches might be said to visualize the dispersal through social plugins of user's data in multiple directions from their source at the bottom, the *Give Me My Data* application uses a white arrow that turns back to the user. Platforms like Facebook encourage users to share information about themselves with their "friends" and "followers." Information may seem innocuous, such as favorite music and movies, but this and other information is valuable in more immediately recognizable ways than date of birth and place of work. Music and movie preferences are monetized in targeted advertising. Facebook followed the model of Twitter by enhancing the newsfeed application, so that the site also becomes a place to gather information on what users read and how they share articles and blogs posts with one another, particularly where editorial comments such as "sigh" or "hurrah," suggest an interpretation of the article or post. The feed has also amplified the appearance of links to "quizzes" that promise to diagnose users according to seemingly meaningless rubrics—"what is your spirit animal?" or "how New York are you?" or "what 1970s sitcom best describes you?" These links can gather data on behavior and taste for "instant personalization" of marketing of goods and services.

Give Me My Data offers users a tool to see, if not claim, their data under Facebook's (frequently amended) privacy rights, which often make seeing one's data impossible. In 2010, the new Facebook interface threatened to "erase" user data, so the app offered a way to save one's data and "refill" one's Facebook profile, which is also useful in cases of identity theft. Users select the data they would like to see and then choose a format in which to see it. Data can be imported into a document or spreadsheet or visualized as a graph or cloud. Users can speculate on how corporations automate their data: sorting it through different filters, running it through different programs, interpreting it for different reasons. The app allows users an opportunity to investigate the types and meanings of information about themselves available outside their control. They are prompted to reflect critically about data they freely and willingly give away to corporation and governments.

The role of US government surveillance on its citizens and foreign nationals became headlines again in June 2013 with the Edward Snowden's release ("leak") of information on the NSA's electronic data-mining program PRISM, which worked in collaboration with transnational corporation and European governments. Unlike journalist and activist Julian Assange's WikiLeaks, Snowden is a Certified Ethical Hacker (CEH), framing his leak of information as potentially more meaningful in terms of exposing the extent to which our privacy has been compromised in the name of security. Unlike the semiprivate interface of social networking, forms of digital communication such as SMS, voice calling, and e-mail are assumed to be the user's private property. Media attention to PRISM revealed the naivety of this assumption. In June 2014, reports circulated that China threatened to punish Apple, Facebook, Google, and Microsoft for spying on its citizens and businesses on behalf of the NSA.[45]

Originally part of *PRISM Breakup*, a series of art and technology events at Eyebeam in New York in October 2013, Grosser's *ScareMail* (United States, 2013; http://bengrosser.com/projects/scaremail/) is a web-browser extension that makes everyday e-mail messages appear "scary" to disrupt the NSA's controversial domestic surveillance program. *ScareMail* attaches a signature to an e-mail message sent through Google's Gmail in the form of an algorithmically generated narrative containing a collection of probable NSA search terms so that innocuous messages seem potentially suspicious. "This 'story,' as Grosser explains, "acts as a trap for NSA programs like PRISM and XKeyscore, forcing them to look at nonsense. Each e-mail's story is unique in an attempt to avoid automated filtering by NSA search systems." *ScareMail* invites us to dare to scare. It also encourages us to think about the scary and constant acts of fingerprinting by surveillance agencies. *ScareMail* takes on the ubiquity of surveillance, particularly in the post–9/11 United States where citizen rights to privacy have come under threat exponentially by state concerns over security. *ScareMail* asks us to question the normalization of compromised privacy as a part of everyday life in the context of a country whose international clout has been historically anchored to its democratic principles. It also reflects upon racial profiling within automated national-security protocols. The user's comfort with having NSA keywords in private e-mails is contingent upon knowledge of their place within racial-profiling schemes.

Contesting from Screens to Streets

Other projects think through digital media in order to convene publics in the streets. The Green Revolution in Iran and Arab Spring in Tunisia, Egypt, Syria, and elsewhere made use of social-networking platforms like Twitter and Facebook, but the uprisings also involved occupying physical streets and squares. Sometimes dismissed as "making noise," activism works to take apart assumptions about the status quo and power. Developed by Nick Knouf, Bruno Vianna, Luis Ayuso, and Mónica Sánchez at the Media Lab in Madrid, *Fluid Nexus* is a decentralized, P2P mobile SMS application operating over Bluetooth.[46] The project seeks to avoid the problems encountered by the Institute for Applied Autonomy's TXTMOB, a SMS system inhibited by limited character spaces and routing though a centralized hub and shut down by the legalities of cell phone proprietary ownership technologies.[47] The project does more than extend the P2P logic of Jonah Brucker-Cohen and Katherine Moriwaki's *UMBRELLA.net* (United States, 2005), which used a wireless network, computer-equipped umbrellas, and light-emitting diodes to visualize transitory connectivity.[48] Instead, *Fluid Nexus* re-imagines documentary as local and migratory activism to mobilize the invisibility of digital networks toward political engagement.

Knouf conceived the project during the summer of 2006 when reading the blog of a Lebanese sound artist during the conflict between Israel and Lebanon.[49] The blog's entries revealed fears of censorship, paranoia over downed networks, and the inherent difficulties of communicating views on events to the outside world. Since mobile phones are more ubiquitous than laptop computers, Knouf contemplated a network to bypass centralized networks, allowing viral transmission of texts through a program linking individual mobile units. Unlike the longer ranger WiFi (90 meters), the shorter range Bluetooth (9 meters) does not require a centralized hub, thereby circumventing some aspects of regulation and closure. Bluetooth has the disadvantage of slower communication times but has the dual advantages of anonymity and avoidance of central servers that record information that could later be subpoenaed by courts. The decision to use Nokia mobile phones and Python programming language reflect the project's commitment to serving the greatest number of potential users. Nokia is the world's most popular brand. Python is a freeware program easily modified for alternative apps. The system functions within a broadcast model, sending information directly from one programmed phone to the next. The project was conceived for areas where communication systems are tightly regulated and censored by the state, as well as for areas affected by disasters that shut down communication networks. The project anticipated the global recycling of Bluetooth-enabled mobile phones from overserved to underserved locations. To use *Fluid Nexus*, the user simply downloads the software on a mobile phone. Once loaded, the user can send messages that are stored on the mobile-phone unit and broadcast via Bluetooth to other mobile phones with the downloaded software. *Fluid Nexus* reroutes short-range wireless connectivity standards like Bluetooth from consumerism and complicity toward activism and countersurveillance. The P2P model of information exchange avoids hierarchy and control. *Fluid Nexus* is part of an emerging documentary modality that recognizes the dangers inherent to documentation when things are not taken apart: fixed archival images risk being repurposed from eyewitness accounts of human-rights violations into visual evidence deployed by oppressive regimes for control.

The Monsantra Project (Canada/United States, 2010) by Wendy DesChene and Jeff Schmuki combines tactical and locative media to promote critical thinking and political action about GMOs. Rifting on the name for a corporation that makes the news mostly for destroying economies and facilitating poverty, *The Monsantra Project* explores the unpredictable and often fatal consequences when GMOs become food. GMO plant hybrids are reengineered by grafting edible plants to robotic, remote-controlled bases. Corporate "grafting" of food production and distribution becomes more clearly visible when this new hybrid evokes critical response as it roams freely in galleries and streets. The PlantBots also can be identified through detailed botanical drawings, available on the website. "Like a B-movie Godzilla, *Monsantra* is a hybrid of imagination, possibility, and reality," explain DesChene and Schmuki.[50]

The project exemplifies how artists/activists have redefined transmedia as a trans-spatial performative process, rather than as a series of fixed media products. It migrates across many different locations, forms, interfaces, and interactions, utilizing a structuring concept of taking their ideas to the streets and to the people, rather than waiting for audiences to come to them. For example, the project runs the Mobile Art Lab, a 5.5-meter trailer where people can come to make plant/robot hybrids. With the artists in white lab coats, the idea is to invite participants in to work the interstices of science, robotics, and environmental issues. *The Monsantra Project* also conducts

Figure 1.2   *The Monsantra Project.*

"Informational Nature Walks" on boardwalks in Florida, mimicking ranger-guided nature walks in state parks. They place their GMO plant/robot hybrids, small remote-controlled machines with green plants sprouting from them, on the boardwalk, creating a border with bright red thick tape. One of the plants in this tour is the "Britneyatacum Permormada," a plant that sings songs by the US pop star Britney Spears, whose career was engineered by transnational media corporations. Further strategies of taking it to the streets involve infiltrating the PlantBots in public areas, ranging from state parks to the streets of Galesburg, Illinois, the corporate headquarters of Monsanto. The artists operate the PlantBot through remote controls as it winds in between people hiking, walking the streets, buying organic produce at a local farmer's market, or touring the landscape of Iceland. Their Moth events exemplify this participatory engagement: tents are erected in the backyard to attract moths next to an outdoor dinner party.

Adopting the poorly designed look of right-wing grassroots associations, Samantha Raut's *Art is Atrocity* (United States, 2011–2012; http://artisatrocity.com/) operates as a visual political satire migrating between the website screen and the streets. It lures central New York State patriotic citizens, with its neoliberal-driven budget cuts to arts, to reflect upon their own assumptions through strategically placed billboards and a website. The tactical-media project calls attention to the erasure of art and music from public school curricula by inviting users to participate in discussions of neoliberal economic policy decisions affecting education in the United States, as evidenced in the archive of responses ranging from real people to people using aliases. This project figures the screens of the fake website and the materiality of the billboards as a visual pun on the word "traffic," here conceived as both website traffic of users and hits to the *Art is Atrocity* website and as real traffic on highways where the billboards exclaiming in bold letters ART IS ATROCITY are placed. Two billboards were mounted close to the largest mall in Syracuse, another at one of the busiest intersections. The movement between the website screens that supply essays on why the arts should be cut that can be read as either a real statement or a satire and the large billboards mimicking political advertisements suggest that politics can only be understood as an amalgam between the real and the fake, the virtual and the material, the small computer screen and the large, legacy media billboard.

Reeducating in the Gallery Space

The digital media projects discussed throughout this book seldom appear in commercial cinemas. More often, they appear in art galleries and museums or at festivals. They occupy a curiously *privileged yet marginalized* space, much like experimental film, traditionally screened in film clubs, museums, and schools, or documentary, screened mostly at festivals and on television. Unlike conventional filmic and ludic practices, other projects migrate between spaces and even occupy several spaces at once. Locative media moves from the physical space of the gallery to the virtual spaces of digital networks. It involves live performance that invites audiences to become participants. By making political interventions within the privileged spaces of galleries, museums, and film festivals, locative media provokes critical self-reflection upon feelings of entitlement to aesthetic or intellectual pleasures. Drawing on performance art convetions by artists such as Marina Abramović, Joseph Beuys, Mona Hatoum, Marta Minujín, Yoko Ono, Nam June Paik, Carolee Schneemann, and Zhang Huan, locative media artists bridge three artificial borders: between inside the gallery and outside in the world; between performer and audience; between art and commerce. It acknowledges complicity instead of offering a pop-art critique of consumerism. Eddo Stern's most recent project, *Money Making Workshop* (United States, 2012), reimagines the board game Monopoly as a five-person, asymmetrical, role-playing game. For digital and locative-media artists, the gallery space transforms into a site for reeducation through affective and embodied forms of knowledge.

Jesvin Yeo's *Singapore Pangram* (Singapore, 2009–present) transports inquiry into the question of national identities, language, and design into gallery. Comprised of a series of printed posters with images related to Singaporean culture, the project opens up the everyday realities of language—in this case, the hidden secret patois of Singlish. The project expands the concept of standard English as it brings Singlish into the open, a language pushed aside as the country marshaled English to position itself as a global city. All the sentences in the project are constructed as pangrams, a sentence using all 26 letters of the English alphabet. Singapore is a port city-state at the southern tip of the Malay peninsula, and, for centuries, a major shipping entrepôt where many cultures intermingled. Singlish jumbles together "East" and "West," mixing English, Bahasa Melayu, Hokkien, Teochew, Cantonese, Tamil, Bengali, and Punjabi. When Lee Kuan Yew became prime minister in the early 1960s, he instituted English as the official language of business and education. Later, in the 2000s, the Singapore government launched the "Speak Good English" campaign to eradicate Singlish and advance standard English as necessary for global business and to insure Singapore's movement into a "first-world" economy.[51]

Singapore Pangram operates within the interstitial zones between the commercial and art world, between the handmade and the digital, and between the image and language. The posters are first hand-drawn with commercial markers, then computerized for custom printing like any commercial graphic element, and finally handmade again with a 3.2 nail punch. The nail punch produces the obscured graphic element: the letters of the Singlish sentences are punched into the poster, not perceptible when looking at the images. The posters hang on special mounts away from the gallery wall. Viewers shine an LED flashlight at the poster. As the light filters through the obscured holes, it projects the sentences on the walls. Appearing in the dark, these illuminated sentences behind the posters suggest how Singlish is underground, pushed aside. The sentences stack vertically, the words

Figure 1.3 *Singapore Pangram.*

piling up, suggesting contemporary Singapore skyscrapers. The color palette infusing *Singapore Pangram* is brightly saturated with rich greens, reds, blues, yellows, and blacks, suggesting the bright sun and rich colors of the tropics. The swirling patterns behind the central image replicate the leaves of tropical plants. For example, one image features tropical black birds with large beaks, sitting on black wires. The sky behind is green, the clouds a lighter green. The sentence literally hand-inscribed into the image, in a typography composed of punches, reads: "A very jude anoneh was attacked by a murder of crows in the quiet zen garden unexpectedly." In Singlish, a *jude anoneh* is a pretty Japanese girl. In another image, four yellow-top black taxis, an emblematic image of Singapore society, float on a black sky. The sentence on the image is "Four yellow top black taxis drive up Jalan Bukit Merah on a quiet lazy night to liak gao." *Liak gao* means peeping tom.

Invisible Life: Flip Flop Journeys (Singapore, 2009–2010) is a research-based practice and installation that materializes the transnational movements of globalization through the commodity of the flip-flop, the ubiquitous footwear worn by the working, unemployed, agrarian classes in warm climates. The flip-flop is the best selling shoe in the world.[52] The installation design asks how to visualize the abstract systems of political economies. Rather than a deductive or polemical argument about globalization, *Invisible Life* operates more as an opening up of inquiry into something one wears but does not think about contextually. An example of an international trend of artists and documentary filmmakers working to unpack supply chains by focusing on one object—such as coffee, fish, cotton, smartphones, mardi-gras beads—as it moves through different phases of production and different countries, *Invisible Life* is a collaboration between Singapore installation artist Michael Tan and UK-based sociologist Caroline Knowles. The installation restores the production and distribution process to flip-flops, showing the people involved as it moves from plants in Fuzhou in China to the streets of Addis Ababa in Ethiopia.

Invisible Life transforms sociological research investigating the contingent, uneven, global movement of flip-flops into a gallery installation that exposes both the product and its process. The subtitle of *Invisible Life* identifies it as an "art sociology investigation." The gallery space requires the spectator to move through the space, shifting between reading text analyzing the production of flip-flops on the walls and looking at images of their manufacture, shipping, selling, and wearing. It flips between conceptual analysis of commodity production and visual immersion into the flip-flop itself. The installation further toggles between scale: large abstract concepts and concrete images of people with flip-flops, large images the size of a wall, and smaller ones the size of a business card.

The installation typically occupies an entire gallery room, a surrounding of flip-flop processes both manufacturing and intellectual. A paragraph analyzing the commodity production and globalization of flip-flops fills one wall at the entrance to the gallery. Then, each wall has one line of black type on a white wall, analyzing and situating the production process, with sentences like flip-flops are "produced through human effort." In the middle of the room, white waist-high cases feature an array of different kinds of flip-flops under Plexiglas, the cabinet evoking how objects from different cultures are displayed in a museum of ethnography, such as the Asian Civilization Museum in Singapore, to encourage viewers to bend over, peer into, and marvel. Above the cabinets, small photographs the size of a business card or MRT (Singapore subway) pass dangle from strings at different lengths. The photographs of factory workers, vendors, flip-flops in markets, piles of rubber, and garbage span China to Ethiopia. These dangling images spin slowly, responding to the movement of people in the gallery itself, never staying in place.

Whereas multichannel installations often invite audiences to contemplate imaginary or distant places, Marina Zurkow's *Paradoxical Sleep* (United States, 2008) invites them to reconsider the gallery space itself in relation to its physical and psychical location.[53] Conceived for the San Jose McEnery Convention Center, *Paradoxical Sleep* consists of display units that resemble CCTV monitors mounted irregularly on walls or from ceilings. Their screens are not hidden for view only by security staff but instead are in plain view by anyone. The space is unremittingly institutional. Exposed raw concrete columns and beams, walls painted in light colors, glass balcony walls, and terrazzo tiling with potted plants, vending machines, and ATMs define the convention center. Each screen of *Paradoxical Sleep* includes a "video portrait" of the building and the nearby Guadalupe River, which appears to overflow into the structure of the building. Zurkow digitally animates a flood by compositing images of the convention center and the river. Most of the screens are mounted to call attention to themselves as a part of a site-specific temporary installations— several small screens are clustered together on a wall or one large screen is suspended over a central corridor. The images on the screens become so compelling that passersby find themselves momentarily disconcerted. Audiences confront images of massive amounts of water, flowing through corridors over parking cones and vending machines on some screens. Other screens show small streams of water that leak or spout from walls.

Instead of feeling psychologically transported away from one's everyday concerns in a contemplative gallery space, audiences find themselves keenly aware of their location. They make mental calculations about the distances between flooded spaces and their current location. For Zurkow, "the screens become magic mirrors, making visible what is invisible to the naked eye: memory, speculation, and projection." People remember past floods, projecting their fears onto the screens or speculating about a path to safety. The project's title refers to one of two states of sleep during which intense brain activity, such as rapid eye movement (REM), accompanies an absence of motor ability. The project evokes feelings that structurally resemble paradoxical sleep: the images on the screens elicit heightened mental awareness accompanied by a lingering sense of physical entrapment inside the convention center. Funded in part through the crowdsourcing platform Kickstarter, Zurkow's site-specific project *Paradoxical Sleep (Industry City)* (United States, 2010) was an installation for Marian Spore, a limited-duration arts space operating in Brooklyn's Sunset Park industrial complex of Industry City from 2009 until 2010. Named after the third wife of the founder of Industry City, the space functions according to a logic of accumulation rather than rotation, with projects added at irregular intervals. Like the earlier project, Zurkow digitally submerged the arts space.

Renate Ferro's installation *Panic Hits Home* (United States, 2007) explores the contiguous histories of panic as it infiltrates psychic spaces. It puts the panic around nuclear warheads from the early 1960s in conversation with anxieties mobilized around terrorism after 9/11. The four-channel video installation features a small wooden house in the center of the gallery. Inside, in high-definition video, interviews with cross-generational subjects recounting their panic, anxiety, and psychic disturbances from each of these two periods 40 years apart, function as a psychoanalytic mapping and exposure of the repetitions and symptoms of trauma. As the spectator enters the blackened house, the interview subjects speak in direct address, repositioning the spectator as an amalgam of witness and therapist. Outside the house, three large-scale, keystoned projections of mass media images of war, nuclear warheads, duck-and-cover drills, bomb shelters, public service advertisements, and Department of Homeland Security (DHS) videos fill the walls. The images function as a cloud around the home, looming in their black and white like approaching storms. Each word of the title, *Panic Hits Home,* operates as a vector for the structure of this installation. The gallery space figures as a bomb shelter. The large-scale mass media images literally hit the white house, a visual pun on the term projection, here meaning both physical and psychic projection. Everything becomes a screen—walls, house, psychic space, interior, exterior, all space, both inside and outside, infused with panic.

Pan-O-matic's *Invisible Threads* (United States, 2007) by Rothenberg and Crouse invites audiences to become participants by ordering custom-made designer jeans from a virtual sweatshop, called Double

Figure 1.4 *Panic Hits Home.*

Happiness Manufacturing, located in the social-networking environment of SL. Rothenberg is interested in facilitating interactive situations that create more engagements with the public to unpack larger issues of the mobilities of global capital. Audiences approach *Invisible Threads*' kiosk storefront, where they place orders for custom-made jeans in the latest fashion styles, including "LowRider" and "Road Kill." The "No Pants Left Behind" style is a parody of the No Child Left Behind Act (2001), which, critics find, exaggerates the structural inequalities in public education in the United States. "Classic" parodies corporate branding strategies, including Coca-cola's 1985 launch of Coca-cola Classic after consumers rejected New Coke as its new formula. "MyPants" parodies successful corporate outsourcing to customers, such as MyMaps for Google Maps. By printing the jeans on cotton canvas, which is glued together, the project parodies the history of jeans, which were promoted as inexpensive and durable items for people who work with their bodies. The designer jeans undo the immigrant ingenuity of Levi Strauss, the Ashkenazi German who founded a company in 1853 that produced durable jeans for the immigrant and working classes.

Invisible Threads also makes a critique of the corporate practices, such as Nike's website for its NIKEiD, which invited Internet shoppers to become "Nike designers" by personalizing Nike's factory-manufactured sports shoes. Mark Andrejevic argues that the campaign was launched in celebration of interactivity as moving toward a fulfillment of the promise of "individuation," "democratization," and "invocation for the nostalgia of lost community."[54] NIKEiD, he finds, effectively transforms interactivity into a means of outsourcing product development while simultaneously increasing the monitoring of its customers, resulting in targeted advertising based on customer preferences. He notes activist challenges to Nike by ordering shoes with tags like "sweatshop" and "remember the toil and labor of the children who made my shoes," neither of which Nike allowed. *Invisible Threads* challenges assumptions about marketing campaigns about "freedom of choice" by asking us to consider our complicity with transnational corporations and neoliberal business practices that limit choices for others. The jeans are produced according to the just-in-time logic of global capitalism whereby factories, along with assembly, packaging, and finishing plants, are geographically dispersed across the planet in order to benefit from the cheapest possible labor. Increased transportation costs to move parts and products across the planet ostensibly are offset by saving in human labor and infrastructures that protect workers and ensure environmental safety.

For *Invisible Threads*, avatars in SL produce patterns for the customized jeans, which are transmitted digitally back to the kiosk storefront, where they are printed onto paper with large-scale printers. Live (human) performers work as pattern cutters and assemblers, using cotton canvas, a glue-gun, and minimal stitching to assemble the jeans. Unable to survive a wash-and-dry cycle—even with delicate hand washing—the jeans are basically disposable, exaggerating the impermanence of the digital but also commenting on common business practices, not unlike Apple Computers, seductively designed and marketed products with their planned obsolesce. The jeans evoke Eva Grunbinger's *Netzbikini* (Germany, 1995; www.evagrubinger.com/netzbikini/), which asked users to become participants by downloading a bikini pattern, then customizing it for wear as a performance of the decentralized structure of the Internet.[55] With *Invisible Threads*, the means of jeans production is overtly nondemocratic, emphasizing neoliberal approaches that include unethical business practices, the exploitation of flexible labor, and links to the military-industrial and prison-industrial complexes. The choice of Hewlett Packard printers points to other aspects of globalization's integration of trade and war since the transnational corporation is one identified by the

Figure 1.5 *Invisible Threads.*

Boycott, Divestment and Sanctions (BDS) campaign for its investment in companies in the occupied territories.

Virtual sweatshops function as a vital but hidden part of the global economy. Virtual migration of outsourced labor from call centers in India and Ireland to cheaper ones in Ghana and the Philippines has increased. "Gold mining" by Chinese sweatshop-workers-as-gamers playing for game points for sale to North-Atlantic and Asia-Pacific gamers has emerged. The production of digital code is outsourced around the globe. In this context, *Invisible Threads* probes the "invisible threads" of just-in-time production and contradictions between the sustainability of human resources and the increasing virtualization of labor. *Invisible Threads* suggests that the work of documentary resides in the labor of collaboration to take things apart. The project developers have created tongue-in-cheek, DIY-style, video entitled, *10 Simple Steps to You Own Virtual Sweatshop,* for "aspiring virtual entrepreneurs."[56] The tag line for the video asks: "Are repressive labor laws and expensive real estate getting in the way of owning your very own sweatshop?" The video explains ways that "anyone" can benefit from neoliberal economic structures by outsourcing work to cheap flexible labor located a safe distance from labor and environmental laws and the work stoppages of on-site protests.

Developed at Eyebeam, *Invisible Threads* has been performed at
New Frontier on Main at the 2008 Sundance Film Festival and at
Synthetic Times: Media Art China 2008 in New York. Rothenberg
and Crouse set up a kiosk with sales racks and other publicity collateral. The project takes apart the seamlessness of online shopping
and the invisibility of sweatshop labor. Indeed, Double Happiness
Manufacturing operates according to an "indentured servant mode"
of labor, paying workers about 90 cents per hour and selling the jeans
for about 40 dollars.[57] Profits from sales are used to pay for SL space
rental as well as salaries of workers in SL and in real life. *Invisible
Threads* creates a participatory space to take apart ways that work
and play, labor and consumption, are refigured through Web 2.0
technologies transforming social networking into telematic manufacturing.[58] The project is mobile and migratory, mixing reality with
networked media, performance with installation.[59] *Invisible Threads*
exposes ways real-world economies affect idealized virtual communities. As web 2.0 technologies move between social relationships and
financial exchanges, *Invisible Threads* produces a collaborative experience that unsettles borders between virtuality and materiality. It is
not a work about producing machinima in SL; rather, it is a project
that transmits and produces collaborative experiences.

Invisible Threads operates according to service aesthetics: the artist
and audience form one-to-one relationships through commodity transactions within service economies of customization and personalization, a radical departure from the relation aesthetics by which the artist
aligns with audience in post-Fordist economies of mass production.[60]
Artistically, Rothenberg is not interested in the production of fixed
images that witness events. Rather, she is invested in the creation of
participatory, interactive situations to create more engagements with the
public to unpack the mobilities of global capital. Rather than documenting a social movement, *Invisible Threads* immerses in the injustices of
digital outsourcing and free trade zones immune from labor laws by creating an accessible project that affiliates with social and political movements. This conjuring of micropublics through tactics of aggregation
and swarming differs from a more fixed view of the documentary project as engaging in an epistemology of representation. Here, images shift,
change, and recede. In *Invisible Threads*, performance, provocation,
and politicization take apart everyday technologies. *Invisible Threads*
breaks down and reconfigures the screen as one endlessly mobile vector.
Invisible Threads challenges the audience to transform from an autonomous spectator to an embodied collaborator migrating between user,
producer, consumer, and critic. It takes things apart.

2

Mapping Open Space to Visualize
Other Knowledges

Mapping orientates and determines ways in which we perceive and understand the world and our place in it. Maps reveal and illuminate, but they also conceal and obfuscate. Early mapping projects like Benjamin Fry's *Anemone* (United States, 1999; http://benfry. com/anemone/) visualize connections between webpages, much like information-clouds visualize keywords today. *Anemone* maps and visualizes using the structure of a tree with branches, revealing connections while concealing context. Digital media also allows for mapping toward the concept of open space that moves away from trees and branches toward rhizomes and nomads. Open space refers to the green commons inside urban areas. Rather than defining and dividing, which are the domain of conventional cartography and historiography, radical and critical forms of cartography and historiography invite new participation and facilitate new questions. By enlisting perspectives frequently ignored or unrecognized, the projects examined in this chapter explore the interfaces and intervals of the digital, abstract, and immaterial with the localized, materialized, and grounded. Mapping projects use data visualization to make visible what might be invisible, such as carbon monoxide, sulfur dioxide, and nitrogen dioxide detected by air-quality sensors, tagged by GPS, and rendered on a Google Earth image of Accra, Ghana, by *Participatory Urbanism* (United States/Ghana, 2006; http:// www.urban-atmospheres.net/), a collaboration between Eric Paulos and the citizens of Accra. Natalie Jeremijenko's open-source *Feral Robotic Dogs* (United States, 2005; www.nyu.edu/projects/xdesign/ feralrobots/) is an automated version of this locative mapping project that mods robotic dogs with emissions sensors.[1]

The projects in the chapter use online platforms to engage us as more than viewers of videos or GIFs, users of websites, or players of video games: they ask us to share with others through social networks and word of mouth. They move virally and attempt to reclaim interactivity as unpredictable and potentially transformative rather than merely a form of monitoring and surveillance by corporations and states. Even as corporations hijack the term interactivity to signify a limited freedom of choice within a predetermined set of possible reactions initiated through human-machine interface, digital media artists, activists, coders, designers, students, and intellectuals interact in virtual and physical places to open space. As viewers, users, and players, we have grown accustomed to thinking within a narrow set of possibilities. Sounds and images appear according to our keystrokes, clicks of the mouse, movements across a track pad, gestures with a controller, or blinks of the eye—but we cannot affect change, particularly change that will affect the experience of others. This kind of reaction-as-interaction remains largely one way, not really altering a somewhat passive experience. User-generated content (UGC) is one means by which we can change the terms of history and contours of a map. The projects discussed in this chapter invite us to imagine and contemplate other ways of interacting, becoming politicized, and activating the social.

Recovering History through Maps

History is written in maps, particularly following the visual turn that saturates us with images. For many of us, the easiest way to locate our place in the world is through apps like Google Maps. We infrequently consider that the base map on the app is a modified version of Gerardus Mercator's sixteenth-century projection of the world, which distorts space so as to facilitate nautical navigation. Visually, the projection gives priority to Europe, exaggerating its size and centralizing its location. Instead of a backward subcontinent of Asia, Europe elevated itself to a continent on its own right. Mercator's projection facilitated European colonialism, initially in commercial terms and later in political terms.[2] Maps, however, have also been used to claim, reclaim, and open space. Mapping becomes an act of power and self-determination. Notable examples include Unintended City Project (UCP) by Unnayan ("development"), a civil organization in Calcutta founded in 1977 with the goal of empowerment and conscientization through what Jai Sen calls "experiments in making visible through mapping those who are traditionally made invisible by mapping."[3] The project focused on making visible communities rendered invisible by the city, thereby denying basic human rights to *batis*-laborer settlements, refugee colonies, and pavement dwellers. For Sen, mapping enables an opening up of thinking about power and counterpower as a different framework of "power-over" and "power-to." Rather than mapping power over minoritized populations, it can entail a mapping of power to such populations. The implication extends to the recovery and transmission of repressed or forgotten histories. In a historical moment of uprisings across the Middle East, North Africa, Latin America, and even Europe and North America, mapping becomes a means to visualize new relationships and political affiliations rendered invisible by cartographic conventions of rationally derived and scientifically objective means of selection, simplification, symbolization, projection, and orientation. Many of the projects discussed initiate open space to community involvement, whereas others consider space for the ways that we experience rather than see it.

Ismail Farouk and Babak Fakhamzadeh's *Soweto Uprisings* (South Africa/Netherlands, 2008; http://sowetouprisings.com) is an example of locative media in a documentary mode that takes shape as a migratory archive through collaboration between artists, programmers, historians, activists, and a local community. A migratory archive moves between platforms and material spaces, continually expanding. Mapping material and historical territories in the virtual environment, *Soweto Uprisings* commemorates a significant moment in South African history in a nonlinear and open format. The project avoids the fixity of physical memorials and in situ installations by utilizing the Internet as a site for ongoing negotiations and contestations over past events and their continued relevance today. The web-application mashup of Google Maps inserts images of key sites in the student uprisings on 16 June 1976. *Soweto Uprisings* follows routes and related events in the African township of Soweto (South Western Township) in Johannesburg during a moment in South African history that would become galvanized by various political groups as a symbol of popular resistance to Apartheid.

Unlike the destructive editing in music or video mashups, web-application mashups leave the underlying code intact, so that applications function. *Soweto Uprisings* actually extends the first mashup of Google Maps when Paul Rademacher at DreamWorks Animation invented *HousingMaps*, an application that mapped the data of housing ads from Craigslist (a classified-advertising website in the United

States) onto Google Maps. Rather than suing him for hacking its software, Google hired him to launch MyMaps in 2007, which allows users to personalize maps. By 2008, there were at least 1468 mashups using the application programming interface (API) for Google Maps.[4] The design for *Soweto Uprisings* aspires to a conception of history that is written collaboratively and remapped onto place through relationality.

Farouk and Fakhamzadeh collaborated with Soweto's first historical museum, the Hector Pieterson Research Project on *Soweto Uprisings*, initially intended to map the actual student routes taken in 1976. It was designed as a community-driven digital archive through which members of the "lost generation" of young South Africans, who sacrificed their education to stand against the Apartheid system, could reclaim and transmit history.[5] The web-application mashup allows users to view individual routes that open to additional information about sites, events, and martyrs; contemporary photographs of key sites along the student routes, such as schools and police stations; and user-contributed testimony or remembrance. It also features RSS feeds filtered through Google keyword searches to track what people around the world are writing about Soweto on blog and websites. The project is even linked to Wikipedia, thereby entering into the world of global information dissemination via the WWW on a platform that itself rejects the authoritative print-press model for a more democratic open-source model.

Soweto Uprisings invites users to read individual routes of protest and resistance mapped onto an image of Soweto from Google Maps with its three standard viewing options: "map" showing political geography, "satellite" showing physical geography, and "hybrid" showing political geography layered atop physical geography. Routes may be selected, so that they appear visually over the map as color-coded polylines. Markers ("balloons" used to provide points along a route) with custom icons (crosses, stars, houses, circles, squares, triangles, etc.) open to additional text and photographic information relating to events of the march, including information about martyrs, also allow users to post comments, which can be read in blogs that also contain RSS feeds.

As both digital archive and critical cartography/historiography, *Soweto Uprisings* mobilizes the open-source potential of the Internet to create a site for a collaborative and migratory model of documentary praxes. The community is invited to contribute content in the form of stories that accumulate to become another layer of unresolved history. The RSS feeds facilitate unwitting collaboration. The meaning of the site's subject, Soweto's history, opens to a broader audience of potential participants than the website's users. Political theorists Michael Hardt and Antonio Negri recognized the Internet as a model for guerrilla networks for the multitude.[6] The accumulation of the comments—one modestly titled, "just one story"—has the effect of opening the history of the uprisings to testimonies from participants that often contradict official versions of this history controlled by groups in power. These comments, in a modest, provisional manner, assemble micropublics. History opens to contestation of African National Congress (ANC) claims to involvements in the organization of the student uprisings. Organized by the Soweto Students' Representative Council's (SSRC) Action Committee and supported by the Black Consciousness Movement (BCM) and Positive Action Campaign (PAC), routes taken by students from various schools toward the police stations to protest the obligatory use of Afrikaans and English in schools create a space for information to be gathered, discussed, and evaluated, rather than memorialized as uncontested, monumentalized history. The project represents a political intervention into the archive and memorialization. As the post-Apartheid state and civic governments begin to follow the so-called global model by memorializing not the actual routes but their symbolic approximates as heritage sites for international tourism, *Soweto Uprisings*'s digital archive becomes a vital means to counter the repurposing of history into consumable goods. Moreover, the political bias of state and civic memorialization of history often marginalizes the role of women and of organizations other than the ANC, such as the PAC-organized route to the Orlando East police station on 23 March 1960, in protest of the Pass Laws.

What inhibit *Soweto Uprisings* are the ongoing realities of digital divides, so that the democratizing potential of the Internet is fuelled by utopic desire. According to a 2005 UNESCO report on knowledge societies, the digital divide is "not one but rather many digital divides" that fracture access to knowledge according to economic resources, geographical asymmetries, generation, gender inequality, language, employment, disabilities, and educational, social, and cultural background.[7] In 2005, when this project was active, only 11 percent of the world's population has access to the Internet, and 82 percent of the world's population represents only 10 percent of this 11 percent with the other 90 percent concentrated in the United States, Canada, Europe, Japan, South Korea, and Australia.[8] Many of the participants in the Soweto uprisings do not have Internet access or Internet literacy. There is also the issue of trust. As the last generation to have lived its childhood under the dehumanizing policies of Apartheid, participants were often hesitant to contribute information that once would have resulted in imprisonment. Nonetheless, *Soweto Uprisings* does propose new ways of interacting with documentary media, navigating history as web environments.[9]

The project's third phase included mapping additional routes and conceptualizing user interface in response to inadequate Internet access within the township, which contributed to limited participation. Since a purely online platform is not sufficient, Farouk and Fakhamzadeh also explored ways to integrate mobile units along the routes. They used Internet cafés developed for the 2010 World Cup and interfaced the project with other services, such as digital scanners and free e-mail accounts. The project further explored the use of existing social networks to encourage participation. Farouk believes that mapping facilitates conceptions of historical documentation that activate spatial dimensions toward visualizations affecting change. The project seeks to give voice to those who participated in the country's future, extending a hacker ethic to *take things apart*—in this instance, the "thing" is the illusions of global consumerism as citizenship through heritage sites. Mapping becomes a means of reclaiming history as process, rather than product—a migratory archive rather than a physical memorial. Participants have found the project extremely emotional and gratifying, releasing thoughts that they have described to Farouk as "lurking in memory." *Soweto Uprisings* deploys an open-archive, community-driven model toward the documentation of history.

Online mapping and digital archives operate as modes of radical historiography to recover and reactivate a past that continues to affect the present and future and that experiences continual threat of erasure by well-intended yet closed civic initiatives. Sylvia Grace Borda's *Eknewtown* (United Kingdom, 2006; http://www.eknewtown.com/), an artist's documentation of the relationship between the natural and built environments in the Scottish town of East Kilbridge, exemplifies this practice. Borda describes the project as "Eugène Atget meets Allan Sekula," referencing a photographer whose mysterious images of modern Paris, largely devoid of humans, enchanted the surrealists, and another photographer whose writing and images critique late modernism's social and economic relationships. The project's main interface is a stylized map of East Kilbridge, which resembles a colorful, simplified tourist map oriented around landmarks. The scale of text that labels areas indicates importance. Color also distinguishes certain neighborhoods marked in browns (e.g., West Mains, East Mains, Greenhills, and Calderwood) from others marked in mossy green (e.g., Nerston, Kelvin, College Milton, and Hairmyres), which blends into the surrounding areas. Icons also indicate Christian churches, woods, and an arts center. When users click on a hyperlinked text or icon, a slide viewer opens with several photographic eye-level images taken by Borda, as well as explanatory text providing historical information on architecture and urban design, particularly as it differed from well-known examples of modernist urban design by Le Corbusier and Walter Gropius.

Proceeding Google Map's street-view app by a number of years, the web-based mapping project includes more than eight thousand digital images, as well as the creative responses of students and teachers. Its mandate is to educate and campaign residents to reconsider saving their architectural heritage. Unlike the tourist-destination sites, there are no commercially available ephemera for residents of East Kilbridge. Self-guided interface permits users to navigate an interactive archive and map of East Kilbridge, located about 15 kilometers from Glasgow. It became Scotland's first New Town in the 1950s. Conceived after the Second World War and constructed as late as the 1990s, the concept of the New Town embraced modernist ideals to create spaces for social living and well-being that camouflage with the environment through an emphasis on light, green space, and open air. By 2006, most New Towns were in process of being altered, demolished, or sold to developers. Popular impressions are that New Towns were a failure in social engineering and urban planning. The project claims modernist architecture and urban design as forms of public art, alongside contemporary arts commissions. Yet it simultaneously questions political will and egalitarianism in housing issues, particularly the utopic desires of European modernism. As Borda explains, the project is designed as a "matrix archive" that allows users to plot their own courses through the documents.[10] An archival mapping project, *Eknewtown* deconstructs the modernist concept of an archive as authoritative and objective by framing of its contents as legible.

Other artists and researchers have utilized the form of the map to convey indigenous perspectives that have been systematically erased and silenced by centuries of settler colonialism in North America, the Middle East, and Oceania. The collaborative *The Visual Meditation of a Complex Narrative: T.G.H. Strehlow's "Journey to Horseshoe Bend"* (Australia, 2008) is a digital hub of archival images and texts that deploys innovative interactive online design with a particular interest to enhance access and participation by the Arrernte (Aranda) people of Ntaria.[11] The work is a collaborative project led by Hart Cohen, Peter Dallow, and Sid Newton (chief investigators), with the Strehlow Research Centre and Arrernte people from Ntaria, Central Australia (partners), with the assistance of Lisa Kaufmann and Rachel Morley (research assistants) funded by the Australian Research Council and based at the University of Western Sydney. The project intends to map visually the complex narrative of T. G. H. Strehlow's memoire of the 1922 "death journey" of Lutheran pastor Carl Strehlow. Utilizing archival photographs, film/video, and other documentation, the project aims to collate and project the narrative elements of the memoire as an online database relevant to the Arrernte community and to an aboriginal sense of place, including specific totemic and ceremonial relationships as well as kinship connections. Geographic maps, genealogy charts, images, documents, media resources, and other online collections are also linked to visual representations of the text. An adaptation of the GoogleMaps fly-through function proposes an alternative interface for access to the database of archival materials. This function is to enhance feedback from the Arrernte community, recorded as oral histories, digitized and hyperlinked to further the specific cultural content of the *Journey to Horseshoe Bend* text. This design suggests what Cohen calls "the cultural work of articulating a modern social existence in a white-dominated civilization, along with an abiding interest in the continuities of tradition that makes cultural practice active, fluid and dynamic."[12]

Other mapping projects ask us to look at the world from perspectives other than the god's-eye view of Google Maps. Faisal Anwar's *MyCityStories* (Canada/Pakistan, 2012; www.mycitystories.com/) develops further an earlier project titled *360EXtEndEd* and invites users to contribute stories about the cities that they call (or have once called) home. The project features stories from neighborhoods whose histories interconnect through the processes of migration impelled in part by colonialism and current globalization—Balmoral (New Zealand), Dubai (United Arab Emirates), Karachi and Lahore (Pakistan), London (United Kingdom), Mississauga (Canada). Now abandoned, Tara Pattenden's *Mapplers* (Australia, 2010; www.mapplers.org) was a collaborative redrawing by hand of the world from emphatically intimate and subjective perspectives, rather than scientific or objective epistemes. The project replaced the supposedly objective views of Google Maps with hand-drawn images through which participants charted their emotional connections to Brisbane. Another workshop applied the project to Helsinki. Like *Soweto Uprisings*, Graham Coreil-Allen's *New Public Sites—Walking Tours—DC* (United States, 2009; http://newpublicsites.org/walking-tours-dc/) offered an intimate tour of the US capital by mapping some of its overlooked and often invisible features. Coreil-Allen uploads to Google Maps images of pavement, piles, gates, and anti-gates within what he names a "disparate zone where the Trinidad neighborhood and the Atlas District overlap."

Other projects map through animation. Whereas animation is often a means to conceal identity in conventional documentary practice, it becomes a means to reveal identity in web-based media. *Flag Metamorphoses* (Germany/Switzerland, 2005–2014; www.thyes.com/flag-metamorphoses/flag-animation.html), for example, is an ongoing participatory archive of short vector-based Flash animations complied by Myriam Thyes. Selections have also been exhibited in galleries and at festivals. The concept of the metamorphoses is to visualize the relationship between two states starting with the flag of one state and ending with the flag of the second state. The process recovers meanings embedded in the symbols that often predate the states the flags themselves symbolize. First introduced at the Fantoche Animation Festival in Baden, Switzerland, the project has been exhibited at festivals in Australia, Brazil, Cameroon, Cuba, Indonesia, United States, and elsewhere. There are presently 30 animations contributed by artists and students from Africa, Europe, East Asia, Latin America, and North America. Each interrogates actual or imagined relations though sounds and images that convey meaning about contacts and conflicts, influences and aspirations. Some speculate on interstate relations that developed during colonialism, others via more recent moments of globalization, and still others do not yet exist. A few of the animations explore larger connections such as the World Cup or Caribbean Carnivals.

"With every new animation we'll understand more points of view," explains Thyes, whether connections between Bolivia and Japan, Eretria and the Bahamas, or Afghanistan and México. The animations open symbolic representations of nation-states to unconventional speculations. Comparably, Graham Thompson's *North-South-East-West 1.0* (Canada/Metis Nation, 2004; www.graham.gs/nsew/index.html) utilizes Macromedia Flash animations, new media installations, streaming media, cell-phone downloads, digital videos, webcasts, and videoconferences to guide audiences through the four directions or four seasons of our lives. Inspired by the meaning of the four sacred directions as taught by the Anishinaabe Peoples of North America, the work tells a story about our lives in terms of four challenges—the challenge to survive, to find a vision, to find a path, and to learn the wisdom of the path of the vision. Such projects open maps to contestation, pointing to features that drop from the lexicons of conventional cartography, conceiving history as fluid and open rather than fixed and settled.

Immersive Mapping with Mobile Apps

Adopting a different approach to opening space to unveil hidden histories through maps, other projects look toward subjective experiences of space as both meaningful and valid forms of knowledge. Such projects are less concerned with challenging the conventional methods of cartography than with engaging us to think critically about such methods. They ask us why we often accept visible and physical features as more meaningful than invisible and psychological features. They summon us to consider different ways space is experienced. Instead of conceptions of space that appear on civic maps that assume a homogeneous experience of equal citizens, these projects ask us to consider different experiences of the same space for people of different ages, sexes, religions, citizenships, or abilities. These projects entreat us to map open space in politically conscious ways. They distinguish themselves from projects that apply insights from affective cartography to reproduce racial stereotypes that silence or erase histories of structural inequality, such as a *SketchFactor* (United States, 2014), a navigational app developed by Allison McGuire and Daniel Harrington that allows users to avoid neighborhoods identified as "sketchy" by culling publically available information and crowdsourcing data.[13] Despite the developers' position that the app does not promote racism because they consulted with community groups, the app lacks a critical framework on "relative sketchiness." The app potentially aggregates racial prejudice by pulling data from user reactions based on the app's prompts. Unlike other user-contributed data sites like *Yelp* for restaurant reviews, the app uses a racially charged term in its title. "Sketchy" means undefined or incomplete, as in a sketch for a police drawing. The term signifies something dangerous or dishonest, often associated with race and poverty. *SketchFactor* thereby moves toward the closed spaces of neoliberalism, much like *GhettoTracker* (United States, 2013), later renamed *The Good Part of Town*, a controversial app that allegedly helped users avoid "unsafe" neighborhoods.[14] By contrast, the projects examined here propose ways of mapping space that are useful while remaining politically responsible. They deploy digital paradigms of recombination and random access to unsettle our sense of space, so that we actually engage with it and feel it. We immerse ourselves in mapping to move around prejudices within conventional thinking.

Babak Fakhamzadeh and Eduardo Cachucho's *Dérive app* (Uganda/Belgium, 2013) runs on the web browser of any smartphone, so that users understand space from an on-the-ground perspective. The app assigns task cards based on Guy Debord's concept of the "dérive," a psychogeographic practice that creates the conditions for an unplanned journey through an urban landscape with the aim of getting lost in order to elicit critical reflection on the space that we inhabit everyday but might not notice or even really see. The field of cartography complicated assumptions that knowledge must be objective or rational to be useful, recognizing the subjective and even irrational as a useful source of information. Affective, emotional, ludic, and subjective mapping reveal meaning that emerges through collaboration or sharing of perspective.[15] Invisible features can be as significant to the ways that we navigate and negotiate space as visible ones. For example, urban areas can evoke all kinds of emotional responses—fondness, nostalgia, apprehension, fear—that might be more relevant to planning a walk between two points than merely the geographic data of their location. Dérives serve as performative and collaborative mappings of space. Participants place themselves in situations that force them to think differently. As Fakhamzadeh and Cachucho explain on the app's website, *Dérive app* was created "to try to nudge those people who are in this repetitive cycle to allow the suggestions and subjectivities of others to infiltrate their urban existences."[16]

The app works by tracking participants' movement on a standard street map. Participants log on and draw task cards from one or more of the decks. They must complete and document through photographs and journal entries each randomized task. The "Urban Deck," for example, includes relatively generic tasks that nonetheless heighten attention and awareness of space: "browse around for an interesting shadow," "wave and smile at the next surveillance camera," "find a crowd," or "find a cat." Other decks have particular significance to

Figure 2.1 *Dérive app.*

particular locations. "Fine a license plate number below 3000," for example, makes sense in Abu Dhabi but is nonsensical in New York. Alternatively, "follow someone walking a dog" is extremely easy in New York but extremely difficult in Abu Dhabi. Comparably, "take a cheap *boda* ride" makes little sense in Paris but a lot of sense in Kampala. Other tasks require specialized knowledge, such as contemplating Abu Dhabi's Egyptian connections or finding someone wearing a *burqa* (leather facemasks) in an era of *sheilas* (fabric headscarves). Fakhamzadeh and Cachucho lead workshops with students at local institutions, which include lectures on urban history and lessons in visualizing tasks. To date, localization decks have been created for Abu Dhabi, Biella (Brazil), Ithaca (United States), Johannesburg, Kampala, New York, Paris, and San Francisco.

Leila Nadir and Cary Peppermint's *Indeterminate Hikes (IH+)* (United States, 2012) is another smartphone app for Android that transforms everyday experience into a revolutionary occasion for learning about the environments that we inhabit but often do not notice. *IH+* provides users with prompts that task them with rethinking their location and their relationship to the location. Reworking associations of hikes with leisurely activities conducted in the wilderness, *IH+* asks users to hike at home—to see, hear, touch, taste, and otherwise experience the wilderness in the everyday all around them. They become indeterminate hikers. When using the app in their home neighborhoods, users learn to see what they overlook on a daily basis. Tasks import terms conventionally disassociated from urban or suburban life, thereby mutating the users' thinking about categories, such as human and nonhuman, natural and artificial. One task might ask a user to sit on the ground and ask a passerby whether they have seen a rabbit; another, to contemplate transient nature of nature and document something that will not exist the following day; still another, to say aloud "non-human animals are people too" in public, locate an animal with a tail and ask the day of the week, then text the response to someone the user loves. Like *Dérive app*, the *IH+* transforms users into participants in what might be considered a never-ending struggle with resisting the temptation to give oneself over entirely to our smartphones. The task cards force us to look away from our mobile screens and notice the world in a critical rather than romanticized way.

Electronic Disturbance Theater 2.0 (EDT 2.0) and b.a.n.g. lab's "safety net" app, *The Transborder Immigrant Tool (TBT)* (United States, 2007), provides lifesaving information, such as directions and the location of water caches, to transborder crossers from México into the United States. Five years after its launch, Ricardo Dominguez was subjected to media scrutiny over the legality of the locative media app by the US Federal Bureau of Investigation (FBI) Office of Cybercrimes, three California Republican Party congresspersons, and the University of California, San Diego, where Dominguez is a professor. In an interview with Dominguez about the controversy surrounding TBT, *IH+* co-creator Nadir observes that EDT 2.0 adopts a practice in which "activists break the law, while artists change the conversation theatrically, by disturbing the law."[17] EDT engages performance as a means to alter thinking about received notions about the illegality of hacking and taking things apart in order to locate ethics within them. The project makes mobile what Heath Bunting and Kayla Brandon's web-based *BorderXing Guide* (United Kingdom, 2002–2003) did by documenting the militarized borders around Europe, so that people could navigate them. It extends the work of Torolab's *The Region of the Transborder Trousers* (México, 2004–2005), which transformed "the endless traffic jams and humiliating searches" of the Tijuana/San Diego commute into "an opportunity for creative experimentation," as Mark Tribe and Reena Jana argue.[18]

EDT 2.0 is a collective that includes Dominguez, Brett Stalbaum, Stefan Wray, and Carmin Karasic. EDT borrows a trespass-and-block-ade tactic that mixes online and on-site performances of electronic civil disobedience (ECD). It draws on Henry David Thoreau's notion of non-acquiescence to civil government. Given EDT's work with the Ejército Zapatista de Liberación Nacional (EZLN or Zapatistas) in México, it is hardly coincidental that EDT should look to Thoreau, whose *Civil Disobedience* (1849) appeared during a tumultuous period in the pre–Civil War United States, which had recently invaded and annexed (reterritorialized) half of its neighbor México. EDT's FloodNet was a collective and recombinant weapon for the EZLN to disrupt access to targeted websites by flooding its host server with requests, including ones asking for pages that do not exist to build bad URLs, in a denial-of-service (DoS) attack.

TBT is open source, encouraging others to apply it to other borders. It runs on inexpensive mobile phones with GPS capacity. The project was partly motivated by the startling statistic of 416 border-crossing deaths between México and the United States reported in 2009. More startling, EDT 2.0/b.a.n.g. lab contrasts this statistic with the reported 98 border-crossing deaths between East Germany and West Germany during the entire 28-year history of the Berlin Wall.[19] For Dominguez, *TBT* is part of a commitment to making ethical-aesthetic gestures and disturbances to the border that divides the Mexican American borderlands. *TBT* engages *affectively* and *effectively* to remix art and activism, often disengaged from each other. Working with the NGOs Water Station Inc. and Border Angels, which leave water caches along the Anza-Borrego area of Southern California for transborder migrants, *TBT* provides vital information for crossing the militarized border.

TBT also provides "poetic audio sustenance" by queering the technology of code to "guide 'the tired, the poor,' the dehydrated— citizens of the world." *TBT* makes the border visible through "critical ecologie(s)/environmentalism(s)" that recognize a "bio-citizenship" or "trans[]citizenship" that crosses between multiple forms of life that are blocked from movement, whether black bears, plants, water, or migrant labor."[20] "The TBT project calls into question the northern cone's imaginary about who has priority and control of who can become a cyborg or 'trans' human," explains Dominguez, making reference to Donna Haraway's *cyborg* and Micha Cárdenas's *transreal*.[21] Thinking through digital media allows for a deterritorialization of history and other forms of knowledge that divide and segregate what are now called transnational histories, such as centuries of migrations within the Mexican American borderlands before the establishment of the Rio Bravo del Norte/Rio Grande as an international border that has been highly militarized. Since the ratification of the North American Free Trade Agreement (NAFTA) in 1994, so-called illegal migrations into the United States have exponentially increased through a systematic dissembling of traditional income sources, such as *milpa* farming, in México.

Resisting Power in Micro-movements

Arts and community centers become sites for other digital media projects that open space by mapping in ways that do not resemble atlases or tourist maps. These centers resonate with the radical reconceptualization of film by Fernando Solanas and Octavio Getino in their manifesto "Towards a Third Cinema," which advocated for audiences not only to become literate in reading film critically but also to become literate in producing their own films.[22] Digital video becomes a means to contest history to reclaim spaces previously denied. Predigital examples include the National Film Board (NFB) of Canada's Challenge for Change program, launched in 1967 to "promote citizen participation in the solution of social problems," especially ones considered important by minoritized groups such as indigenous nations, as well as the various experiments by the French Unit in Montréal with *cinéma direct* (direct cinema). Indigenous media centers throughout Latin America and Oceania have taken advantage of relatively inexpensive and user-friendly analogue and now digital cameras and editing software to make visible and audible voices that have been ignored, marginalized, and delegitimized. Most significantly, the video becomes a means of transmitting knowledge from generation to generation, sometimes without allowing outsiders to know about this knowledge. Other centers have used digital media to claim a right to modernity. Even micro-movements can affect enormous changes.

Started in 1982, Scribe Video Center is a nonprofit media arts center providing media production instruction to Philadelphia-area residents in the United States. Scribe views media production as a tool for community groups and individuals to explore personal, social, political, and cultural issues. Rather than a top-down, individualistic, and argumentative, single authorial vision, their epic project *Precious Places Community History Project* (United States, 2005) advances a collaborative model, where community participants become active authors rather than passive subjects. Scribe's community media and oral history project, *Precious Places*, a video anthology of 19 eight-minute documentaries exploring the historical memories in public spaces, buildings, parks, street corners, churches, and monuments, intervenes into misrepresentations of development. The videos employ a realist documentary style of interviews and cutaways, advancing collective storytelling as an active historical enterprise. These polyvocalities counter cities as places for high-end hotels, symphonies, theaters, and expensive restaurants.

To *Badlands and Back Again*, for example, was produced by the Fair Hill Cemetery activist group. The video engages micro-movements to answer problematics regarding the ethics between subject, maker, and audience. It shows how a partnership between Philadelphia Quakers and concerned local African American and Latina/o American residents transformed a historic cemetery from a garbage-dumping ground into a community safe green space. Although early feminist and anti-slavery activists are buried in the cemetery, this community knowledge was lost. Fair Hill had disintegrated into a drug-pushers haven. The Quakers and community groups cleaned the cemetery, disposing both refuse and drug dealing. Community members contend this reclamation project twins land and history. A diverse range of organizations participated: African Cultural Art Forum, Community Leadership Institute, Mount Moriah Preservation Society, Germantown Historical Society, Odunde, and West Girard Community Council. With some assistance from academic historians based in Philadelphia, *Precious Places* documents particular locations through residents' oral histories, a response to development initiatives destroying both communities and their histories. *Precious Places* moves documentary toward networked, collaborative micro-interactions between neighborhoods, places, filmmakers, scholars, and histories. *Precious Places* embodies polyvocalities and microhistories to reclaim the archive, history, and memory through the production of new micromemories.

Precious Places rewires development from the perspective of communities and restoring lost histories to particular blocks. These microhistories reframe public places and individuals as community. They suggest collective effort can rejuvenate community spaces through oral histories and actions. In *Putting the Nice Back in the Town*, the Neighborhood Advisory Committee restores the area with participant voices narrating the block. Although documentary history heroicizes individual authorship, an equally long collaborative tradition exists, extending from Robert Flaherty's *Nanook of the*

North (United States, 1922) through the Workers Film and Photo Leagues of the 1930s to community media operations like Appalshop, Kartemquin, and Paper Tiger Television. *Precious Places* extends this collaborative community media legacy. It reclaims Philadelphia histories from churches of the Underground Railroad, a community garden called Las Parcelas, or Mount Zion Baptist Church. *Precious Places* materializes diverse, microhistorical, collaborative neighborhoods amid the press of development. One of Scribe's latest projects is *Muslim Voices of Philadelphia* (United States, 2014) under Louis Massiah. The project gives voice to the diversity of Philadelphia's historical African American Muslim community.

Helen De Michiel's *Lunch Love Community* (United States, 2014) addresses another area of where US democracy fails to provide for its citizens: public school lunch programs. The short videos, ranging from three to ten minutes, feature the cooks, parents, teachers, and children in the Berkeley public schools as they work to move toward more nutritious school food. The videos are mounted on the *Lunch Love Community* website, designed in orange, red, and green colors evoking fresh vegetables and ripe fruit. The exhibition of these short videos combines the website, insertion of the videos in links in various forms of social media related to food politics and policies, and public exhibition in specially designed media socials. The project operates on a philosophy mobilizing the micro, as each episode title in this mosaic of voices suggests a different prism through which to consider children, schools, and food, rather than a doctrinaire argument: *The Whole World in Small Seed; Flamin Hot Cheetos; The Parent Factor; The Labor of Lunch; But Is It Replicable; If They Cook It, They Will Eat It; Feeding the Body Politic*. Each episode shares a similar visual style with a focus on lush, richly colored close-ups of children, teachers, cooks working with plants and food. They were designed for mobile phones, tablets, as well as theaters. The people and the food are integrated, constantly touching, moving, and working with vegetables. The episodes foreground different groups in the schools telling their stories, rather than experts or politicians, an example of both citizen science and grassroots engagement. In *Flamin Hot Cheetos*, a teacher asks her elementary school students to analyze the ingredients on junk food packages, and then creates an experiment to see how long a Cheeto (a food product made from corn and flavored to taste like cheese) would burn, showing its chemical structure.

Collaborating with parents, teachers, children, and schools in Berkeley, California, the project developed out of the Berkeley Unified

School Districts' 1999 groundbreaking food policy to provide locally grown organic food in the schools. Berkeley was a pioneer in the movement for healthy food for students. Rather than a long form deductively argued documentary with a narrative arc and a central character, *Lunch Love Community* presents a series of micro-stories featuring a wide array of everyday people involved in school food, including parents, cooks, teachers, politicians, and health advocates. Rather than an argument about school food reform, the project creates a fluid, constantly changing open space for convening of collaborative publics to discuss these issues in what De Michiel has called "media socials," designed for dialogue rather than for indoctrination. The episodes are never exhibited in theaters or at festivals as a continuous stream. Instead, De Michiel adapts a customized exhibition practice for each community, working with local cooks, schools, teachers, and food-reform advocates to not only decide which episodes in which order, but to craft an interactive event. De Michiel insists that screenings include speakers from the local community, stopping after each episode for dialogue with the speaker and the audience, emphasizing process and engagement with particular local issues like nutrition or food reform.

Founded in 2000, the Jakarta-based Raung Rupa is an art collective that produces exhibitions, festivals, workshops, art labs, books, magazines, and an online journal. Drawing upon ideas from the social sciences, politics, and technology, it concerns itself with thinking through media about urban issues in contemporary Indonesia. In 2004, it launched *Jakarta 32°c*, the first biannual visual art exhibits by students; in 2003, it inaugurated *OK. Video*, the first biannual Jakarta International Video Festival. The collective also has a Video Art Development (*Pengembangan Seni Video*) whose goal includes producing audiences for nonmainstream audiovisual work, particularly video art, and produce the festival's themed editions: *OK. Video* (2003), *Sub-versi* or *Sub/version* (2005), *Milisi* or *Militia* (2007), *Comedy* (2009), *Flesh* (2011), and *Muslihat* or *Deception* (2013). The most recent takes its name from the practice of "making the impossible possible" through tricks, tactics, and strategies. It outsmarts technology by adding another function, extending its life, reworking its aesthetics, or reflecting upon the presence of media technologies in our lives. The theme resonates with the hacker ethic of taking things apart in the North Atlantic and the *jugadu* ("make do") solutions in South Asia, discussed in chapter 1. However, the vast political changes and neoliberal structural adjustments in Indonesia prompts specifically local applications of this innovative and improvisational practice. Marking its tenth anniversary in 2010, Raung Rupa mounted *Celebrating Ten Years of Raung Rupa: Expanding Space and Public* (Merentang Ruang dan Publik), an exhibition at the Indonesian National Gallery and *ruru.zip*, an exhibition in collaboration with the Yogyakarta-based Indonesian Visual Art Archive (IVAA). Compiling ten years of data and memorabilia, the exhibition also interprets it. As one of the curators and a former editor at Raung Rupa's *Karbon Journal*, Farah Wardani explains, the collaborative discussion between herself and cocurator Ugeng T. Moetidjo, with the founders of Raung Rupa, allowed for a filtering and restructuring of the archive to trace the development of the collective from an artists' initiative into art and urban activists.[23]

An important aspect of Raung Rupa's work is its engagement with the urban space of Jakarta after the 1998 resignation of Suharto, Indonesia's US-backed authoritarian president, which brought to an end 31 years of New Order. As cultural anthropologist Doreen Lee explains, the production of images of youth (*pemuda*) was a significant part of the history of activism in the post-Suharto *Reformasi* ("reform" in Bahasa Indonesian) movement for democracy, particularly in the contributions of 1998 Indonesian Student Movement with its "politically transgressive yet increasingly popular forms of expression." Their success in mobilizing activists, she argues, "lies in their imminent reproducibility; at once ephemeral, easily forgotten, and remade the next day, the production and reception of photographs, slogans, signs, and t-shirts resembled already wide-spread consumption practices belonging to urban youth culture."[24] In this larger political context, Raung Rupa's exhibitions, performances, and workshops have contributed toward a remapping of Jakarta to open space for the production of audiences.

Raung Rupa's *10 Tahun Seni Video Indonesia 2000–2010* exhibited ten years of video art, including work by internationally regarded artists, such as Krisna Murti and Tintin Wulia, and installations of video art by collectives such as Forum Lantang. The video art takes the locality of Jakarta as a nodal point for economics, politics, and technologies. Forum Lenteng's *Andy Bertanya/Andy Aska* (Indonesia, 2003), for example, looks at "illegal" advertising around Jakarta. By looking at the language of informal posters for domestic help, painting lessons, and other services, as well as paying attention to the language of negotiations for such services—often in a humorous way—the video expands the ways that we can think about the rapidly growing urban space of Jakarta. Similarly, Ari Satria Darma's *Iqra* (Indonesia, 2005) animates the lettering on signage, so that it appears to peel and float away, along with wires, strings, graffiti, and images of fish, leaving behind a static gray world. At moments, it appears as though the letters will form an alternative message in the sky. With advertisements and promotions suddenly blank, spaces in the commercially driven Bandugan Hilir part of Central Jakarta are opened to a different interpretation of neoliberal reform and its restructuring of social relations. The evocative and equivocal video won awards at the ASEAN Short Film Festival in 2006 and ASEAN New Media Art Competition in 2008.

Bagasworo Aryaningtyas's *Bilal* (Indonesia, 2005) shows a young man with a very tall punk Mohawk haircut lip-sync to a muezzin's voice giving a televised *azan* or *adhan* (call to prayer). Krisna Murti's *Beach Time* (Indonesia, 2003) shows slow-motion video of women in *hijab* at the beach. Although these videos might seem surprising for their "unexpected" content to audiences outside of Indonesia, they document everyday life in ways that ask us to look and listen more attentively, subtly challenging orientalist visual imaginaries while also registering the rise of Islam in post-Suharto Indonesia. Martin Kristianto's *Dangdut Kopolo* (Indonesia, 2003) compiles video of the boom of *dangdut* music and the erotic dancing of *kampong* stars from East Java that circulated primarily on pirated DVDs. The video asks us to think about the public debates on morality and ethics that emerged during the boom, as well as the possibilities for independent media distribution. Mahardika Yudha's *Sunrise Jive* (Indonesia, 2005) looks back at the New Order's Senam Kesegaran Jamanl (Gymnastics for Health) program of Friday morning exercise mandated in schools and governmental institutions. In the video, some workers cheerfully follow the music and exercise outside a factory, while others largely ignore it. Other videos translate with greater facility across cultures, such as Hatiz's *Alam: Syuhada* (Indonesia, 2005), which is staged as an interview with a young man on a public bus. The video screened at the Oberhausen Short Film Festival (Internationale Kurzfilmtage Oberhausen, Germany) in 2006 with Aryaningtyas's *Bilal* in its "Unreal Asia" section in 2009.

Tintin Wulia's five-minute stop animation *Everything's OK* (Indonesia, 2002) becomes a point of departure for debate on unsustainable urbanization. A solitary figure rests in a field with trees. The entire environment is white. The camera takes images from various sides of the scene, giving a rhythm to the shots that matches the fluttering on the white cloth that serves as the ground. Suddenly, a human hand appears and plants a small house near the trees, an act quickly followed by the arrival of other houses. Eventually, larger buildings encircle the houses and trees, blocking light and their view. As they skyline grows, so too does pollution. The hand dabs charcoal-color paint onto the pristine white buildings. Later, three other hands join the first one, showering the city in miniature US currency before erecting billboards that advertise gated communities in the suburbs. Finally, the hand lays another sheet of white ground over the first. Atop, another solitary figure rests in a field with trees. The short video conveys urban history.[25] As in many places around the globe, neoliberal reforms in Indonesia have resulted in greater pollution, further entrenchments of corruption, and the erosion of public space. Wulia's first video, *Violence against Fruits* (Indonesia, 2000) makes a contribution to establishing Indonesian video art as politically committed through a simple dialogue between a male and female voice as a *kaki* (a fruit originally from China) is sliced and eaten.

Andry Mochammad's *Just Do It* (Indonesia, 2005) animates illustrations for Chinese children's conduct books, beginning with one retitled "Beautiful Day: Piracy Environment.05." Figures engage in conversations nearly incomprehensible on the audio playback but subtitled in Bahasa Indonesian. Mochammad only animates head, hands, and mouths, so that the images and their movement seem antirealist. In one scene, a family sits around a dining table only to flood it with vomit. The video foregrounds low production values, furthering its exploration of the notion of replicas and fakes in an era of highly policed intellectual property and rampant consumerism. The English words "JUST," "DO," and "IT" flash everywhere until they shift from the globally recognizable branding motto into an invocation to do anything one likes, including piracy. Nike's "JUST DO IT" trademark appears once more in white text on a black screen followed by the Nike swoosh logo, which bursts into flames like a poorly maintained sweatshop. It breaks, and a small child exits, referencing the use of child labor in sweatshops. The following images show a photograph of a young child inspecting a Nike trainer. The text reads: "Work it. Nikefactory. Open in Vietnam and Indonesia." Nike's motto of consumerism as self-empowerment to do anything— "just do it"—is reduced to a slogan for the disempowerment of factory workers—"work it"—through unskilled repetitive labor, low salaries, and often great risk to health.

As the images appear on screen, the video's audio track becomes increasingly dissonant. The video concluded with an English-language message in all caps that appears one word at a time on the screen: "Just Do It Support Your Local Piracy Don't Believe The High Brand Look At The New Market Keep Smart With Software Piracy Against The Global Brand." The following screens include a command—"Do not eat the brand / and make new brand"—followed by slightly modified ("pirated") logos for brand names such as Adidas, Aiwa, BMW, Canon, Casio, Coca-cola, Daewood, Epson, Honda, Hugo Boss, JVC, Kenwood, and L.G., familiar in night markets throughout Southeast Asia. Hewlett-Packard's *hp* logo becomes *dy*, a homonym for "die"; Levi's, eviL's; Shell, hellS. The final text reads: "We are still alive / happy and not stupid." The video satirically rejects the mechanisms by which we are trained to respect copyright through education. It is also a celebration of open spaces where content can be reused. Rather than end credits, the video concludes with the simple explanation: "All video take from DVD Piracy." Mochammad's video points to open spaces through piracy.

In general, the video art scene in Jakarta differs from comparable experimental media scenes in East Asia, Europe, and North America, which often locate their politics in avant-garde elitism. The Jakarta scene seeks to open discussion to larger publics. These videos stage and record events that sometimes serve as antirealist historical documents, pointing to ways that affective meaning can be as meaningful as visual evidence anchored in a faith in photographic indexicality. Indonesian video art becomes an important site for negotiating contradictory desires of the postcolonial condition. Thinking through digital media can entail the production of new images to produce new audiences, as in the case of Scribe, or it can entail the recycling of images, including ones ripped from DVDs. Removing corporate encryption through color-correction software, space is opened for the pleasures of contestation and dissonance. Mochammad is a visual artist from the West Java capital of Bandung, site for the 1955 Asian-African Conference (aka Bandung Conference), which united 25 recently decolonized countries against colonialism and neocolonialism in the nonaligned movement against domination by China, Soviet Union, and United States. The conference established a declaration of values that included respect for human rights, sovereignty, and equality—all of which have been greatly eroded by IMF-led neoliberal reforms that arrived in Indonesia after the 1997–1998 economic crisis. Bandung was also the site for the fiftieth anniversary of the conference in 2005. Indonesian video artists have witnessed enormous changes that restructure social relations, a subject evident in the documentaries by Leonard Retel Helmrich, discussed in the following chapter, as well as digital video by non-Indonesian artists, such as *Shrivel* (Canada, 2005), about a Paris-inspired gated community, part of Oliver Husain's trilogy on Shanghai, Jakarta, and Hyderabad.

Distributing Connections

Artists, coders, activists, students, and intellectuals come together to think through digital media to produce audiences in open spaces that are both physical and virtual through distributed and cellular networks. Such projects use maps to locate new connections and unmarked commons, often at moments of crisis. They galvanize ingenuity and self-motivation. They infect us with inspiration toward productive possibilities within systems designed for monitoring and surveillance masked as interactivity. One of the most historically significant instance of Google Map mashups was conceived in response to lawyer and activist Ory Okolloh's post on her blog *Kenyan Pundit* after Mwai Kibaki was announced winner in the 2007 Kenyan presidential elections and leading opposition candidate Raila Odinga claimed that ballots had been rigged. The violence unfolded as part of tensions traced to the political and social structures formalized under British colonialism, which gave land and resources to a colonial elite upon Kenya's independence in 1963. Like other former colonies of the North Atlantic empires—British, Dutch, French, Portuguese, Spanish, and US—colonial corruption continued in Kenya, further exacerbating structural inequalities and consolidating social prejudices. The violence in 2007 and 2008 left more than a thousand dead and more than half a million displaced. Kenya's democratic laws and media were practically suspended. Unlike the 2011 democratic uprisings in Tunisia and Egypt, where blogs and social-media platforms became a significant means to relay information, Kenya's Internet penetration was estimated at only 8 percent. Its mobile-phone penetration, however, was greater than 40 percent. In May 2008, Ushahidi developed a web-application mashup for crowdmapping that interfaced with mobile technologies.[26] In contrast to conventional documentary that often recovers history by digging into archives, Ushahidi documents urgent contemporary events through data visualization. Documentation becomes a mode of urgent activism. Only five months before Ushahidi's creation, Okolloh had posted her question: "Any techies out there willing to do a mashup of where the violence and destruction is occurring using Google Maps?"

David Kobia and Juliana Rotich in Kenya, along with Erik Hersman in the United States, joined Okolloh to form Ushahidi ("witness" or "testimony" in Swahili). They developed a platform that would allow Kenyans and others to report and map incidents of violence via SMS or a web browser. Messages are fact-checked and stored on a secure server. Reports are tagged with metadata, including priority (e.g., urgent) title, description, category (e.g., fire, looting, rape), and GPS coordinates that map onto Google Maps. The platform permits data to be compiled into reports for activists, relief workers, healthcare providers, and NGOs. Raised in an impoverished part of Kenya, Okolloh is committed to the use of digital technologies that assist Kenyans in changing their circumstances. After winning awards for applications of technologies toward social change, the Ushahidi platform was launched in a 2.0 version, which has been used to collect and visualize data in various conflict zones: it monitored elections in India and México; organized relief efforts in Haïti, Pakistan, and Thailand; and tracked sexual harassment in Egypt and crime in Indonesia. Ushahidi has also created iHub, Nairobi's Innovation Hub where coders gather to produce web and mobile resources to meet community needs, offer technology consultant service to global clients, share perspectives at regularly scheduled hackathons, and learn together through speaker sessions, workshops, and mentoring at Tech4Africa in Nairobi, Lagos, and Cape Town. Ushahidi has also developed BRCK, a rugged portable router that allows Internet access during power outages.

Ushahidi maps open space for social causes often ignored by state and local agencies, along with transnational corporations, for a variety of reasons. Its innovations and ethics of open-source continue to inspire and empower others to think through digital media. The results are sometimes ephemeral, but their ramifications are long lasting. The Monsoon Collective in Kathmandu, Nepal, for example, was a month-long enterprise that emerged from the need for information on public transportation that is reliable, easy to understand, and electronically available. Organized by Prabhas Pokharel and fellow students at Kathmandu University—Robert Ochshorn, Sakar Pudasaini, Suveg Pandey, Shirish Pokharel, and Anshu Khadka—the collective was a "hack/make space," whose Yatayat web, SMS, Android apps interpret the unwieldy paper schedules for the Kathmandu Valley Public Transport authority.[27] In 2012, Pudasaini launched Karkhana, a space for experimentation and collaboration, focusing on hacker/

maker solutions for local needs and a sustainable future. Its learning lab, KL Cubed, offers hands-on instruction in critical skills for the twenty-first century. Other collectives and spaces, including online collaborations take place, suggest possibilities for remapping the world. Geopolitical borders are less inhibiting than firewalls and data-mining software. Physical walls and checkpoints, however, are an everyday part of life in many parts of the world. The Israeli "separation" wall in the occupied West Bank erodes Palestinian national identity as a "security threat." In the absence of substantive support from the international community, Palestinian artists have a long tradition of thinking through media, including the guerilla filmmaking of the Palestinian Liberation Organization (PLO) during the 1960s and 1970s. With the movement away from violent toward nonviolent protest, anticolonial thinking through digital media includes the production of infographics distributed through social media. *Visualizing Palestine* (Palestine/Israel, 2012–present) responds to the erasure of Palestine through European colonialism during the Nakba ("catastrophe" in Arabic) through continued occupation by the state of Israel, including what Saree Makdisi calls the "erasure of erasure."[28] The project developed after TEDxRamallah. Like most other licensed TEDx events, which are designed to showcase the "power of ideas to change attitudes, lives and ultimately, the world," TEDxRamallah was inaccessible to many Palestinians living in the West Bank due to Israeli checkpoints.[29]

In part, the *Visualizing Palestine* collective responds to Israeli state policies of *hasbara* (literally, "explaining") that attempt to promote Israel against what is seen as "negative" press, particularly following the Intifada (1987–1993) and Second Intifada (2000–2005) in Gaza and the West Bank. Israel aggressively promotes itself as "the only democracy in the Middle East" despite well-known policies of discrimination, not only against Palestinian Christians and Muslims but also against Mizrahi (Arab) and Ethiopian Jews. Israeli exceptionalism is also evident in the promotion of Tel Aviv as uniquely queer friendly in an otherwise homophobic region through tourism and a "Tel Aviv Pride Tumblr."[30] "Pinkwashing," as Jewish American LBGT activist Sarah Schulman writes in her analysis of Brand Israeli campaigns, "is the cynical use of queer people's hard-won gains by the Israeli government in an attempt to re-brand themselves as progressive, while continuing to violate international law and the human rights of Palestinians."[31] *Visualizing Palestine* is one of several new media projects, including the *Electronic Intifada* (2001–present), offering news analysis by activists, journalists, and intellectuals, including Omar Barghouti, Joseph Massad, and Ilan Pappé. Such media is dedicated to reminding English-language audiences that Palestine has been occupied for more than 60 years and that many Palestinians continue to live as second-class citizens of Israel and as refugees in Lebanon, Jordan, and other states. Resembling Robert Stam's "media jujitsu," *Visualizing Palestine* attempts to control the narrative on the Palestinian struggles in the wake of Israeli *hasbara*.[32]

Describing itself as an "intersection of communication, social sciences, technology, design and urban studies for social justice," *Visualizing Palestine*'s purpose is to create "creative visuals to describe a factual rights-based narrative of Palestine/Israel." *Visualizing Palestine*'s infographics are displayed on its website and through social media like Flickr and are featured in news streams from *Al Jazeera English*, *Huffington Post*, *Jadaliyya*, *PolicyMic*, and *The Daily Beast*. They have been translated into Arabic, French, and Korean. Its designs are elegant and effective, including an infographic on the design process, which includes eight steps:

1. identify new directions and ideas;
2. get the raw data and validate sources;
3. make it into a compelling story;
4. translate it into a brief;
5. bring in designers to express it visually;
6. review the work to ensure quality;
7. publish the work online; and
8. trace its impact and virality.

The overall aim is to amplify emotional appeal in order to shift perceptions by taking bland data and transforming it into dynamic information.

Identity Crisis: The Israeli ID System (Palestine/Israel, 2014), for example, visualizes the layers of identities that determine where someone can live or work and whether they can vote since the Naksa ("setback" in Arabic) of 1967. The upper layer of 5.9 million Jewish Israeli citizens occupy almost the entire landmass of Palestine/Israel. Their only prohibition is that they cannot live in Gaza or 40 percent of the West Bank. The 1.3 million Palestinian citizens of Israel constitute the next highest layer: they are allowed to vote, but they cannot live in 68 percent of Israeli towns. The 300 thousand East Jerusalem Palestinians cannot vote and, if they leave East Jerusalem, can have their ID revoked. The 2.3 million West Bank Palestinians cannot vote and cannot live in the 40 percent of the West Bank occupied

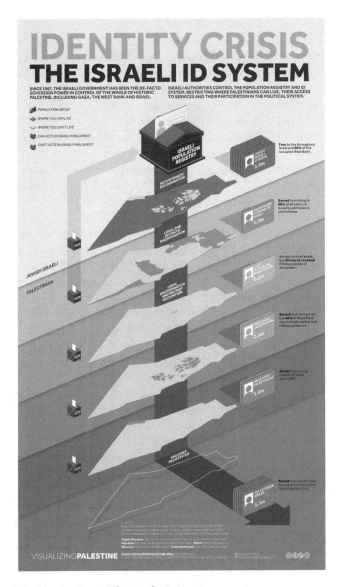

Figure 2.2   *Identity Crisis: The Israeli ID System.*

by Israel, and the 1.6 million Gaza Palestinians cannot vote and have not been allowed to leave Gaza since 2007. The infographic also includes a shadowy underlayer of 5.7 million Palestinians who are barred from returning: they are excluded by the system of occupation. Moreover, the infographic visualizes the nonexistence of the Green Line or pre-1967 borders that mark the boundary between Israel and Palestine under the 1949 Armistice Agreements. Palestinians are contained to increasingly smaller territories that are disconnected from one another. *Segregated Road System* (Palestine/Israel, 2012) examines the color-coded license plates that determine freedom of movement in Palestine/Israel, where the best highways are reserved for Jewish Israelis, so that Palestinians must often spend considerably more time moving from one place to another, even without checkpoints. The infographic visualizes precisely how closed, policed, militarized, and confining the space of Palestine/Israel can be based on racial/ethnic and religious classification.

Other infographics examine the role of Lebanon and the United States. *Palestinian Labour Force in Lebanon: Restricted Professions* (Palestine/Israel, 2013) treats the condition of Palestinian refugees in Lebanon, where Iqbal Assad—the world's youngest doctor—cannot practice medicine. She must go to the United States because "foreigners," including refugees who were born and have lived in Lebanon for more than 60 years and hold no other passports, are barred from professions like medicine, law, and engineering. The infographic is illustrated with simple blue-and-white figures and the shapes of Lebanon and the United States. Key phrases are accented in green. Others deal with issues of administrative detentions, segregation of public buses, the continued construction of walls and barriers in the middle of the West Bank, mortality rates for babies born at military checkpoints, contaminated water in Gaza, Israeli settlements in the West Bank since the 1993 Oslo Accord, hunger strikes to protest arrest without charge, and US military aid to Israel, much of which is used against Palestinians.

The inforgraphics often attempt to communicate to US audiences. *Uprooted: 800,000 Olives Trees Uprooted, 33 Central Parks* (Palestine/Israel, 2014) conveys a sense of the scale of Israeli destruction of Palestinian olive trees, an act whose economic and symbolic consequences are signified by layering an image of Caterpillar bulldozers razing olive orchards in New York's Central Park. The loss is visualized in simple graphics of trees uprooted, US dollars lost, and families affected. *Visualizing Palestine*'s interpretation of the film *5 Broken Cameras/Khamas Kamarat Mhattamah/Hamesh Matslemot Shvurot* (Palestine/Israel/France/Netherlands, 2011; dir. Emad Burnat and Guy Davidi) also addresses a US audience. Although funded in part by both the New Fund for Cinema and Television (NFCT) and the Israeli Film Fund (IFF) and directed by an Israeli filmmaker, the film was nominated as a Palestinian film for an Oscar from Hollywood. The film documents the history of nonviolent protests against illegal Israeli occupation of Palestinian lands through the first-person account of a Palestinian protagonist in Bil'an, West Bank. The infographic provides a broader context of occupation that is not included in the Oscar-friendly film, including the construction of Israeli settlements, Israeli Defense Force (IDF) violence of teargasing protestors and razing olive orchards, and international declarations against such actions. *Visualizing Palestine* thus uses social media to map an open space for discussion of one of the most misunderstood topics by Hollywood fans, who might not understand the historical context of the conflict. The infographics remap what has historically been cast as "long-standing" cultural antagonism between "Arabs and Jews," which are reproduced throughout US media.

Like TEDx talks, infographics are a powerful means to communicate dissonant ideas virally to the Millennials—the generation that followed Generation X—born in the 1980s to 2000s for whom digital technologies were never really new. In various ways, increasing criticism of the occupation among US university students can be linked to new media projects like *Visualizing Palestine*, which was conceived by Ramzi Jaber shortly after he graduated from McGill University in Montréal. *Visualizing Palestine* is a powerful example of thinking collaboratively through digital media to produce audiences on social-media platforms to affect political change on behalf of human rights. Created by the human-rights organization Witness, *The Hub* (http://hub.witness.org) was an online venue for organizing action human rights organizations, grassroots activists, and citizen eyewitnesses around the world. With its simple motto—"See it. Film it. Change it."—*The Hub* aimed at affecting social change. Agnieszka Pokrywka's *Central Eastern European Media Art Chart* (Poland, 2000–present; http://ceemac2000plus.blogspot.com/) maps media organizations, institutions, and practitioners in this region. Evoking an in-flight route map in the back of airline magazines, the project charts these featured organizations and individuals, collating a regional media ecology database. In different contexts, these digital media projects map open space for a moment when life is increasingly precarious.

Negotiating Borders and Checkpoints

Maps usually indicate geopolitical borders, but they do not customarily indicate checkpoints, including the ones that monitor anyone or anything that crosses a militarized border. Checkpoints mark spatial and temporal crossings that are not only physical and referential but are also experiential and referred. Although they are embedded in geographical and historical debates that often seem utterly objective, they can feel deeply subjective. Some checkpoints mark violent moments in everyday life like going to work when it involves crossing into a free trade zone or going to school in an occupied territory. Other checkpoints establish peaceful moments like birthdays, holidays, and anniversaries; the sound of a personal alarm clock in the morning; or calls to prayers that punctuate the day.

Checkpoints also register along distributed networks, through user-ID verification as well as firewalls. Political theorists have suggested that an epoch of disciplinary control is giving way to one of regulated control in a centerless, yet hierarchical, distribution of power that functions like distributed networks of what was once called the Information Superhighway. Despite efforts of transnational media corporations to co-opt political movements as "Twitter Revolutions" or "Facebook Revolutions," movements often emerge in the streets when communication networks are blocked and when news media seem unready or unwilling to dispatch investigative reporters or even broadcast information. Checkpoints take forms other than microblogging through copyrighted social-networking software. Checkpoints are everywhere—in the airwaves and on our hard drives. Artists, intellectuals, coders, activists, and students respond with innovation and circumvention. States and corporations strike deals for exclusive power and absolute copyrights, while hackers and modders crack and unlock systems for the commons.

While checkpoints are often defined by the racism and violence of surveillance as security, Valerie Hind's *The Maiden Voyages Project* (United States/Egypt/Iran/Jordan/Palestine, 2010; www.maidenvoyagesproject.com/index.html) is a collaborative project with women in Egypt, Iran, Jordan, and Palestine in which checkpoints become a scheduled day per month to communicate their thoughts on being a woman among other women. A voluntary and collaborative checkpoint maps difference with a feminist commons. In her own words, Hird wanted "to recognize that women can have a shared experience within the rhythms and routines of daily life and still be very different women from very distinct cultures." The women recorded aspects of their lives on a set day of the month for the period of a year. All but one of the women chose to remain anonymous to Hind. Along with Hind's own entries, the project collates the landscapes of daily routines, intimate reflections, and dreams of five women who share certain experiences, expectations, and aspirations and yet also share important differences. Hind's collaborators trusted her to interpret, illustrate, and animate their personal thoughts. For audiences unfamiliar with the Middle East and North Africa (MENA) regions, this open-access project brings what Hind defines as a "measure of reality" into discourses dominated by US media.

Of Hind's four collaborators, two are Muslim and two are Christian (Coptic or Catholic). Two are students—one in university, the other, in graduate school. The other two are teachers—one at primary and secondary school, the other, at university. The women chose the music that accompanies their diaries, which are shaped by their individual locations. Much of the diary by the Palestinian S. K., for example, is dominated by crossing Israeli checkpoints in the West Bank. Getting permission for an Easter celebration in April is not guaranteed. By contrast, the Jordanian K. K.'s diary entry for April begins the "getting ready for my day" and ends with "getting ready for bed," in May about her mother's visit to Riyadh, Saudi Arabia. These monthly communications cut though the firewall of misinformation about the MENA erected by transnational media corporations based in places like Australia, Europe, Japan, and North America. Even in more progressive venues, such as international film festivals, MENA is often reduced to orientalist, chaotic tropes of war, poverty, religious fundamentalism, and the oppression of women. Hind's communications with the women also cut through misinformation about "Amreeka," that is, the myths about "America" that circulate in Egypt, Iran, Jordan, and Palestine. These myths range from the American Dream of success (often in exile) to familiar associations of death and injustice through US wars and historical support for oppressive regimes, which began to shift only after the uprising in 2010, as well as unconditional support for Israel.

Myriam Thyes's *Magnify Malta* (Germany, 2012; www.thyes.com/political-symbols/magnify-malta/index.html) is a multi-platform art project that explores the implications of globalization for the state of Malta, a small island state in the middle of the Mediterranean Sea, which, like Lampedusa (Italy), has become a primary entry point into Fortress Europe. Within close proximity to Africa and Europe, Malta experiences the push of geopolitics and neoliberal economics on transnational migrations, particularly as refugees flee different parts of Africa where economies have been destroyed by free trade and structural adjustments after decolonization. Examining such

human traffic through its borders, *Magnify Malta* ponders the implications of migration for Maltese culture, society, and labor market.
Since Malta joined the European Union (EU) in 2004, East African
refugees have been arriving in rowboats in increasing numbers. At the
same time that the arid island is witnessing a construction boom with
speculatory hotels that often stand empty for long periods, the refugees live in custody in refugee camps of condemned buildings, tents,
and in one case, an aircraft hangar. Some await deportation. The EU
accepts a limited number of refugees. Of them, a few find work in
Malta in construction or, less frequently, in tourism.

Thyes's project is composed of a downloadable archive of photographs and photomontages. They capture aspects of Malta from
the construction sites of luxury hotels to the tent village of the Hal
Far refugee camp. One image shows colorful rowboats sitting on the
beach and anchored near the coast in the Birzebbuga Freeport with
equally colorful containers for shipping in the background. The juxtaposition of containers and rowboats evokes comparison between the
infrastructure that facilitates transnational mobility for goods under
free trade and the vulnerabilities that inhibit transnational mobility
for people, whose vessels are often haphazard, makeshift, and contingent. Another image shows a yacht and a replica of a medieval galley ship in Grand Harbour, offering another view into transnational
mobility. An image titled "Grand Harbour, yacht (looking like a war
ship) and refugee woman" shows a woman, standing with her arms
folded across her chest, in front of a yacht and a smaller boat. The aesthetics of her clothing—a pink floral-patterned dress, brown blouse,
and blue and white scarf over her head—stand apart from the sterile
tones of the boats. She looks away from the boats.

Other images evoke religious ritual manifest in stone in the many
churches and statues of saints of the deeply devout Catholicism practiced by the Maltese. On the one hand, Malta takes in more refugees than she is genuinely capable of accommodating; on the other
hand, for all the vitality of faith in the island population, racism is
on the increase as it is throughout the EU. Malta's battle-ridden history as a bastion between European, Turkish, and Arab civilizations
becomes visible in the traces of the Order of the Knights of St. John.
From the sixteenth to the eighteenth centuries, many combatants
and galley slaves of all parties lost their lives in naval battles in the
Mediterranean. Today, many refugees drown in that same sea on
their way from Africa to Europe. In all aspects, Malta is like a small
model of migration—a metaphor for Europe. The project *magnifies*

Figure 2.3 *Magnify Malta.*

the small state, so that the complexities of the EU and the legacies of European colonialism in Africa become visible.

Encounters with Planetary Change

Graham Huggan and Helen Tiffin argue "the conjunction of postcolonialism and ecocriticism has begun to prove mutually illuminating in terms of, say, colonial genesis and continuing human inequalities and environmental abuses," yet "the two areas have often been in conflict."[33] Although climate change remains controversial in states like the Canada and the United States, which refuse to endorse international agreements like the Kyoto Protocol to reduce emissions of greenhouses gases, many states have already embarked on transitions to renewable energies, notably Germany, Iceland, Norway, Portugal, and Spain.[34] Connections between energy consumption online and off-line are sometimes deceptive. Considered the first state that will disappear due to climate change, Tuvalu has leased use of its attractive top-level domain (.tv) in order to assist with the transition of its citizens via mass emigration to places that will not be flooded by rising tides in the Pacific Ocean, a subject considered in the feature-length documentary *The Disappearing of Tuvalu: Trouble in Paradise*

(France/United States, 2006; dir. Christopher Horner and Giliane Le Gallic). Average avatars in Second Life consume more energy that average humans in Brazil, pointing to ways that ecocritical thinking challenges neoliberal thinking. Ecocritical art examines other affects of the Anthropocene, including the ecologically disastrous effects of insecticides like neonicotinoid that contribute to mass deaths of honeybees, industrial farming practices linked to bovine spongiform encephalopathy (BSE, or "mad cow disease"), and other epizootic crises, as well as the unknown and undisclosed effects of GMOs. Like other projects discussed throughout this book, the ones in this section consider our everyday encounters with harmful planetary change affected by human progress.

Christina McPhee's *La Conchita mon amour* (United States, 2005; www.christinamcphee.net/la_conchita.html) studies the struggles of life in the beach community of La Conchita in California after it was inundated by debris flow after a devastating mudslide. Caused by increased intense winter rains, an effect of climate change, this digital video and photography project documents vernacular shrines to the dead built by surviving residents off Highway 1 in California, when governmental assistance for victims of cyclical recursion of disaster is not forthcoming. The project's photos continue this memorializing through the vernacular of everyday and homemade objects by compositing and layering shrines iconography and destroyed, disintegrating natural environments. In *Banana Memorial*, groundcover and wildflowers are digitally composited with black mud. In *California Republic*, US flags and prayer flags are reduced to ribbon-like status, layered over a black background evoking mud and torrential rain. The digital compositing of these images, where layers fall into and merge with each other, doubles the collapse of the land in mudslides. One triptych image is in fact titled *Collapse Mechanism*, creating continuity between environmental disaster and an aesthetic of destruction. McPhee's project evokes Alain Resnais's film, *Hiroshima mon amour* (France/Japan 1959), based on the screenplay by Marguerite Duras, on the lingering devastation and anguish of human-made ecological disasters, like the US atomic bombs dropped on Hiroshima and Nagasaki in August 1945, which contaminated humans, animals, plants, land, and water for generations.

Nicole Antebi's *Geography of Reclamation: An Essay in Three Parts* (United States, 2012; https://vimeo.com/49290133) splices together traditions of the essay film and animation to describe how humans have altered rivers. The hand-drawn compass shown at the beginning of the film intimates that geography is not the spectacle beyond us, but something of smaller scale, which we can enter. Describing a beige globe she purchased, the voiceover notes that the water was beige, "a non-color, neutral." The voiceover points out that the Romantics figured the landscape as sublime. The film then charts a path through water in the opposite direction, one that is partisan and not neutral, political and not sublime, but interventionist, both in destroying rivers and canyons as well as protecting them. The film engages ways that economic interests shape the very form of the planet, and simultaneously proposes that art and activism can again reshape the planet after the trauma of dams. With its chalky pastel drawings washed over by blue or early-cinema iris techniques, the film offers the smaller scale of the drawing, invoking botanical prints or a biologist's field diary.

Exploring environmentalism through the intersection of the work of David Brower from the Sierra Club, Floyd Dominy from the Bureau of Land Management, and Robert Smithson, the land artist, *Geography of Reclamation* layers competing ideas that shaped the course of history as much as the policies, activism, and art of these three men shaped the course of the waterways within the Colorado River Basin in the western United States. The short animated essay is structured by the counterpoint of three voices, concluding with queries about preserving Smithson's *Spiral Jetty* (1970), an earthwork constructed of mud, salt, and rocks that the artist hoped would disappear naturally but is now faced with the threat of oil drilling.

With *Pine Point*, Kenneth White (United States, 2007/2009) uses the event of a young couple's trip to the seashore as a setting for their engagement photographs to explore the relationships between technology and nature, work and leisure, space and time. The carefully composed shots, along with the short video's ambient soundtrack of waves breaking softly on the sands of the beach, reveal what stands to be lost without increased attention to environmentalism. Comparably, *Anima* (United States, 2009; www.mnartists.org/work.do?rid=122455 or http://www.youtube.com/watch?v=f4SLtL-0KIE) by Jim Grafsgaard with PJ Tracy takes a journey in extreme close-up over the surface of Grafsgaard's painting *Geo Grande*. The digital video takes a panoramic view of the systems and energies of planetary ecology, particularly an imaginary biological community of microbial and fractal forms. The animation offers space for a meditation on experiences of time and space, relationships of scale, and energies of color, motion, and breath. It considers ways that organic metropoli regenerate and mutate in response to their destruction by humans.

Survival and food figure in digital visions of sustainability. Bryan Konefsky's *Chicken Delight* (United States, 2006) and Artur Augustynowicz's two remixed films, *Meat Cutter* (Canada, c. 2006) and *Cheese Burger* (Canada, c. 2006) highlight the unsustainable and unappetizing methods of modern food production. While often tongue-in-cheek, these videos traverse the multiple ways in which we either sustain or contaminate the environment. They suggest that the Anthropocene is not pastoral, but violent: food production as an act of rage and aggression. Thinking of food beyond hunger pangs, *Chicken Delight* examines food production that results in harm instead of sustenance. Touching on issues such as irradiated chicken and cannibalistic lobsters, *Chicken Delight* is a deeply satirical look at human-made environmental disasters, deterioration of health, and growths of tumors. By appropriating and repurposing media images and found footages of food production, advertising, and food-related television programs, *Meat Cutter* and *Cheese Burger* remediate the processes of food production. Referencing situationist-inspired ways to pilfer and mash images, these films show animals being killed and ground up to take their place on non-vegetarian tables.

Mapping Databases

A significant difference between analogue and digital media is the capacity for random access to digital files. Digital databases magnify this capacity. They suggest new routes through data to locate information, often yielding more complex, contextualized explanatory structures of knowledge than the linear and causal ones that have been the foundation of analogue documentary and narrative. Digital media maps open space by activating database structures and random access memory (RAM) as a means of producing variegated knowledges. *Permanent Transit: net.remix* (Afghanistan/United States, 2004; www.kabul-reconstructions.net/transit) is a database road movie about the anxieties of continual migration, the shifting identities of the multiple-generation refugees, and the state of statelessness.[35] Originally conceived as a single-channel gallery installation, the video was shot in 2001 and edited in 2002. Filmed through the windows of planes, buildings, and vehicles in various countries, the 12 screens of *Permanent Transit: net.remix* alongside the fragmented soundtracks reimagine documentary and narrative practice according to digital recombinatory databases. The web-based project is part of a larger initiative. Created by Mariam Ghani in collaboration with programmer Ed Potter, *Kabul: Reconstructions* (Afghanistan/United States, 2003–2005) was an ongoing collaborative, community-based, interactive, and accumulative enterprise designed as a series of open-ended databases and systems that grow through the input of the artist, collaborators, community members, and audiences. The project became an interactive documentary and public dialogue to document reconstruction projects in Kabul at yearly intervals. By adopting both a conventional documentary mode (representing) and a less conventional mode (dialoguing), the project documents multiple perspectives of particular situations, emphasizing movements toward collaborative, open-ended knowledge rather than single perspectives or closed structures constructing and transmitting knowledge.

Moreover, the project was open to actual interaction: users could post questions on any topic, which the team would research and answer, thereby moving definitions of interactivity beyond the industrial-defined notions of clicking on hypertext or choosing options. Questions ranged from ones about daily Internet usage in Kabul and other cities to the role of women in the field of technology after the US occupation of Afghanistan, as well as inquiries about finding work in Kabul.[36] The first two sections of *Kabul: Reconstructions*, which were active from March 2003 to March 2006 and are archived on the website, include data about Kabul's reconstruction gleaned from the official networks of international media coverage, as well as data about the reconstruction transmitted via Afghani diasporic and exilic networks in response to questions posted on the website by users. The third and fourth sections of the project turn their attention to the constitutional assembly and national election, posing questions about the "architectures of democracy proposed and promoted through the reconstruction efforts during that window of possibility which now seems to be closing." The project deploys Internet communications P2P technologies to disrupt the authority of centralized models of distribution.

Permanent Transit: net.remix by Ghani and Potter with poet Zohra Saed and composer Qasim Naqvi considers the instability of states of being through migration in response to political events. It is a database documentary about the anxieties and recoveries, disorientations and reorientations, associated with the continual migrations of expatriates, exiles, refugees, immigrants, and itinerants. Shot on digital video through the windows of planes, buildings, and vehicles on location in Armenia, Italy, Jordan, Lebanon, the Netherlands, Palestine, Russia, Syria, Turkey, the United Kingdom, and the United States, looped video in QuickTime windows and fragmented sound of the 12 windows of *Permanent Transit: net.remix* result in "experimental documentary reconstituted as a documented experiment."[37] It is designed to relocate viewers from state-bound lives to the crossroads experienced by the "hybrid generation" of stateless populations that Ghani defines as "difficult, absurd, productive zone where locations and cultures blur, intersect, overlap and exchange," while political borders reify. Experience, memory, and identity are not merely fragmented, as articulated by postcolonial theories. Instead, experience, memory, and identity are distanced, blocked, and often mediated in self-alienating ways that find description in views through the glass of windows of moving vehicles and temporary lodgings. The images resonated with documentary images in McPhee's *La Conchita mon amour*, which, as Sharon Lin Tay has argued, are infused with subjective evocations, thereby displacing indexicality as a primary mode of making meaning from visual representation.[38]

To enter *Permanent Transit: net.remix*, the user opens a browser divided into a dozen windows, manipulating the content by clicking on the mix button to download one single-channel video after another from the video subset of the database, as well as the play and pause buttons of the media player in each window. Sound tracks are selected by algorithm from the audio subset of the database. In ten of the 12 windows, the short videos loop automatically. The audio track plays only once. The seventh and tenth windows contain text that appears and disappears in sections. The only window that does not automatically loop is the first window, which contains the title in white capital lettering against a black screen. The letters rotate through the alphabet faintly behind the words "permanent transit" as images appear and disappear in clusters in a visual representation of the transience of memories and sensory impressions. The audio-track of the title window generates anticipation of change suggested by the rapid beat of percussion instruments, punctuated by the occasional clanking noise of a metal instrument.

Fidelity of visual representation to experience comes into question. Indeed, sound often compensates for the people and places that vision cannot produce. Handshakes and hugs find approximate substitutes in long-distance telephone conversations, so that the sound of voices fills in the gaps left by the absence of faces. The documentary explores substitutions and partial equivalences of being in a state of permanent transit where environments seemingly always shift under-foot. Structured as a database, *Permanent Transit: net.remix* would seem to question the very assumptions of database search engines to produce meaningful results. Although the videos document travel through 11 states, images of these disparate places are seen only through the windows of vehicles and locations of transit. Cultural and political constructions of an East and a West collapse when the visual markers of the familiar and foreign are largely obliterated in partial views. Memories of one flight splinter into memories of a thousand flights. "What was the order of cities?" asks Saed's text; "Beirut...Bag hdad...Damascus...New York...Baghdad again...Amman...New York. In the ellipses we find only war." Memories become sites for contestation between generations.

As an unreliable structuring narrative for the piece, Rula Ghani recounts her memories of Syrian comedian Doreid Laham's absurdist tale of a man trapped in a no-man's-land during the Lebanese Civil War (1975–1990). The gaps in Ghani's memory of Laham's tale, orig-inally televised in 1981 but only remembered and recorded decades later, are evocative of the project's attempts to document what is lost everyday. "How many windows can we look from? How many roof-tops await our return?" asks Saed's text alongside the images. The clicking and chiming of clocks in the waiting rooms of airports, bus depots, railway stations, and checkpoints comes to replace the call to prayers once heard from the local mosque. In another segment, sounds of prayers mix with sounds of traffic as a woman eats a meal by a win-dow. "God and radio hold hands in the eternity of no-man zones," suggest Saed's text at one point. Although "bells, work, clock—all cut up the day as neatly as a traffic jam," little relives the sense of being in a state of "permanent waiting," emphasized by looped video across a multiplicity of screens. *Permanent Transit: net.remix* also explores possibilities for recuperation of identity and grounding: "There are borders, there are checkpoints, and there are our mother's stories to undo them all with one twist of a tale and a gentle laugh like glass breaking." To break the glass of the windows that stand as barriers between modes and sites of permanent transit suggests a substitute for home, particularly for families whose individual members may have strikingly different memories of home due to histories of movement across borders. For the hybrid generation, the sound of the mother's voice is perhaps all that binds identity.

Perhaps the most sobering feature of *Permanent Transit: net. remix*'s documentation of the disorientations of expatriates, exiles, refugees, immigrants, and itinerants is its remix feature that shuffles images. New images appear, old images disappear. The same images may surface more than once within the grid structure of the windows. The user's ability to remix the videos and audio, paired at random by the project algorithm, suggests meaning cannot be contained within linear temporalities. Rather, it spills over into circular loops and is mapped onto multiple screens that suggest spatial and experiential relationships. According to Ghani, there is only a one–in-four chance that audio and video will align as they were recorded. Ultimately, images are interchangeable due to their representational transience. Memories cannot be anchored to fixed locations of home and homeland: identity is diffused and subject to atrophy. The absolute presence of the images guarantees nothing, so that "we are all in imminent danger of becoming merely ghosts in the machine" in Vivian Sobchack's terms.[39] The project mobilizes the database structure of the Internet and digital video's ability to loop endlessly to reconfigure documentary via temporal and relational dimensions not possible with analogue technologies that demand linear structures.

Educating visitors about the hidden military heritage of the United States, Owen Mundy's Camp LaJolla (United States/Germany, 2011; http://camplajolla.org/) is a multi-faceted research and performance project that features a database, a gallery installation, a mock national park brochure, a taxonomy, and a golf cart tour that records the relationship between the University of California San Diego and the military-academic industrial complex. Repurposing an interface analogous to military reconnaissance, the project deploys geographical coordinates to map the historical nodal points for military contractors, such as General Atomics and Northrup Grumman on the campus. Avi Rosen's 3 Generation Lullaby (United Kingdom, 2003), by contrast, composites three generations singing into one compressed image. Parallel Space #1 (United Kingdom, 2007) defies linearity through a dissonant virtuality.

Other databases are not project-specific, such as GPS databases that allow us to locate ourselves—and be located by others—on a global grid. In GPS drawing practices, human subjects are equipped with matchbox-sized GPS loggers that record their geographical location at short intervals as the subjects move along a calculated route. When the drawings are imported into data-visualization software like Google Earth, they are rendered in color pixels and polylines from a bird's-eye perspective. This "bird," however, is metaphorical: Google Earth likely looks nothing like space seen through the optical perspective of an actual bird. *Farm Animal Drawing Generator* (Austria, 2008; www.gebseng.com/09_farm_animal_drawing_generator) by Gebhard Sengmüller mobilizes auto-generative properties of GPS drawing to map a farm in Salzburg from the perspective of six cows and two goats by attaching GPS loggers to their bodies to record their movements. Rather than approximating the vision of cows and goats, the project permits a glimpse into their sense of spatiality in a state of containment on the small Austrian farm. The movements of these animals can be screened as animations or large-format print-outs, which suggest a very different way to conceive territorial divisions of space than the map, satellite, and terrain option of Google Maps. Since the animals are not free to roam away from the farm, the animations and images reveal their state of imprisonment. Yet they also document areas of the field that are determined by the animals themselves, as well as the proximities of their interactions with each other, without translating these coordinates into human ones. The digital drawings recontextualize tracked movements, making them remarkably unhelpful for anyone interested in surveillance or understanding the animals' movements. By rendering the context of animal migrations illegible, the project engages an emergent form of interspecies ethics. *Farm Animal Drawing Generator* maps in ways that humans cannot fully understand, thereby decentering the anthropocentric logic that stabilizes cartography. The project responds to one of the central inquiries in the field of Animal Studies, specifically Randy Malamud's question of "how we might overlay our maps upon their maps to directly compare our sense versus their sense of geographical space."[40] In other words, how we might map open space with and alongside nonhuman species.

3

Documenting Databases and Mobilizing Cameras

This chapter turns to projects that think about and through the digital structures of data and databases, and the mobility of digital cameras. These projects explore how digital media disrupts conventional structures by prompting a rethinking of the concept of documenting that foregrounds spatiality over temporality, relationality over causality, and automated functions over auteurist choice. We draw on Christiane Paul's description of a shift "from 'mapping' to 'tagging' as the new paradigm of dynamic classification, context creation, and meaning production" in digital media.[1] Digital technologies not only map our anatomy, they tag our identity. We are becoming digital through biometrics (e.g., dates of birth, shoe sizes) in state and corporate databases and digital profiles in social media. Our digital identities exist as data in databases, which suggests that we can document ourselves or be documented by someone else, including an artificial intelligence (AI)-enabled bot, without ever having to appear on camera. Comparably, mobile cameras and sensors also allow movements that are not constrained to human perspectives or abilities. More profound than a majestic crane-shot in the latest Hollywood blockbuster, mobile cameras can be harnessed to document spatial relations for further analysis. Remote sensing from airplanes, satellites, and drones documents our lives from a distance. Processing images with mobile cameras extends into processing images with nonlinear editing software. "Slow motion, tinting, distortions and intense layering turn images into discursive elements rather than the depiction of facts," writes Ursula Biemann, so that "material space" becomes "technologized, dislocated, dematerialized and prepared for a different reading."[2] Her video essays avoid "documenting realities" in favor of "organizing complexities."[3] Her video essays are subjective, but they are not personal in the sense of individualistic and egocentric. They engage the world, including its digital structures, and see meaning as a process of assemblage, much like the mobile cameras of Leonard Retel Helmrich, discussed below. Databases and cameras are engaged as participants in performances rather than mindless technologies for human expression.

Adapting Marsha Kinder's concept of "database narratives," in which a surplus of information emphasizes a "dual process of selection and combination," we argue that documenting through digital media unsettles analogue assumptions about documentary from fixed modes (expository, observational, personal) and toward open modes (collaborative, reflexive, interactive).[4] "Digital information and data sets exist as processes that are not necessarily visible or graspable— processes that can be visualized in multiple ways and manifested in multiple materialities," writes Paul. "At the same time, data sets have a direct influence on how societies are shaped (from economics to politics) and therefore on the subject, body and identity."[5] Katherine Hayles suggests that the arts and humanities might benefit from thinking through databases, much like researchers in the sciences and social sciences work from a common set of data, creating "different front-ends from the same data, thus encouraging collaboration in data collection, storing, and analysis."[6] Artists, activists, students, scholars, and coders have conceived and implemented projects according to digital structures of tagging, visualizing, and filtering data in databases. The structure of digital data and metadata asks us to think differently. We are accustomed to linking, filtering, navigating, and orienting information since we have been partially trained by AI to do so. We engage in a kind of thinking with machines as part of our everyday experience with "smart" technologies. Examples include auto-format in word processing, auto-focus on cameras, suggested items on news aggregators or shopping sites, and computerized opponents in video games. In part, automation through AI is programmed to anticipate human choices based on data that has been collected, tagged, and stored in a database of past choices. When the data is processed through filters, for example, information appears.

Digital media moves from images on chemical-based celluloid and magnetic-grounded analogue video to images digitally coded and rendered. Images are coded into data (from the Latin *datum*, meaning "something given") and metadata (instructions for how data will be processed) that is organized and structured in databases rendered into information through automated sequences of simple operations of decoding data.[7] Images are no longer indexical traces of reality or direct representation of continuous movements. Images recorded or stored on celluloid are visible even when the reel is not running through the projector. By placing filmstrips on an optical table, images can be isolated. Digital media is different. Its images can only be seen or heard then they are played back on a computer, so that all representations are performances of codecs (*compressor-dec*ompressors or *c*oder-*dec*oders) running to make sounds and images, rather than an indexical trace through audio or visual evidence.

Digital images provide a means to advance discussion of documentary beyond claims to mediation ("realism") and immediacy ("truth"), signaling the limitations of visual evidence. Documentary, then, moves as a concept from evidence-based "push" media (celluloid, video, even visual display of GUI) toward act-based "pull" media (user acts, hyperlinks, algorithms). As Biemann makes evident in her media practice, the role of the maker can become one of preparing data for multiple readings rather than expressing individual opinion; in other words, practice can become radically collaborative. The digitization of audio and visual images into code that can be accessed randomly, labeled and sorted, then distributed (relatively) instantaneously, prompts reflection upon the historical and cultural assumptions that determine and manage meaning for many of the key terms (e.g., evidence, witnessing, testimony) associated with documentary. A defining characteristic of digital media is its ability to organize information as data tagged with metadata in databases, so that information may be rendered into a theoretically infinite number of discreet sequences via user acts and algorithmic operations. Meaning is not fixed as it is on celluloid; rather, meaning is malleable, destabilizing the certainties of positivist constructions of knowledge and opening meaning for ongoing debate. Digital structures, then, offer a means to address controversial subjects, such as environmental catastrophe and species extinction triggered by modern progress or displacements and deaths of millions through neoliberal economic and military policies, in ways that open meaning to debate rather than attempt to circumscribe the contours of meaning.

Although proliferation gave way to consolidation as commercial interests appropriated the DIY aesthetic, the potential of media produced and distributed via consumer-grade technologies like mobile phones remains an important component in the formation of digital media ecologies. Activist media emphasizes its primary concern with enacting policy change and dislodges expectations of impartiality and balance, which have been naturalized by analogue documentary practice since the early twentieth century. Mobile-phone movies have the potential to dislodge expectations of high production values without the apolitical relativisms of DIY discourses. Media-activism programs use mobile cameras to train nonprofessionals to document human-rights and environmental-safety violations committed by transnational corporations, as is the subject of *Maquilapolis: City of Factories* (United States/México, 2006; dir. Vicky Funari and Sergio de la Torre) about female workers in the finishing plants (*maquiladoras*) of the NAFTA's free zones. Professional documentarians have also mobilized mobile cameras to organize complexities, as in Leonard Retel Helmrich's concept of Single Shot Cinema, discussed below.

From its etymological roots in the word *documentaire*, roughly translating into English as "travelogue," documentary film foregrounds its ability to present (or transport) audio and visual images ("documents") across time and space. Historically, documentary film constructs meaning through the temporal sequencing audiovisual images onto reels of celluloid, or onto analogue and magnetic tapes. Since digital images are not recorded as a direct representation of a continuous process, they are produced as a process of encoding information as data and metadata that can be searched, selected, combined, and converted back into an analogue signal that can be displayed on a screen and played through a speaker.[8] Vivian Sobchack argues that presence in electronic (digital) media is "absolute presence" or "being-in-itself."[9] Rather than a presence confined to the past, as with photographic media, or a presence forever constituting itself as presence, as with cinematic media, the absolute presence of digital media is a centerless, network-like structure of instant simulation and desire, rather than in nostalgia for the past or anticipation for the future, so that qualities of the photographic and the cinematic are schematized into discrete pixels and bits of information, "each bit being-in-itself even as it is part of a system."[10] Digitality, then, implies an opening to ways of conceiving one's place in the world that is not constrained to the linearity of most analogue formats and has the potential to challenge the historical legacies that have deployed such technologies as they have intersected with colonialism, racism, ethnocentrism, sexism, class oppression, homophobia, religious fundamentalism, and war. They foreground meaning as always in process, as something that can be subjected to another layer of analysis and interpretation rather than something fixed and settled. Structures tend to be modular rather than linear: meaning is produced by relationality rather than causality. Content is reconfigured via RAM that permits immediate access to any part of the "new media object."[11] New media emphasizes programmability, so that interactivity operates in ways that exceed the reading strategies offered by reception theory (i.e., interpretation of different meaning from a single text).[12] Users manipulate information, actively exploring hyperlinked web pages and performing other acts. In particular, the database model facilitates selection and recombination of documents, thereby offering a mode of documentary that more closely resembles an archive, which, in Michel Foucault's terms, "defines at the onset the system of its enunciability" and "causes a multiplicity of statements to emerge, as so many things to be dealt with and manipulated."[13] More than a system of display and distribution, then, the database becomes a mode for Internet-based documentary where meaning is subjected to endless re-combinations, operating within a simultaneously constructive and destructive "archive fever" that Jacques Derrida has described.[14]

Like analogue video archives, online digital archives are open to receive new documents, suggesting the meaning is a constant process of accumulation. Unlike their analogue counterparts, however, online digital archives mobilize the random access of digital code and the remote access of digital networks as a means to facilitate collaboration between humans and machines in this process. Polyvocal, unstable, and contested meanings, rather than fixed ones, become a means of politicizing online and off-line environments. Digital media that documents databases refigure conventions of collaborative and self-conscious documentary. The absolute presence of digital media suggests a potential for emphasis on meanings that differ from causalities explained by temporal and spatial coordinates to relationalities based upon a database format of potentially endless recombinations. Digital media that itself documents databases prompt recognition that meaning is always polyvocal, unstable, and contested—always present in a moment of transition toward movement and contestation. Web-browser–based projects, for example, use plug-ins to add an additional layer over those that constitute the original webpage. As Mary Flanagan argues, they "critique, contextualize, or activate what is happening in the networked space 'below,'" emphasizing ways that "the system cannot be separated from the material of the digital media nor from the structure of the shared space on the Web and the shared labor those spaces represent."[15] These projects make visible digital structures of data and the digital network of the Internet as context. "The context of exchanges infuses the content itself," as Flanagan explains, "for the content reflects the exchange in the form of compression, edits, identifying marks, [and] sampling rates."[16] Meaning becomes mobile in the sense of contingent and provisional—that is, speculative rather than conclusive.

Repurposing Databases

The archive and the database are not fixed, but ever expanding repositories for knowledge production. Digital media artists have fashioned databases from repurposed commercial media. In *Every Shot/Every Episode* (United States, 2000), Jennifer and Kevin McCoy sample scenes from a television police drama *Starsky & Hutch* (United States, 1975–1979).[17] Grouped under 278 tags, such as "every sexy outfit" or "every racial stereotype," the sequences are burned on VCDs. As installation, the VCDs are placed on a shelf; visitors select a disc. The McCoys assign tags, transforming narrative-driven Hollywood media into nonnarrative digital media. Projects satirizing professional standards anchor critiques of inequalities in jagged glitches and crufts rather than seamless interfaces and realism. Mark Napier's *The Shredder* (United States, 1998) and *Digital Landfill* (United States, 1998) are earlier projects that engage imperfection by allowing users to select webpages for aggregators to "shred" into colorful digital debris.[18] Remixing data and metadata, design and content are no longer fixed but unstable and in flux.

Fernando Velázquez's *Your Life, Our Movie* (Uruguay, 2008; www.yourlifeourmovie.org/) is an algorithmic image-search program that visualizes "your life" by harvesting images from Flickr's public databases and generating a montage movie. The project explores the ways we interface with automated machine acts to organize data into information. Automation functions according to metadata, such as the commonly used tags for images in Flickr. Although the meaning of tags such as "tree," "sky," and "bird" might seem relatively fixed, when the project searches for them, slippages in signification are visualized. The project reveals ways that automated tasks unsettle ostensibly seamless technologies. *Your Life, Our Movie* identifies and selects images by tags. It produces new meanings by editing them together algorithmically. Compare the movies produced by entering words like "border," "nafta," or "usa" versus entering words like "river," "zapatista," and "palestine." Working with Bruno Favaretto and Francisco Lapetina, Velázquez created another iteration of *Your Life, Our Movie* as a gallery installation with three large screens. By repurposing images from databases, the project asks us to think about our complicity with surveillance systems that search user-generated and tagged content—our gifting of our digital identities and digital lives to corporations.

Ripping and recombining source material from a number of online databases, Ben Baker-Smith's *Infinite Glitch* (United States, 2011; www.infiniteglitch.com) generates a continual flow of sounds and images by scraping sounds and images from publically accessible websites. It modifies them through glitch effects of digital compression formats, source coding, and bit-rate reduction, organized according to automated collage effects. As a live performance, *Infinite Glitch* documents, animates, and comments upon the ever-changing mediascape of the Internet. The loss of information in each digital image serves as a potential marker for the loss of information in other areas of life. More significantly, the relatively unregulated and ever-increasing stream of media files uploaded by users every second represents a flood of data in comparison with broadcasting's regulated and measurable flow of images. The sometimes-incomprehensible sounds and images generated by *Infinite Glitch* points to limitations in our critical methods and theories to make sense of networked media.

By countermining major search engines such as AOL, Google, and Yahoo!, Owen Mundy's *Keyword Intervention* (United States, 2007; www.keywordintervention.com) visualizes the popular words and phrases by repurposing automated search functions. Inspired by the form and content of the *mandala*, the circular form that encourages focused attention and contemplation of impermanence in Hindu and Buddhist practices, the project represents the information cosmos in human terms while acknowledging the transitory aspects of material forms. By exploring an "imaginary line between commerce and culture," the project reveals the predominant use of these commercial search engines for information on celebrities, especially "nude pics" or "suicide." By mining these terms, the project's webpage itself is aggregated to the top hits of the search engines, pointing to ways that the Internet can function as a closed system. Like the other projects in this section, *Keyword Intervention* works to perform the operations of the database in ways that make us less naively complicit. In some cases, algorithmic operations are initiated by humans; in other cases, human input is not even necessary.

Visualizing Metadata

If digital structures operate according to modular and fractal logics, then recombination becomes a primary means for making meaning. Thinking through digital media suggests a way to recombine everyday terms, so they redefine themselves in relation to digital technologies and distributed networks. Juxtapositions open counterpositions. Unlike the analogue media content, digital media content is not immediately recognizable as content. Data is bound to metadata, code that carries instructions for rendering visual and audio content. By making metadata viable and audible, digital media projects interrupt the illusions of seamlessness within the interface. Metadata frames the data in databases and gives it meaning as information to produce knowledge. Given the rapid automation of tagging through software like facial-recognition programs, documenting earlier automated digital technologies situates AI as both the object and subject of documentary modes.

Eduardo Navas's *Goobalization* (United States, 2005–2007; www.navasse.net/goobalization/index.htm) is a series of short animations that remix images retrieved through the Google search engine.[19] The project's four search terms—"surveillance," "difference," "resistance," and "globalization"—expose complex online power struggles. *Goobalization* documents ubiquitous corporate logos. Like Cocacolaization and McDonaldization, Navas's title takes the brand name of the globally dominant Internet search engine corporation, Google, to name the process of WTO integration and interdependence: globalization. At the time, Google declared its mission to organize "the world's information and make it universally accessible and useful." It is also a publicly traded corporation specializing in online advertising that generates revenue in billions of US dollars. Google targets search engine users with Geo-ID, locating them by IP address and targeting them with advertisements based on browser history. Advertisements automatically display in local languages, reflecting user complicity with the automated monitoring/surveillance.[20]

Rejecting narrow analogue definitions of documentary, *Goobalization* documents and animates search-engine machine acts. Rather than conceiving images in an indexical relationship to reality, the project considers visual evidence as mediated iconicity. Images begin in an assigned frame space (upper left corner for "surveillance," for example), then fade in and out, spurring discomfort between the concepts and familiar media objects. Navas programs the images to appear in proximity to his key terms—"surveillance" in the upper left; "difference," upper right; "resistance," lower left; and "globalization," lower right. This design prompts contemplation about Google search engine algorithms and how search engines construct meaning through interaction with human users. As the images appear on screen, their juxtapositions expose complex power struggles, disrupting Google search results' hierarchy, highlighting the production of meaning in the process of filtering data. Images fade in and out at different intervals. The user experiences uncomfortable proximity between the incompatible social, economic, cultural, political, and ideological processes of globalization and the mundane acts of a Google search.

Goobalization does not hack or modify the Google search engine. Rather, it makes visible its logic, interrogating what highly contested key terms might produce. At the time, Google boasted that its search engine is "untainted" by human involvement or paid advertisement. Its patented "hypertext-matching analysis" and "page rank" algorithms decreased search calculation time. An open-content model allows copying and modifying of information. The Google search engine relied on human users to index data via tags ("image labels"). In its own example, an image of a large tropical seabird in flight against a blue sky receives higher points for the labels "sky" (background image), "bird" (foreground image), "soaring" (action), and "frigate bird" (more detailed description). The tags link keywords to visual images. Google's labor micro-outsourcing recalls Amazon's electronic freelance platform, Mechanical Turk (MTurk), satirized in Laborers of Love discussed in chapter 1.

As critical praxis, Goobalization mimics the database logic of Google search engines while adapting web-application mashup logic, extending sampling in music remixes during the 1970s. Navas argues Web 2.0 mashups are designed "to subvert applications to perform something they could not do otherwise by themselves."[21] CrimeChicago.org, for example, overlayed data from the Chicago Police Department onto Google Maps, mapping according to date, type, and location. The site revealed race, ethnicity, and class biases in Chicago, Los Angeles, and New York, where "driving while black" or "walking while black" can be a crime. Other mashups convey information about the violence over the 2007 Kenyan elections, discussed in chapter 2, and the 2011 uprising of the Arab Spring. Unlike hacks or mods, mashups combine existing technologies, leaving underlying code intact. Web-application mashups materially copy data and constantly update, utilizing Internet open archives, random access, and search filters. At first glance *Goobalization* appears to adopt a mashup strategy. Rejecting Google's conceits of objectivity and consensus, *Goobalization* defines globalization, surveillance, resistance, and difference politically. For Navas, globalization expresses transnational corporate control over international activity that amplifies inequalities between haves and have-nots. He identifies surveillance as a complementary term describing a primary mode by which globalization is enacted upon the bodies and online activities of the world's populations. Corporations, governments, and certified ethical hackers deploy surveillance for purposes ranging from commercial exploitation to political control. Navas understands resistance to suggest critical positions that interrogate structures of power that simultaneously mobilize and are enabled by difference. Navas's selection and compositing of images complicate initial suppositions of simple binaries—and foreground his subjective responses to these key terms.

Goobalization-I, for example, opens with a black-and-white image of "surveillance," depicting a woman tourist taking a photograph of a man swinging from a lamppost, above a color image as "resistance" depicting the Zapatistas (EZLN), known for their interventionist mobilization of Internet technologies through DoS, discussed in chapter 2. As the images fade in and out, composite images are formed momentarily in the overlapping areas between the four key terms. Plants merge with men holding machine guns. In *Goobalization-III*, "difference" is represented with a stock advertising image of US multiculturalism (smiling African American, East Asian American, European American, Latino/a American faces, yet predictably no Native American ones). An image of a pair of Gap jeans labeled "made in a sweatshop" represents "globalization." The images shift to a logo for a reforestation movement for "difference" whose text ("you can make a difference") is quickly covered by an image of three smiling waitresses wearing Hooters chain of fast-food restaurants' trademark tight singlet for "globalization."

The animations imbricate purportedly oppositional discourses. The series animates how agents of globalization appropriate antiglobalization discourses, as well as the inverse. The digital structure determines meaning more than the actual content of the images, updating Soviet montage and Third Cinema political avant-garde strategies. The overlapping images challenge the conventions of expository documentary where text (in voiceover, intertitles, or subtitles) reigns and argument is paramount.[22] By mimicking an actual mashup that selects images based upon Google's own rankings, the *Goobalization* animations pose questions about ways information is labeled and tagged in databases and processed through search engines. It proposes meaning as polyvocal, unstable, contested, and ethically urgent. Leandro Araujo's *Reações Visuais (Visual Reactions)* (Brazil, 2009–present; www.superficie.org/reacoesvisuais) visualizes urban Brazilian soundscapes as moving digital images through software. An urban art project, it explores the interplay between the embodied and metadata, demonstrating that the ambient possesses a structure, processed Sonic episodes of sirens, singing, and yelling alter the image. Performance art, public intervention, and technology education for the poor, *Reações Visuais* employs an audio archive recorded during street encounters with hip-hop movement aficionados, evangelic priests, and prostitutes. For example, a sequence begins with the location of the recording and time: Guaicurus Street, Belo Horizone, Brazil, 28 May 2009, 18h30–23h50, identifying this episode as a nighttime encounter. Special software translates the sound into a digital image, a red background with black lines in constant movement in three dimensions. All audio and image files are translated yet again into public performances with projection, computers, drums, and marimba. Documenting becomes process.

Amy Szczepanski and Evan Meaney's *Null_Sets* (United States, 2012; http://evanmeaney.com/ns/) translates user input of digitized text into algorithmically generated digital images when users click on the command "jpegify." Whether a Roland Barthes's *Image Music Text* (1977), Mary Shelley's *Frankenstein* (1818), an X chromosome, or the US Digital Millennium Copyright Act (1998), the program renders texts as data and then translates that data into bands of neon colors and pixilated color fields. This digital visualization points to the potentials of reworking information available to anyone with uncensored access to the open-access (or nearly open-access) digital libraries. *Null_Sets* pushes mid-1990 cyberutopian dreams of unlimited access to the limit, generating another library of color fields from books. Exploring gaps between data and information, *Null_Sets* renders large-scale data translation into visualizations of the size and architecture of words, concepts, and writing. *Null_Sets* engages the utopic notions of digitized data across distributed networks like Project Gutenberg and Google's libraries by allowing users to enter titles of books that routed through a Flickr photostream. If these libraries function like micro-utopias across distributed networks, then *Null_Sets* asks what it means when all information is no longer rendered in legible form, so that difference becomes negligible and nonmeasurable.

The interactions between technology and subjects are often repressed in considerations of visualizations of metadata, which concentrate on representations. In *Law of Attraction* (Canada, 2006; www.ramieblatt. com/lawofattractiondemo.html), Ramie Blatt explores relationships between the user and artificial life, speculating on how the mouse and cursor activate group activities in a life world. A nest of gray ant- or spermatozoa-like creatures appears on the white computer screen, jittering constantly. When they sense the movement of the user's mouse, they follow and swarm around the cursor, like flies to food. Blatt's *Mirror Series no. 3: I See (the) You* (Canada, 2006; www.ramieblatt. com/iseetheyoudemo.html) explores notions of self-perception: the pixelated images on the screen move with the observer's response to these images. As small dashes move around the white screen, the click of the cursor produces a portrait in red outlines. Images on the computer screen embody a mirrored reflection of the self, as generated by AI.

Nadine Hilbert and Gast Bouschet's *The Trustfiles* (Belgium/ Luxembourg, 2001–2007; www.bouschet-hilbert.org/previously/the-trustfiles/) questions perceptual ambiguities and written-word impartialities to dismantle codes of power where words conceal and reveal. Hilbert produces sound; Bouschet, photographs and videos. Words are scraped from websites to construct the project's own database. Drawing upon mystical traditions combining the letters and numbers of sacred texts to move beyond the literal, the project mixes the visual and auditory, prompting the user to investigate incomplete transmitted information imbedded in this project.[23] "Trust is the glue in the structure of power" write curators Javier Martinez Luque and Izaskun Etxebarria Madinabeitia, which "succinctly sums up the driving force running through the piece."[24] Moreover, the project poses questions about trust in data processing.

Derived from the German word for a border, which separates two areas and cannot be crossed, *Grenze* (France, 2004–2007; www. grenze.org) by Patrick Fontana with Emeric Aelters and Pierre-Yves Fave is a series of visual readings of Karl Marx's *Grundrisse* manuscripts (1857–1861) and *Capital* (1867) informed by the philosophical writings of Giorgio Agamben, Antonio Negri, and Jacques Rancière. Videos are generated from "artificial units of development" (AUD), corresponding to fragments from Marx. Dynamic animation of objects is rendered once in 2D, then in 3D, and finally as sound and images, always remaining open to other interpretations. 2D animations reproduce "idiotic motions"; 3D animations, "more complex real and metaphoric movements." In perpetual transformation, the cube-capital visualizes collisions between opposites. Showing invisible machine acts, these projects make visible the impossibility of differentiating metadata and data. As the archive frames the meaning of its documents, the database frames the meaning of its data and metadata.

Processing Sound Archives

Much like Craig Baldwin and other experimental filmmakers who used found footage to challenge copyright and advocate for creativity in the arts, artists have used found sound for comparable purposes, ranging from Negativland's live performances and recordings since 1979 to contemporary remix programs available online via community radio, such as Jonny Farrow's *Distract and Disable Program* (United States, 2011–present; http://distractanddisable.blogspot. com/). These projects highlight sound as an archival element. These projects invert the relationship between sound and image, positioning the acoustic as a primary conceptual driver. They operate as sound archives, but they configure the archive as a malleable, ever-expanding site that both collects and generates. Helmut Draxler defines sound as mediation between "music and noise" and between "art and everyday life."[25] As collection systems, these projects create new ways to organize, search, or listen; they produce new contiguities and connections. As generative systems, some of these projects provide ways to produce new sounds by layering and shifting tonal qualities, creating software to respond to natural sounds. Mobilizing conceptual systems, software programs or mixing boards, these projects process sound, conceptualizing it as mobile, changeable, and relational. These projects focus on sounds found in daily life, making space for voices or creating music by combining sonic fields. These projects create what R. Murray Shafer has described as a soundscape, "events heard not objects seen."[26] Some of these projects, like *Blood Sugar* about heroin addicts and *La Buena vida* about Latin American politics, emphasize the voices of participants, demonstrating knowledge production outside of experts. Other projects, such as *samesamebutdifferent*, *aux2mondes*, and *thefluteintheworld*, propose that natural or ambient sounds, often blocked out, be reinstalled as critical sonic topographies.

Sharon Daniel's *Blood Sugar* (United States, 2010; http:// bloodandsugar.net) offers an audio archive of conversations with current and former injection-drug users who Daniel met at a needle exchange in an HIV-prevention program near where she was living in 2000. The project processes not only sounds, but also Daniel's own collaborative process with the users. She describes *Blood Sugar* as part of her ongoing interest in using the Internet as a means of forwarding dialogues between "People" (capital *P*) with full and uncontested access to the rights and privileges of citizenship and "people" (lower-case *p*) with partial or contested access. *Blood Sugar* takes its name from combining the word "blood" (vital fluid) with the slang expression "sugar" for heroin, so as to "tip the delicate balance of biology and disturb the social equilibrium" and therein remap thinking about social exclusion and addiction. Daniel collaborated with programmer Erik Loyer on the site's design.

thefLuteintheworLdthefLuteistheworLd (United States, 1995) is one of Henry Gwiazda's many sonic works that remix field recordings and sound effects to amplify the intrinsic musical qualities of everyday noises. Gwiazda's other projects are designed as installations experienced from speakers with particular specifications about where the body is positioned. This virtual-audio project, evoking *musique concrète* (concrete music), is designed to be listened on headphones because it uses panning between sounds sources (the left and right ear) as a structural motif. Comparably, *thefLuteintheworLdthefLuteistheworLd* engulfs its listener in a landscape that combines music with ambient noise of walking, scissors, sirens, water, and trucks. Thor and Runar Magnusson's *SameSameButDifferent v.02* (Iceland, 2003; www.zen59732.zen.co.uk/ssbd_snapshots/) generates a new musical work every five to eight minutes from field recordings of Icelandic nature. Such sonic productions via algorithm, composed in real time by machine acts, challenge the format of traditional radio and sound production. Miming the natural archives of Icelandic nature sounds, *SameSameButDifferent v.02* generates new sound combinations at each hearing, and transmits a proliferation of Icelandic aural imaginaries over the Internet.

A collaborative project between Nicolas Malevé, Pascal Mélédandri, Chantal Dumas, and Isabelle Massu, with grants from Le Centre national de la cinématographie in Paris and La Compagnie in Marseilles, *aux2mondes* (France, 2006; www.aux2mondes.org/aux2mondes) is an Internet audio project that links commentaries to process a nonnarrative story based upon the user's interest and intuition. The project concerns representation and "human linkage," drawing from interview audio recordings linked by keywords. The interface traces their

progress, so that the project "resists the voyeurism inherent in representation and returns the user to her or his own self-interest." Catherine
Clover's *Untitled (FLEFF)* (United Kingdom/Australia, 2007; www.
ciclover.com/info.html) constitutes an ongoing investigation into aural
patterning. Working with incidental and misheard sounds that fade
into the recesses of consciousness, this work heightens the listener's
aural sense by isolating found sounds and field recordings. Frequency
and repetition evoke a sense of place. Highway sounds overpower, pro-
pelling careful listening for the most delicate bird and insect noises. The
work consciously evokes what Paul Carter has termed "the sonorous
identification with foreign surroundings" by processing sounds that are
supposedly part of the everyday, and then elevating them to the status
of cultural place markers.

In addition to LANs for wireless Internet connections, we are
also connected by and imbedded in wireless telecommunications.
Jody Zellen's *Disembodied Voices* (United States, 2004; www.dis-
embodiedvoices.com/) explores the semiprivate nature of cell phone
conversations, making visible the audible fragments of invisible communications networks in our everyday environment. *Disembodied
Voices* considers communication within public spaces, specifically
private cell-phone conversations, which render half-dialogues public
since they are audible to anyone within the range. Zellen develops
the cell phone as a "metaphor for the new translocal of connected,
disembodied voices, linked across space invisibly—forming an unseen
network of wanderers, always within reach yet nowhere in sight."
The project offers users the ability to select between female and
male voices, speaking languages such as Arabic, Cantonese, English,
French, German, Indonesian, and Spanish, as they explore ways that
private conversations enter into and change the sonic dimensions of
public and semipublic spaces.

La Buena vida (The Good Life) by Carlos Motta (Colombia/
United States, 2005–2010; http://carlosmotta.com/text/the-good-life-
la-buena-vida-by-carlos-motta-2008/) is an audio database about the
ongoing processes of democratization in Latin America in responce
to foreign interventionist policies initiated by the United States. The
project presents an archive of voices across Latin America, processing the experiences and ideas of people as they live through political and economic change. Along with installations of the project, its
online archive allows searching a digital database of more than 360
video interviews conducted between 2005 and 2008 with pedestrians
on the streets of Bogotá Buenos Aires, Caracas, Guatemala, La Paz,

Managua, México DF, Panamá, Santiago, San Salvador, São Paulo, and Tegucigalpa. Topics covered include perceptions of US foreign policy, democracy, leadership, and governance. The project includes an extensive website, critical texts by artists (Naeem Mohaiemen, Oliver Ressler) and writers (Tatiana Flores, Maria Mercedes), a chronology of Latin American politics between 2005 and 2010, a searchable Internet archive of the videos, and also analogue components in a 12-screen installation and a book. The project explores questions of democracy, leadership, and governance across Latin America, pointing to differences and similarities as points of contention.

Drawing upon conceptual and methodological models by filmmakers Fernando "Pino" Solanas and Octavio Getino, and by educator Paulo Freire, *La Buena vida* performs what Motta describes as a "need for a systematization of inquiry (political, social and historical) and rejection of abuse, manipulation and violence" that "doesn't attempt to impose another hegemonic world view, but rather to magnify unheard voices and opinions about the complex set of relations that have maintained the majority of our continent poor and under-represented." It functions as a new media reformulation of Third Cinema by creating a polyphonic platform of everyday people voicing analysis of neocolonialism and democratic reforms. It also extends the city symphony mode of documentary: it interviews all its subjects in public spaces, on the streets, discussing these complex relationships between different issues of foreign policy, democracy, and economics. The structure of the interview is the same each time, with subjects framed in medium close-up, and speaking in direct address to the camera.

La Buena vida rejects the notion that documentary advances one point of view and one argument by emphasizing the endlessly searchable and remixable modularity of documentation. On the video page, all 360 videos appear as a mosaic. About one-third of the videos are translated into English. The videos are searchable by the six questions that Motta asked each subject as well as language, gender, age, city, occupation, and themes, producing different archival experiences and different sets of relationships across different categories and subject positions. When clicked on, each video page also features a list itemizing city, name, age, occupation, date, and duration. The videos range in length from three minutes to five minutes. *La Buena vida* generates an archive of voices from Latin America, suggesting that Latin America is not one large landmass with a unified set of ideologies, but instead a polyphony of points of view and different class and gender perspectives.

Undoing Consumer Complicity

In addition to visualizing metadata that determine the kinds of meanings produced by digital technologies, other projects intervene IRL ("in real life"), to borrow an early chatroom acronym. The projects that we analyze draw on earlier interventionist art, such as *etoy.CORPORATION* (Switzerland, 1994–present), an ongoing performance that recently entered its twentieth year as a registered company. The project first came to notice in 1996 when it deployed *Digital Hack*, a search-engine hack, which redirected browsers from eToys to the eToy website.[27] Although the project does not question online shopping as an interactive means for corporations to collect data and outsource service labor to the customer, the project came to wide attention in 1999 when a US corporation, eToys, attempted to take over the domain name. Known as "toywar," eToys sued eToy for trademark infringement to which eToy responded with coordinated DoS attacks on the eToys website. Organizing (swarming) nonmembers, eToy's performance caused the stock price of eToys to drop from USD 67 to USD 15, reducing its capitalization by USD 4.5 million.[28] eToy intervenes IRL by delivering its trademark orange studio-and-exhibition units, "TANKS" (12 × 6 meter standardized shipping containers), which contain the project's "mobile and multifunctional living and production system including studios, hotels, conference rooms, storage space, workshops, sarcophagus etc." TANKS have appeared in cities such as Amsterdam, Berlin, Madrid, New York, San Francisco, Tokyo, Torino, and Zürich. eToy's ongoing intervention into reeducating customers shares much in common with digital media that intervenes into user complicity with data-gathering corporations such as Amazon and Facebook. Around the world, digital media artists produce work that moves from the abstract realms of distributed networks into the concrete realms of localized sites. It refuses to allow us to hide in a darkened cinematheque and dream of the revolution to come. Instead, it engages us in small ways, prompting us to rethink, respond, and, when possible, redo. We sometimes forget where the work ends and we begin.

The conflations of work and play, private and public, commodification and participation are perhaps nowhere more apparent than in so-called free services on offer by transnational corporations like

Google and Facebook. Ulises Mejias points out Google scans e-mails and documents "to collect more information about us, their users," which it then sells through targeted advertising. The social act of sending an e-mail is "almost invisibly transformed into a revenue-creating opportunity for a corporation."[29] The Internet becomes both "playground and factory," as Trebor Scholz argues about digital labor.[30] YouTube uses automated content identification software to scan videos uploaded to its free platform, sending matches with copyrighted content to the copyright holder, which has the option of blocking, monitoring, or monetizing the content by inserting advertising links to iTunes. With UGC containing copyrighted material, Mejias notes that the labor in producing content and making it go viral is "translated into real profit for corporations (Sony, Google, its advertisers, etc.) without them having to do much in return."[31]

Paolo Cirio and Alessandro Ludovico's *Face to Facebook* (Italy, 2011; www.face-to-facebook.net) reveals the monetization of UGC by looking to the social-networking platform Facebook. The user profile, network of friends, preferences of "likes" and "shares" becomes a digital self freely given to the corporation to sell, as Cirio and Ludovico's project makes evident. *Face to Facebook* asks users to rethink aspects of their personal identities they give away to Facebook. As hundreds of millions of Facebook users attempt to negotiate the corporation's ever-changing privacy settings, the project stages an occasion for reflection about user complicity. *Face to Facebook* scrapes public data from one million Facebook profiles, filters them with face-recognition software, sorts them by expression, and them posts them to a dating-service website called *Lovely-Faces*.

The project uses a customized software to categorize faces as "climber," "easy going," "funny," "mild," "sly," or "smug," suggesting the absence of control that Facebook users ultimately have over how their profile pictures are understood by AI—despite assumptions of individuality and self-expression. The shock of finding oneself on offer for online dating, promoted and advertised to potential buyer by one's own Facebook profile photo, is intended to elicit reflection about social networking as a for-profit industry. "Their mission is not to help people create better social relationships or to help them improve their self-positioning," explain Cirio and Ludovico; "their mission is to make money." *Face to Facebook* visualizes ways that we give away very private parts of our digital identities—that is, our faces—to corporations that sell products and services to us through targeted advertising.

Figure 3.1 *Face to Facebook.*

Since Facebook promotes itself as "free and always will be," *Face to Facebook* also asks users to think about ways that they pay for the service by constantly updating their information for corporations whose privacy policies are constantly in flux. Web scraping is a process of data extraction from websites, performed by a bot much like copy-and-paste by a human user. It is often used to gather prices for price-comparison charts on the websites of online vendors. *Face to Facebook*'s joke about scraping and rating profile photos relies on user knowledge about Facebook creator Mark Zuckerberg's claims to have scraped personal data on students from the Harvard University database. Our digital identities on Facebook also represent crowd-sourced targeting for Facebook, that is, a means of collecting data about groups of people who share common interests and desires, which are reflected back to them in targeted advertising. Facebook responded to the project with several cease-and-desist letters, resulting in *Lovely-Faces* being taken down after only ten days, though not before it had been covered by news outlets including CNN and *USA Today* in the United States, *Haaretz* in Israel, and *Der Spiegel* in Germany. Upon request, Cirio and Ludovico would remove profile photos from *Lovely-Faces*. As hactivists, Cirio and Ludovico critique customer complicity with the near-monopolization of corporations. *Face to Facebook* is the third of *The Hacking Monopolism*

Trilogy that began with *Google Will Eat Itself* (Italy, 2005) and *Amazon Noir* (Italy, 2006).

Other projects elicit interventions into our individual lives. Rebecca Mushtare's *Self-Disclosed* (United States, 2010; http://selfdisclosed. com/about.php) is a web-browser "formWatcher" add-on that allows users to visualize personal information they might ordinarily upload to any number of forms on websites as part of shopping, social networking, and renewing subscriptions and licenses online. By asking users to input data that constitute a digital identity (name, date of birth, race/ethnicity, address, e-mail address, mother's maiden name) sorted for identity verification upon return for services or information. Digital identities can also be stolen: protecting one's personal data is a first line of defense against identity theft. Mushtare asks users to consider their personal data as a sort of currency by tracking and registering transactions, such as downloading instant coupons or accessing instant messaging they have paid for with their personal-data identity. Much like budgeting software, the project allows users to visualize their personal-data spending and gifting in order to track it. Categories of personal-data—biological, contact, genealogical, geographical, governmental, professional, and so forth—are visualized in different colors for legibility, so that their intersections at different nodes, representing websites, offer user access to another kind of data about themselves that typically passes as invisible. The visualization depicts the relationships of users to institutions and businesses. The formWatcher add-on also allows users to see when webpages are collecting data from the user's computer or receiving it from an external server. The add-on does not keep users' personal data but rather gets them to reflect upon when they are giving their personal data to other entities that are keeping it. Mushtare's interests range from code to fibers, particularly as they intersect with sex and gender. She has reproduces personal-data visualization from *Self-Disclosed* on wallets and tote bags.

Gaming Documentary

Although many scholars dismiss the notion of interactivity as simply user reactivity within a vast network of choices, David Hogarth argues "interactive technologies could extend and deepen modes of engagement" and "may allow new forms of dialogue with documentary form, undermining authoritative (and authoritarian) modes of communication along the way."[32] He extends Trinh T. Minh-ha's assertion that there is no such thing as documentary, whether a cat-egory of material, a genre, an approach, or a set of techniques.[33] Trinh argues "the present situation of critical inquiry seems much less one of attacking the illusion of reality as one of displacing and emptying out the establishment of totality."[34] Transcending observa-tional, expository, self-reflexive, and interactive modes of documen-tary, video game form can reposition audience and events in ways that exceed the discursive spaces contained on a single screen or within the fixed site of installations.

Available in Espanglish and English, Alex Rivera's web-based *LowDrone: The Transnational Hopper* (United States, 2005; http://lowdrone.com/) puts the user in the driver's seat of a drone pointed in the direction of the fence marking the militarized border between Baja California in México and southern California in the United States. *LowDrone* engaged political education through play. The Mexican American borderlands is a highly irregularly regulated inter-national border flanked by free zones carved into México for maquill-ladoras and marked by fences and walls constructed by the United States. Historically, more than 50 percent of México was occupied and annexed by the United States in 1848, a history evoked in the Mexican American expression "we didn't cross the border, the bor-der crossed us." The international border was selectively enforced long before post-NAFTA policies like Operation Gatekeeper (1994), which was "successful" not in preventing undocumented migration but in rerouting migration from San Diego into the more dangerous inland territories of Arizona, where controversial stop-and-identify laws (interpreted as a form of racial profiling) prevail.[35] The free trade of NAFTA escalated the destruction of *milpa* farming in México, driving migrations to the maquilladoras, prostitution, and narcotics trafficking. Migrants are pushed by neoliberal economic policies that facilitate free trade and free zones to move to "al otro lado" ("the other side") for work in agricultural fields, construction sites, hotel and private homes, and superstores like Wal-Mart.

With *LowDrone*, the user manipulates a model of a gold 1937 Ford coupe, equipped with gyroscopes, thermal sensors, and a wireless video system, trying to avoid the US Border Control to become a "transnational hopper"—a term playfully reworking the anti-immigration expression "border hopper." The project situates the user's relationship with the US border militarization within the history of technologies such as the invention of lowriders in 1940 by Mexican American youth, the outlawing of lowriders in 1957 by the governor of California, the invention of the first radio-controlled drone in 1935, or the invention of the first drone by anti-immigrant vigilantes in 2002. Like counter-gaming, the goal is not to win by reaching the other side but rather to learn by contemplating the difficulties of getting across. The project acknowledges the nonsensical dimensions of militarized border that previously may have seemed normal to some users.

Taking invisible surveillance technologies, including everyday wearable technologies as its point of departure, Mez Breeze and Andy Campbell's #PRISOM (Australia/United Kingdom, 2013; http://prisom.me) asks players to think about the embodied and ethical dimensions of privacy and social logistics. #PRISOM examines online realities since Edward Snowden's exposure of classified documents as evidence of the participation of Apple, AOL, Google, Facebook, Microsoft, Paltalk, Skype, Yahoo!, and YouTube in the NSA's PRISM data-mining program. Players are immersed in the Head-Mounted Display 3D immersive project, navigating the synthetic game environment by engaging with objects, scenarios, and texts that question the player's culpability in surveillance programs embedded in communications technologies. The Glass City of infinite surveillance becomes a prison rendered through prisms into a visual interface evoking Jeremy Bentham's infamous Panopticon.

Although first-person shooter (FPS) video games often make headlines in the United States after mass shootings at educational institutions and shopping malls—Virginia Tech in 2007, Town Center (Colorado) in 2012—they less frequently make headlines in relation to war. Matthieu Cherubini's *Afghan War Diary* (Switzerland, 2010; www.afghan-war-diary.com) uses data from the server of Valve Corporation's online multiplayer war game *Counter Strike* (United States, 2000) to trigger a search through the 75 thousand secret military reports from the US invasion of Afghanistan made public by WikiLeaks in its Afghan War Diary (2004–2010), then mapping them onto Google Earth display. The project visualizes links between gameplay assassination or "frags" and actual military assassinations.

Built from the source engine of *Half-Life* (United States, 1998), *Counter Strike* is an FPS game in which players join either terrorists or counterterrorists teams. Typical tasks within the game are planting bombs, taking hostages, or assassinating VIPs. Unlike *Counter Strike* or Google Earth, the user has no control over events. The project situates users as passive witnesses to never-ending carnage. There is nothing the user can do apart from closing the browser to end the continual barrage of information: names of players who have "killed someone" are followed with place names in Afghanistan with "enemy actions" and number killed. Information is preceded by a date and time stamp; for example, "2014–07–19 17:43:57 dob killed someone" with "2004–03–05 00:00:00 Kandahar–Heart Highway Other (Other) 9 deaths" or "2014–07–19 17:49:30 KoMaDy *^@^* killed someone" with "2004–08–02 00:00:00 Lashkar Gah Explosive Hazard (IED Explosion) 2 deaths." In light of information of civilian casualties and increased instability in Afghanistan, Cherubini's project unsettles US military language of IEDs and "hostiles." Once killed by an opponent, players become spectators. In *Afghan War Diary*, we are all spectators, suggesting that we are all already dead.

With Wei-Ming Ho's *The Art-Qaeda Project* (Taiwan, 2011; www.vimeo.com/artqaeda), media adventurers engage in guerrilla art action to capture discursive imagery and sounds of the city. Documentation for the site-specific performances shows the interactions between images projected onto buildings and trees by a mobile high-power projector and the urban environments that contain and sustain us. The project poaches statistics and symbols, such as the Environmental Sustainability Index (ESI), which tracks elements of environmental sustainability, including resource endowments and pollution levels, and Morse Code, which translates the alphabet into on/off tones that can be deciphered without a decoding device. Through *The Art-Qaeda Project*, the media adventurers question the value of received information in an era of fears of surveillance inflected with paranoia over terrorism. The project migrates through urban spaces, engaging passersby as participants in a game of decoding information.

Hacking the Control of CCTV Cameras

During the 1960s and 1970s, spies in thrillers attached tiny cameras or microphones to their lapels to record sounds and images surreptitiously. Today, wearable technologies are commonplace. Cameras have become ubiquitous, from the ones we carry with us on our smartphones to the ones that follow our every movement via closed-circuit television (CCTV) systems. Hidden, camouflaged, and other CCTV cameras monitor our movements in unmarked checkpoints of everyday urban and highway life, amassing data on us for databases controlled by states and corporations. They are promoted as security measures, such as the ones guarding ATMs, but they are often understood as technologies of surveillance, such as the ones that issue traffic tickets to speeding drivers.

The Institute for Applied Autonomy (IAA)'s *iSee* (United States, 1998–2002) was developed in response to the USA PATRIOT Act, as security cameras increasingly came under public scrutiny for mining data from the everyday lives of citizens. Even places traditionally known for their relative tolerance of difference, such as Manhattan, become places governed by suspicion and fear, whose violence was aggravated by the normalization of racial profiling policies in the guise of security since CCTV systems only work (i.e., filter and sort) by knowing in advance who looks or acts suspicious. *iSee* is a tactical-cartography project that includes a web-based application that uses CCTV surveillance cameras in urban environments in tactical cartography that maps of "paths of least surveillance" by maneuvering around "unregulated security monitors."[36] Users select a starting location and destination, and the program generates the path of least surveillance through an unregulated network of CCTV at ATMs and traffic signals. The project is fully open source, running on Linux. *iSee* updates a set of data points on CCTV cameras compiled in 1998 (yet outdated by 2002) by the New York State Civil Liberties Union. Although the CCTV cameras have ostensibly been applied to protect everyone, the IAA maintains that particular groups are more vulnerable due to video surveillance in public spaces, including social groups minoritized by race/ethnicity and religion, women, youth, homeless, activists—and "everyone else." One of the primary concerns is that the legal ownership of images from CCTV footage remains largely undecided, as *iSee*'s website explains. Footage from "spy cams" in public toilets can appear on television without the consent of the subjects "caught on tape."[37]

IAA describes its work as "applied critical theory," an example of thinking about and through digital media. Whether focusing on robotics or automation, IAA moves toward a critical engineering technology culture, with a sense of humor to engage audiences as participants, if for nothing more than determining whether its projects are "real." In the case of *iSee*, tactical cartography becomes an "inversionist practice that creates disruptions within existing systems of power and control" by privileging critical social engagement toward "spatial representations that confront power, promote social justice and are intended to have operational power."[38] They are "symbolic resistances" that are "concerned with temporary destabilization rather than permanent transformation." They are ephemeral and event-driven, existing only as long as they are effective—then vanishing.[39] "On the one hand, they are pedagogical devices that provoke public discussion of critical issues. This conception of work fits neatly within the confines of 'art practice,'" explains IAA. "At the same time, our projects are functional tools that dissidents can actually use. In this regard, our work has more to do with engineering (or at least hacker) practice."[40]

In the tradition of critical cartography, such as Unnayan's mapping marginal land settlements and unintended cities during the 1970s, *iSee* focused on the dual task of rendering proliferation of video surveillance legible and creating an empirical basis for challenging policy. Decentralization and privatization have contributed to no public records of surveillance cameras and remote monitoring services that are literally off the map, such as the BluServo network discussed below in relation to *The Texas Border*.[41] The *iSee* project included camera-mapping workshops for grassroots campaign to put CCTV networks on a map for a round of community-based analysis that would move beyond the typical considerations of cost and efficacy. The project revealed that CCTV cameras in Manhattan tended to be located in financial districts and commercial areas rather than residential neighborhoods, particularly lower-income ones, pointing to the privileging of public funding for security to protect "property not people."[42] "Maps don't merely represent space," the IAA observes. "They shape arguments; they set the discursive boundaries and identify objects to be considered," so that projects like *iSee* allow mappers "to claim their rights to set the rules of debate and to provide interpretations of local events with both authority and a contingency equal to official representation."[43] IAA raised three ways to reconfigure surveillance systems: (1) providing people with ways to avoid their control; (2) putting control over the systems in public control; and (3) deploying CCTV cameras in public spaces to allow for public oversight of the footage.[44]

Broadcasting live video from the BluServo network of surveillance cameras along the Texas border with México, Joana Moll and Héliodoro Santos Sanchez's *The Texas Border* (Spain/México, 2010; www.janavirgin.com/the_texas_border/index.html) documents failed attempts to cross the militarized border resulting from reports from BluServo's users to the Texas Border Sheriff's Coalition. Advertising itself as a "public-private partnership that deploys Virtual Community Watch," BlueServo is a real-time surveillance program that crowdsources the police work of regulating drug and human trafficking to untrained users as a social-networking activity. *The*

Texas Border visualizes ways that BluServo trains a user to become a "Virtual Texas Deputy^{SM}," who manipulate mediated images in a video game–like interface and submit anonymous reports about suspicious activity by e-mail. As Moll notes, the website's success with 203 thousand user volunteers and 165 million hits amounts to almost one million hours of free labor for the Sheriff's Coalition. The website effectively outsources police work in a kind of role-playing game in which users act according to a model of vigilante justice mediated through Hollywood film and television about the so-called Wild West during the colonial era or so-called border hopping in commercial news media today. BlueServo also has a presence on Facebook, so that its users could report suspicious activity and mysterious items in real-time discussions with representatives of the Sheriff's Coalition, occasionally consulting Google Earth to determine whether the activities that they spot are on the US or Mexican side of the border.

The Texas Border renegotiates the complexities of the Mexican American borderland, recognizing it as one of the primary battlegrounds in the US War on Terror. US policy historically focused on selective repatriation through the Deportation Act (1929) and Operation Wetback (1954). With the reinvention of the border as a mechanism of neoliberal economics under NAFTA, policy shifted from apprehension to deterrence, inspired in part by 1993's Operation Blockade (later, Operation Hold the Line), developed by regional Border Patrol supervisor in El Paso, whose specific goal was to intimidate "would-be-illegal entrants" by stationing agents visibly near border.[45] With wireless surveillance cameras connected to the Internet, the borderlands are mediated through satellite-image display software. After an initial expenditure of USD 1.3 billion between 2006 and 2010, the US Department of Homeland Security (DHS) abandoned the Virtual Fence Program (aka SBInet) under the Secure Border Initiative, which proposed a vast network of sensors, cameras, and radar towers through the southwestern United States. Earlier projects included the Integrated Surveillance Intelligence System (ISIS), later renamed America's Shield Initiative (ASI) launched by the Immigration and Naturalization Service (INS), the predecessor to the DHS, in 1997.

Other private border-watch communities have been organized by militia and by individuals, such as wireless-systems businessman Jon Healy, who founded *TechnoPatriots* in 2007 to police the Arizona border, allowing users as far away as New York to become "armchair warriors." Healy launched the site after learning that his competitors were underbidding him because they employed undocumented

labor.[46] Although it might sound ad hoc, the highly selective enforcement of the laws about transborder crossing has been the modus
operandi since the first policing of the border against Chinese immigrants in 1882. Other current and former websites include *American
Border Patrol*, *Wireless Border Cams*, right-wing political activist
Jim Gilchrist's *The Minuteman Project* that announces, among other
things on its homepage, that "U.S. citizenship shouldn't be about
money, influence, or election results" and "Americans shouldn't have
to compete against low-wage illegal workers!"[47] As Moll argues, *The
Texas Border* makes visible this infosphere of everyday acts of war
and offers the possibility of political action through countersurveillance. The project has also been exhibited as a large-scale installation at venues including *antiAtlas des frontières* in Aix-en-Provence
(France) in 2013.

Surveillance as security can made visible in auto-generative work,
such as Robert Spahr's *Crufts*, which scrapes images and texts from
the Internet and recombines them into a politically conscious form of
glitch art. Spahr's work draws information from governmental websites and databases to initiate acts of rejecting predetermined meaning and exposing the invisible structures of digital media, such as
the significance of metadata, and digitally mediated everyday life,
such as the countless images of ourselves captured by CCTV surveillance cameras. "Organized under the umbrella concept of *Cruft*,"
explains Spahr, "I take apart, juxtapose, recycle, and interrupt the
relentless flow of media to reveal a relationship in which we don't
simply consume media, but are also consumed by it."[48] Conceiving a
practice that draws upon "collage, remix, automation, indeterminacy,
and randomness," his projects move between and combine aspects of
computational art, performance, installation, and object making. His
aim is one of interrupting our frequent complicity with technologies
of surveillance.

Crufts uses computational algorithms to scrape the Internet for
images that are recombined in digital collage. His code operates as
an autonomous machine that instigates its own customized program
of web surveillance. *Cliff Dwellers (Drone Study #4)* (United States,
2014–present; www.robertspahr.com/crufts/cliffdwellers/) harvests
images from a CCTV camera in New York, as part of larger project *Machine Vision: Images of Drone Landscapes* (United States,
2014) on the hidden technologies and algorithms that constitute a
machine vision of the world.[49] An ongoing project, *Machine Vision*
repurposes footage from CCTV cameras and other media to create

images that pose questions about our role within a complex of war, surveillance, and automation inspired by Snowdon's whistleblowing on the role of corporations like Apple, Facebook, Google, and Microsoft in facilitating NSA surveillance on US citizens through automated systems. "Our personal lives and images are looked at by automated machines, shared by computational processes and controlled by hidden algorithm," writes Spahr, suggesting a frightening moment when state aspirations for "total information awareness" have aligned with "capitalism's need to consume itself at all cost."[50]

For *Cliff Dwellers (Drone Study #4)*, Spahr adapts the title from "cliff dwelling," a term that describes the practice of carving dwellings into cliffs, particularly as it was practiced by indigenous nations in what is now Canada, México, and the United States. For Spahr, cliff dwellings are an antiquated technology that precedes ones like fax machines, gaming consoles, and personal computers. Aesthetically attractive, the digital collages generated at two-hour intervals have highly saturated color and soft focus that render their photographic detail imprecise and illegible. Although their photographic imprecision provides little information on the subjects of the CCTV cameras—and potentially erases information useful in identifying people on the street, the images do provide useful information to us about ways that CCTV cameras are used in New York. The high-angle shots of streets with pedestrians show a machine-eye view of a world in which everyone is considered a potential victim or suspect in crime, as well as ways that automated technologies can fail to deliver data. Sometimes the images exist only as word, noting that the particular camera is being serviced. An archive contains multiple images for every day since 08 January 2014, offering a visualization of the much more massive state and corporate databases of images taken by CCTV cameras.

Negotiating Mobile Phones

India is a cutting-edge site for mobile phones. Henry Jenkins notes the first feature film distributed via mobile phone was *Rok Sako To Rok Lo/Stop Me, If You Can* (India, 2004; dir. Arindam Chowdhuri), screened via EDGE-enabled phone in Bangalore, Hyderabad, Mumbai, and New Delhi.[51] As media industries explore greater mobile phones profits and market penetration, artists and collectives have worked toward more socially conscious ends. Through a joint venture with Indian and French organizations, Laurent Sauerwein attempted to launch an emergent nonprofit cell phone movie experimental research center. Taking its name from Pondywood after the commercial film industry in Puducherry (formerly, Pondicherry) in the south Indian state of Tamil Nadu, the NGO proposed "small videos can make a big difference." Although the center has not yet materialized, Sauerwein did teach a course in Auroville as part of the American University in Paris (AUP)'s first Sustainable Development Practicum in 2008/2009.[52] Two AUP students, Cody Merrit and Jacqueline Segal, shot on a Nokia N-95 and examined the ecological footprint of CO_2 emissions. The three-minute film features shots of traffic-congested Puducherry, intercut with shots of tree planting to offset carbon emissions.[53] Despite this potential, Pondywood, with its historical French colonial architecture often figured as exotic, has fared better as an alternative shooting location for films like *Jism* (India, 2003; dir. Amit Saxena) and *Life of Pi* (United States/Taiwan/ United Kingdom/Canada/India, 2012; dir. Ang Lee), and television, including *Alexandra David-Néel: J'irai au pays des neiges* (France, 2012; dir. Joël Farges).[54]

The first Indian Festival of Cellphone Cinema was launched in 2008 by the Asian Academy of Film and Television (AAFT) and received submissions from Bhutan, Dominica, Haïti, Iran, Iraq, Kazakhstan, Kenya, Malaysia, Nigeria, and the United States.[55] The festival was conceived by Karl Bardosh, professor at New York University in the United States, and Sandeep Marwah, director of AAFT and founder and managing director of Marwah Studios in Noida Film City in the New Okhla Industrial Development Authority (aka "Noida") in the national capital region of Uttar Pradesh about 20 kilometers south of New Delhi. Bardosh and Marwah shot three feature films on cell phones before launching the festival. Rebranded as the International Film Festival of Cell Phone Cinema, the festival had its seventh edition in January 2014. The number of submissions swelled from 58 in 2008 to 450 in 2013.[56] For Bardosh, the festival and cell phone movies "make cinema and the art an accessible non-discriminating platform."[57] His ambition is part of a broader enthusiasm for the democratizing potential of inexpensive digital technologies. Anyone, the aspirations dictated, could make media and distribute it online through a proliferation of websites hosting amateur video.

In the context of the on-going Syrian civil war (2011–present), protestors against the Ba'ath Party are sometimes shot by the army or police for taking photographs or shooting video with their smartphones. To become a Syrian filmmaker is often to become a martyr.

Helga Tawil-Souri uses the expression "Tora Bora filmmaking" to describe how Palestinian artists move around impossible-to-cross checkpoints of colonial occupation in Israel/Palestine.[58] Consumer-grade cameras used to document human rights violations range from *5 Broken Cameras* discussed in relation to *Visualizing Palestine* in chapter 2, to *Silvered Water, Syrian Self-portrait* (France/Syria, 2014; dir. Ossama Mohammed) on the siege of Homs. Taysir Batniji's *Transit* (Palestine/France, 2004) examines the endless delays in crossing between Egypt and Gaza in a clandestine image slideshow. Emily Jacir's *Crossing Surda (A Record of Going to and from Work)* (Palestine, 2002) documents the racially and sexually charged humiliations when Palestinians attempt to cross an Israeli checkpoint inside the occupied West Bank during daily commutes between home and work with a camera camouflaged inside her bag. For *ex libris* (United States/Palestine, 2010–2012), Jacir photographed more than 30 thousand books stolen from Palestinian homes during the Nakba in 1948 with her mobile-phone camera.[59] Six thousand of these books are kept in the Jewish National Library, marked "A.P." for "abandoned property," the same designation legitimizing the appropriation of Palestinian property. Both of Jacir's projects use mobile phones and cameras to document what has been forbidden. In this sense, mobile-phone cameras open documenting to erased histories.

Max Schleser's *Max with a Kaitei* (United Kingdom/Germany, 2005–2008; http://uk.youtube.com/watch?v=1jc2iLI5Mx0) is an experimental documentary made on two mobile phones, allowing reflections on documentary that move beyond the ones predicated on 16mm, Super8, video, and digital cameras. Schleser experiments with the formal and epistemological possibilities for documentary with the small cameras included on mobile devices intended for multiple purposes. He manipulates the phone's limited settings and codecs to determine the possibilities for rethinking "film." The project is part of a larger one that explores the "mobile-mentary" (mobile documentary) as a form for small mobile screen productions (*kaitei* roughly translates from Japanese as "handheld" but is also used for mobile phone). It proliferates an alternative mode of documentary filmmaking that has the potential to transform the mediascape through the convergence of wireless communication technologies and conventional lens-based media. At the same time, cameras on smartphones are bundled with tracking software such as GPS, so that taking snapshots and uploading them to social-networking sites becomes an exercise in becoming tracked, much like phoning on a cellular network.

The "selfie," a self-portrait typically taken with a mobile-phone camera for posting to social media, has become politicized in the era of militarized borders controlled not only by Israel but also by the European Union and the United States, such as the stories of so-called illegal immigration from Central America aboard "the beast" (colloquial expression the freight trains onto which migrants travel clandestinely) that are posted on Facebook.[60] *Selfiecity* (United States, 2014; http://selfiecity.net/) takes the computational function of digital media as a means to analyze and visualize the practice of selfie self-portraiture. The Digital Thought Facility (DTF), a collaborative team established in 2013 by Daniel Goddemeyer at the School of Visual Arts in New York, conceived and executed the project. The team participates across a number of labs, such as the Present Technologies Lab and the Speculative Futures Lab. DTF members also work on independent projects for transnational corporations like Microsoft. In collaboration with Lev Manovich's Software Studies Initiative, founded in 2007 at the University of California San Diego, the Present Technologies Lab devised a project aimed at "uncovering the human stories behind the anonymity of Amazon.com Mechanical Turk" (MTurk). The Speculative Futures Lab examines the future impact of technologies, such as their role in reshaping public spaces.[61] *Selfiecity* extends this research.

The project examines the phenomenon of self-portraits, typically taken with a web or mobile-phone cameras, and posted on social media platforms. The project follows some of the objectives of automated facial-expression analysis, which differs from automated facial-recognition technologies by looking at affective qualities of the face, such as head tilt or smile, rather than so-called objective qualities, such as distance between pupils or width of mouth, to confirm or verify identity. Kelly Gates describes Paul Ekman and Wallace Friesen's Facial Action Coding System (FACS) as a "gold standard" system for facial-expression analysis, noting it aspires "to make human affective behaviors more calculable, to open them to precise measurement and classification, thereby making them more amenable to forms of intervention, manipulation, and control."[62] These systems look at unofficial images rather than official ones, such as passport photographs, where smiling is often discouraged. *Selfiecity*, however, also departs from this model by examining ways people self-represent through selfies via Instagram, a mobile photo-sharing service launched in 2010 that promotes itself as a way to "capture and share the world's moments."

Seflies are characterized by particular angles, often high-angle shots from an extended arm visible in the portrait, and by particular formats, such as views inverted by photographing oneself in a mirror. Selfies typically have an aspect ratio specific to mobile-phone cameras: portrait rather than landscape view. Selfies are considered a form of self-expression and self-reinvention. In some cultures, they include the subject's face or body—including genitalia, as often comes to public attention in US political scandals involving nude selfies as a part of "sexting." In others, faces are obscured for privacy or modesty. Like any kind of nonprofessional photography and UGC, selfie protocols vary enormously; intentionality is difficult to discern. *Selfiecity* works from the assumption that selfies are self-indulgent means of self-promotion, operating on a celebrity model of having one's selfies go viral as a means of securing market position in the highly competitive industry of reality television. This iteration of the project, thus, is not concerned with appropriations of such practices around the world, including ones that parody or satirize it. The project does not address, for example, the role of transnational appropriations of photography, as in David and Judith MacDougall's transcultural documentary *Photo Wallahs* (Australia, 1991) on practices of self-fashioning in tourism and studio photography at hill stations in India to Awam Amkpa's recent work on self-fashioning in contemporary Nigeria and South Africa.[63]

Selfiecity attempts to make sense of selfies through four key sections: "finding," demographics data on people taking *selfies* in its five-city study of Bangkok, Berlin, Moscow, New York, and São Paulo; "imagepoints," visualizations of comparative analyses of photos; "selfexploratory," a navigational tool through the database of 3200 photos that allows users to filter them by preset categories; and "essays," historical analyses of the art and technology of photography, critical analyses of the function of images in social media, and others. Although the cultural range of sites is not particularly diverse, minor differences do emerge. The imagepoints visualizations, however, work to flatten these differences even further into universalizations that attempt to establish direct relationships between head tilting and emotion. In one of the essays posted on the *Selfiecity* website, Liz Loch notes the binary terms for sex (i.e., male or female) impose meaning on subjects whose of self-definition by gender (e.g., butch, femme) are erased, so that the project actually lags behind commercial social-media sites that include transgender, cisgender, and gender queer as options.[64] She also refers to studies that question the use of exploitative platforms like MTurk and its alienated labor pool in academic work, which sustains a "tendency to trivialize tagging and data entry work." On the automated functions, Loch points to Gates's study of facial recognition technology and surveillance.[65] Despite these very significant reservations, Loch finds the project useful for thinking about user-generated content and datification of human subjects, such as the use of hashtags #selfie or #me in combination with automated GIS tagging.

The project is also useful for thinking through digital media about digital media. It points to limitations in both human-judgment and automated analysis of visual images, for example. The initial stage of analysis of 120 thousand Instagram photos is outsourced to MTurk workers; the second stage includes running the top one thousand photos for each city through automatic facial-analysis software to estimate positions for the subject's eyes, nose, and mouth; and the final stage has the team manually examine the tagged results of 640 photos for each site. By computing information from the data, the project attempts to establish finding, such as the relative rarity of selfies among photos in general and cultural assumptions about age, sex, and city; yet in so doing, the project points to the archival drive that philosophers like Derrida have argued are also drives to the archive's own self-destruction.[66] The "interactive" practice of producing, publishing, and tagging selfies in an open database becomes an act of complicity with corporate and state monitoring.

Other projects investigate the political economies of mobile phones, encouraging us to think about our contribution to global e-waste. Rifting on Disney's animated feature universalized white male *Toy Story* (United States, 1995; dir. John Lasseter) in which a cowboy doll named Woody finds himself feeling antiquated after the arrival of a new spaceman doll named Buzz, Molleindustria's *Phone Story* (Italy, 2011; www.phonestory.org/) questions the material waste that accumulates through consumerism. In an ever-widening culture of disposable gadgets, it looks at end-of-life for phones in relation to end-of-life for the exploited workers whose under- or unpaid labor makes these gadgets inexpensive. The project asks consumers to consider questions of ethical and environmental responsibility typically not included in industry-driven campaigns. The project also underscores ways that mobile phones are mobile: they move across borders not only during packaging, shipping, consumer sales, but also during preproduction of raw materials, production of parts, assembly into products, and afterlives as e-waste.

About 60 percent of the world's population owns a mobile phone, yet there is a great deal of variety among these devices. Most people still look to Japan and South Korea for the leading edge of mobile technologies, which later filter down to other markets. Samsung's smartwatches have recently been launched. UAE is considered the most saturated state with 208.65 subscriptions per hundred residents—or two phones per person—in contrast with Burma/Myanmar, which has less than 0.74 subscriptions per hundred residents.[67] In the UAE, residents, both nationals and expatriates from Australia, Europe, Middle East, North Africa, North America, South Asia, and Southeast Asia, replace phones once every six months. In Europe, residents typically replace their smartphones once every 18 months.[68] Such statistics, however, are not representative of the world where the average life of a handset is seven years.[69] Although mobile phones are considered a status symbol in Dubai, Seoul, Singapore, or Tokyo, they are considered a basic necessity in much of the world where landlines are either not available, prohibitively expensive, or have extremely long waiting periods for installation, such as the least-developed parts of Nepal and China. In the 19 least-developed African states, 75 percent of phone use is mobile.[70]

Once outdated, these devices cycle through secondary markets, yet only a very small percentage are refurbished through take-back schemes for use by new customers or disassembled for recycling for traffic cones, metal, gold, and jewellery. A number of formal and informal structures exist to facilitate reuse and recycling. In places with strong recycling traditions such as Egypt, mobile devises are seldom included in take-back schemes but are taken apart for recycling. Attention to education on hazardous materials is important, such as a French partnership program in Sénégal or end-of-life phones. Companies have been founded to assist reuse and recycling, including Fonebak, which collects phones in Europe and sends them to its refurbishment facility in Romania for African and Asian resale markets. ReCellular collects in Canada and the United States for refurbishment in China, Latin America, and the United States for resale in the Dominican Republic, Hong Kong, and even parts of the United States.[71]

Despite efforts by manufacturers to dematerialize (i.e., use less material), substitute less-hazardous substances, and reduce the amount of mixed materials to minimize the amount of e-waste, mobile phones account for an estimated 50 metric kilotons of e-waste with about 125 million mobile phones discarded each year.[72] About

85 percent of electronics are not recycled but go directly into land-fill, where toxic chemicals, including a large amount of lead, poison the environment. Hardware accessories and components, such as batteries, headsets, decorative cases, charging stations, and cables are seldom compatible with newer models, increasing the amount of e-waste, sometimes dumped with other household waste. Recycling through environmentally conscious companies like Fonebak and ReCellular is encouraging, but the vast majority of discarded devices travel through labyrinthine layers of contractors, subcontractors, sub-subcontractors, and sub-sub-subcontractors. Compliance and accountability are nearly impossible because companies bypass bilat-eral and multilateral agreements on e-waste trade. Reusable items like servers and phones are mixed with junk like CRT (cathode ray tube) monitors in a system resembling the Hollywood studio system's block booking that bundles desirable hits with undesirable flops, thereby blocking theatrical screens from independent films. Mixing waste into e-waste is like bundling content.

The thriving market for sending discarded phones to Nigeria has been called an *unfair* trade in e-waste since 75 percent of the electron-ics are obsolete and cannot be refurbished.[73] The phones are dumped into landfills and swamps, where toxic metals (e.g., lead, cadmium, mercury) contaminate lands and water, or are burned, sending car-cinogenic dioxins and polyaromatic hydrocarbons from plastics into the air. With increasing attention to e-waste in Africa's largest port of Lagos, traffic now migrates to Cairo, Dar es Salaam, and Mombasa.[74] Egypt, Kenya, Nigeria, Tanzania, Cambodia, China, India, Indonesia, Pakistan, and Thailand are top e-waste destinations. The illegal trade contribute to what has been termed an "e-waste tsunami in China."[75] The United States is one of the largest producers of e-waste, yet it refuses to ratify the Basel Convention (1989). This convention aims to reduce hazardous waste, promote environmentally sound disposal, and restrict and regulate transboundary movements of hazardous wastes.[76] It aspires to help developing countries defend themselves from the toxic e-waste of developed countries. Toxic materials are dumped in someone else's "backyard."

Phone Story is smartphone app that contains four games that take apart the lure of smartphone elegant design and inexpensive price. It reveals their production from the extraction of coltan in Congo and outsourced labor in China through their planned obsolescence and eventual return to the earth as e-waste in Pakistan. The app promotes itself as being "banned from the [Apple] App Store." Apple dropped the app from its iTunes store four days after its release, initiating numerous articles on the political economies of smartphones. As tactical media, the app was banned for violating Apple rules concerning "depictions of child abuse (code 15.2), objectionable or crude content (16.1) and promises to turn over a portion of the money to charity (21.1 and 21.2)."[77] The four mini-games ask players to (1) manipulate armed guards, so that miners continue to mine coltan; (2) catch suicidal Foxconn workers as they hurl themselves from the factory; (3) lure consumers into Apple stores to purchase newly released merchandise; and (4) forward e-waste to workers for breakdown. The games chart mobile phones moving through hazardous work environments. The objectionable feature of the game was the Foxconn suicide mini-game, which showcased the suicides of more than 20 workers within a period of a few months an Apple's supplier factory in Shenzhen. Rather than addressing 36-hour shifts and working poverty in special economic zones (SEZs), Foxconn installed safety nets to catch workers leaping from the factory's roof—an ethically questionable response to correcting working conditions.

Phone Story's website explains each of its four subgames. The section on coltan contextualizes the mineral extraction within the 15-year history of civil war in Congo, where military groups enslave prisoners of war, mostly children, to mine minerals exported through transit countries to avoid the stigma of being labeled as "conflict minerals." Coltan is processed by East Asian-owned refineries, then sold on the world market to companies such as Apple, Intel, Hewlett Packard, Nintendo, and Nokia. "Directly or not, we are all involved in this complex illegal traffic," the website concludes. The page also includes links to strategies consumers can adopt. The website's extensive amount of text and reading materials is familiar to players of *World of Warcraft* (United States, 2004–present) and other single- and multi-player computer games. *Phone Story* can be played online or downloaded for PC or Mac. In Story Mode, the app, exhorts: "don't pretend you are not complicit." The project offers insights into consumer complicity with corporate business practices.

Rigging Mobile Cameras

To assure corporate control, classical Hollywood producers conceived every shot in advance, to contain directorial agency and meaning. In contrast, thinking through digital media opens filmmaking to the complexities of life's meanings from multiple points of view and perspectives. Conceived by award-winning documentarian during an underwater shoot, Leonard Retel Helmrich's concept of Single Shot Cinema revolutionizes how we can think about documentary practice. Departing from the industry conventions of highly constructed conventional documentaries—an A-roll of talking heads in close-up as evidence and a B-roll of space and place in long shots and long takes as context—Single Shot Cinema has the camera entering events by taking advantage of inexpensive digital video. By eliminating large crews of technicians—along with other cost-prohibitive limitations, such as film stock, camera rentals, and film processing—documentary filmmaking can discard controlled shooting ratios. The concept reimagines and reinvigorates the filmmaking process.

In Siegfried Kracauer's famous distinction between realist and formative tendencies, he looks to the Lumière brothers' actuality films (actualités) as proto-documentaries for ways that they appear to reveal life caught unawares, somewhat in the manner of Dziga Vertov's camera-eye (kino-oki).[78] Despite fanciful stories of audiences running for cover from black-and-white images of trains pulling into stations, audiences were actually astonished by the discrepancies between the Lumières' animated images and personal experiences of perceptual reality, as Tom Gunning notes.[79] Nonetheless, the images did resemble reality more than the later visual rayographic experiments by Man Ray. The Lumière actualities were nonetheless carefully composed 50-second recordings of actions that were often planned in advance and even rehearsed. The position of the camera for some of the best-known films, Sortie d'usine/Workers Leaving the Lumière Factory (France, 1895) and Arrivé du train en gare/Arrival of a Train at La Ciotat (France, 1895), were composed to allow the illusion of 3D depth, following photographic conventions developed earlier. Creative and intellectual work begins—and to some extent ends—during the profilmic moment of these predominantly one-shot films. Production and postproduction follow a preset course. Rather than continuing this practice of careful setups in pursuit of illusions of realism, including the highly stylized ones in classical Hollywood's invisible style, Single Shot Cinema opens filmmaking, so that creative and intellectual thinking can occur throughout the process from preproduction through production into postproduction. Recording sounds and images becomes a means of investigation and analysis in the moment, that is, with a flexibility to allow for consideration of context and contingency for change. The concept minimizes the necessity for multiple takes.

The core idea of the concept is the constant movement of the camera at different speeds and at different distances from its subjects, so that video conveys meaning through affect bundled with content. In this sense, it departs from the aggressive practice of cinema verité (*cinéma vérité*) and the passive practice of direct cinema (*cinéma direct*), both of which seek to conceal the presence of the filmmaker behind the semblance of objective images. For Helmrich, documentary is less about objectivity and evidence than it is about subjectivity and feeling, but this reconfiguration of documentary after the affective turn is not merely a kind of first-person or personal documentary. It emphasizes social context in a rigorously analytical way that is conveyed through visual images, narratives, and affect.

With SteadyWings, Helmrich invented a means for the camera to move freely through space on land like the underwater camera moves through water: fluidly, uninhibitedly, and without the aesthetic shakiness of handheld camerawork that has come to be associated with the constructed realities of reality television. He and Willem Doevendans conceived and designed SteadyWings to "provide extreme flexibility without the loss of stability." The camera mount is held in the camera operator's hands and can be folded to allow movement through tight spaces. The stabilizer system differs from Garrett Brown's Steadicam, developed back in the mid-1970s, which required camera operators to wear a "vest" (harness) to which the camera, battery pack, monitor, and stabilizer are mounted, thereby limiting the range of motion that even light-weight digital cameras could make. SteadyWings allows for camera operators to pass the camera back and forth, permitting the camera to float through windows, for example. Helmrich combines techniques from puppetry and tai chi to facilitate movement through space. His newer stabilizer, Orbit, allows enhanced flexibility and stability.[80] His latest inquiry into thinking through digital media involves taking this new consumer-grade 3D digital technology to an area of intellectual inquiry rarely experienced in the latest wave of 3D filmmaking. Much like Wim Wenders's 3D documentary *Pina* (Germany/France, 2011) suggested a means to liberate dance-on-film from the analogue conventions of commercial dance photography, which often rendered dancers into mere objects under the photographer's controlling gaze, Helmrich's invention promises to allow documentary to visualize entry into the lives of its subject in ways previously unrealized.

While these concepts and inventions can be applied as process and tricks in commercial filmmaking, Helmrich deploys them as a creative and intellectual means. His three films about the devoutly Christian Rumijah Sjamsuddins, her son Bakti, and his orphaned niece Tari avoid the technical formalism of longitudinal documentaries, such as Michael Apted's *Up* series (United Kingdom, 1964–present) for television.[81] Instead of focusing on exceptional individuals, even if cast as unexceptional, Helmrich's films situate the family within the context of the vast changes to Indonesia over the past decade. A friend of Helmrich's late mother, Rumijah still lived in a village, only moving to Jakarta more than a decade after appearing in the initial film. *De Stand van de Zaon/The Eye of the Sun* (Indonesia/Netherlands, 2001) examines Indonesia during a moment when student protests culminated with the resignation of Suharto and the end to the authoritarian New Order (1965–1998); *Stand van de maan/The Shape of the Moon* (Indonesia/Netherlands, 2004), when fundamentalism was on the rise in Indonesia within the context of global social changes about the meaning of Islam in a post–9/11 world; and *Stand ven de Sterren/Position Among the Stars* (Netherlands, 2010), when recent neoliberal economic policies that have widened the gulf between an ever-contracting group of global rich and an ever-expanding group of global poor.[82]

In each film, Helmrich uses digital media as a means of thinking about and through his subject and the ethical, political, and intellectual questions that making films about a family raises. Although a long sequence of a young boy named Bagus, running through the street in a Batman t-shirt and cape while trailing clothing from a hanger over this shoulder, is often discussed by film critics as the most memorable in *Position among the Stars*, Helmrich's extreme close-ups of action through the prism of dewdrops on a rice stalk becomes a visual metaphor for his thematic explorations, not only into the complexities of life, but also in ways that space has been conceived cinematically.

In *Shape of the Moon*, Bakti's decision to convert to Islam is visualized in a scene in which he walks over a railway bridge over a deep green gorge. Helmrich rode a dolly across a railroad bridge with a digital camera mounted onto a bamboo pole ("crane") in order to capture an aerial shot of a young man (not Bakti) who crosses a deep ravine by walking across the bridge.[83] The five-minute scene was done in one take and later edited for the film. Screened in a theater, the shot is both breathtaking and disquieting: audiences tend to leap from their seats at one point when the editing of the footage suggests that the young man may have lost his footing. Understood in the context

Figure 3.2   *Stand ven de Sterren/Position among the Stars.*

of the film's exploration of Islam soon after the United States declared its War on Terror, which critics often describe as a thinly veiled War on Islam, the shot becomes for Helmrich a figurative image of *Sirat al-Mustaqim* ("right path" or "bridge of life"). The scene conveys Islam in relation to one man's act of faith, rather than anonymous acts of fanaticism that are often conveyed in foreign media. Bakti's conversion is motivated by love for his Muslim fiancée, not by religious fundamentalism or political aspirations.[84]

In *Promised Paradise* (Indonesia/Netherlands, 2006), Helmrich explores terrorism in relation to the Bali bombings in 2002 and 2005 that were attributed to Jemaah Islamiah ("Islamic Congregation"), a militant group that is attempting to establish an Islamic caliphate in Southeast Asia and is considered a terrorist organization with cells in Indonesia, Malaysia, the Philippines, Singapore, and Thailand. The film opens with a scene of Agus Nur Amal, a traditional Indonesian puppeteer and modern performance artist known under his stage name of PM Toh, as he entertains children in Acehnese storytelling genre (*dangedria*) that illustrates the story with realist objects in an abstract way.[85] In this case, Amal performs a reenactment of the destruction of the World Trade Center (WTC) towers in New York. His battery-operated gyrating Osama bin Laden doll directly addresses the children as images of suicide bombings in Indonesia undercut the comedy of the WTC scene. If thinking about the Nazi holocaust in documentary as *exceptional* can prevent audiences from recognizing other holocausts, including the genocide of indigenous nations and enslavement of Africans necessary for the economic foundations of US democracy, then this scene in *Promised Paradise* unsettles US exceptionalism in 9/11 discourse. *Promised Paradise* explores reasons that people would pursue martyrdom through religiously motivated suicide bombings. Traveling to the Denpasar prison in Bali, Amal has a conversation with one of the surviving perpetrators of the 2002 bombing, Imam Samudra, that Helmrich constructs by intercutting his own video of Amal posing questions to Samudra with prerecorded video of Samudra reciting readymade answers. Helmrich's film is edited to suggest that the video was purchased on the gray market.

By thinking through digital media, Helmrich has become "the first two-time winner of the top prize at the International Documentary Film Festival Amsterdam."[86] Single Shot Cinema, SteadyWings, and Orbit move filmmaking forward by providing models for thinking through digital media. Images are more visually interesting and more intellectually complex, perhaps suggesting why Helmrich's concept and technologies might be considered a threat to Hollywood models of film production, which employ a hierarchal division of labor that affords accountants, lawyers, and marketing executives decision-making power over armies of (often outsourced) technicians in order to control content. Given the significance of Helmrich's ingenious thinking through digital media, he has been awarded top prizes at the most prestigious documentary film festivals and has been invited to offer workshops around the world. Hollywood-style assembly line film production is a cost-prohibitive and antiquated model for filmmaking that developed almost a century ago yet continues to be employed in many film schools, where non-teaching staff sometimes outnumbers faculty, thereby limiting the types of knowledge production possible in the classroom. Single Shot Cinema is a sustainable alternative that promises to open filmmaking to perspectives previously silenced and erased.

Although students are sometimes resistant to the concept, they grow confident to allow camera movement, rather than focus or framing, to serve as their primary means of defining and advancing a story, which will later be refined through editing. The goal, Helmrich explains, is to get them to think more holistically about ways that everything, whether in-frame or out-of-frame, is connected. When they begin to notice small details in the environment around or behind their actors, they begin to think about the world differently. They start thinking in terms of connections, rather than separations, which can produce compelling stories as well as make important statements about social topics. In this way, the very choice of subject becomes important.

In many film schools around the globe, students are instructed to look inward to themselves, so that the filmmaking becomes mode of personal or individualist expression that frames the filmmaker as a unique human being from a romanticized notion of nineteenth-century humanism. In contrast, Single Shot Cinema asks students to look outward at the world and notice connections between self and other. When students learn to think through media about topics that have relevance to huge populations like climate change and species extinction, they begin to notice connections that are meaningful to others rather than personal observations whose significance is confined to themselves, their friends, families, and teachers. In his trilogy, such connections can be seen. The microcosm of the Sjamsuddins reflects the macrocosm of Indonesia as free-market economic policies threaten to alter family dynamics permanently. Helmrich's concept of Single Shot Cinema trains us to notice interconnections and the precarity of life.

4

Tactical Engagement through Gaming and Narrowcasting

Lev Manovich explains that interaction is an *obvious* function of the computer that should not be confused with precomputer audience interaction in the form of reading audiovisual information and interpreting meaning.[1] Digital media, then, functions within closed systems, not outside them. This chapter examines two types of interaction that are potentially not overdetermined by corporate and state surveillance of data gathering. Here, interaction functions as critical or tactial engagement. We analyze digital media that forwards the ideals of tactical media that Rita Raley has described that engage in strategic micropolitics rather than grand revolutions.[2] We examine digital media projects that include counter-gaming, machinima (3D animation shot in a game engine), video performances, and documentaries that appeal to affective and subjective forms of knowledge and reject assumptions that objectivity and evidence are the only valid forms. Identities are not fixed but performed, that is, contingent upon politics rather than place. We also probe narrowcasting, which reconfigures the push of broadcasting on commercial networks in the direction of P2P models, somewhat like the "spreadability" described by Henry Jenkins.[3] Given restrictions on both print and online access to journal articles, Katherine Hayles argues that academic work largely has "a negligible audience and a nugatory communicative function."[4] The same might be said for animation, documentary, experimental, interactive, and narrative media that do not circulate within the system of exhibition networks in theaters, cable, VOD, and DVD controlled by transnational media corporations (TMCs). These forms of media do not benefit from generous state sponsorship as in Europe. Nor do they benefit from the well-established distribution and exhibition networks of TMCs that themselves benefit from the economic and military power of particular states. They often escape notice by anyone not specifically searching for them. They can, however, convene micro-publics through tactical engagement. By expanding the range of perspectives, narrowcasting on platforms promoted through social media allows a larger multiplicity of ideas that sometimes go viral and thereby possibly change ways of thinking. We discuss these two modes of tactical engagement—gaming and narrowcasting—in tandem. Both offer ways to open debate on marginalized, discredited, ignored, and often controversial voices. They provoke. At times, they speculate; at other times, they foreground irresolution. They mobilize strategies of desire in different ways than commercial films and video games. Such modes of tactical engagement do not suggest an "outside" to a larger system but instead call attention to alternatives within the system.

The democratic promise of interaction is matched by one of participation. While the myths hold some truth, they largely mask ways digital networks have been used to contain and control the types of interactions and participations in which we engage. Ulises Mejias argues that digital networks function within a capitalist order, which "reproduces inequity through participation." Digital networks become "a mechanism for disenfranchisement through involvement and for increasing voluntary social participation while simultaneously maintaining and deepening inequalities." Thus, while the Internet broadens participation, it exacerbates disparity through various strategies, such as the commodification and privatization of social space and enhanced surveillance of dissenters.[5] He contends that P2P networks, where "all nodes can simultaneously play the role of server and client as needed," are really no more than "a decentralized network structure *superimposed* over a centralized network structure." Participating in a digital commons is really partaking in an "alternative to the capitalist economy that cannot exist without the capitalist economy."[6] He notes exploitation is the very basis for P2P sharing because "the production for the electronic circuitry used for P2P is still dependent on the surplus labor of the Congolese miner or the Mexican *maquiladora* worker." In Matteo Pasquinelli's words, there is "no acknowledgment of the offline labour sustaining the online world" according to "a *class divide* that precedes the *digital divide*."[7] Comparably, the concept of spreadability has been criticized as a non-centralized model since it "seems to frame a procapitalist approach as neutral."[8] In addition to the anticommerical practices of piracy, we consider practices that might be unabashedly commercial and unapologetically capitalist yet work around forms of power that include state censorship and intellectual property. As we discuss below, Saudi production companies such as UTurn narrowcast web serials on YouTube and promote them on Facebook and Twitter to suggest models for appropriating platforms controlled by TMCs. By thinking in terms of comparison, particularly multiple modernities rather than a universalizing modernity, the frameworks for evaluation shift to allow formerly marginalized, ignored, or silenced groups to use TMC-controlled platforms and technologies to different ends. Comparably, Nollywood film producers have also used YouTube as a free—both for themselves and for their audiences—distribution platform, which counters the so-called dominant distribution practices of Hollywood in much the same way direct-to-video via "wheelbarrows" had in past decades. In other words, Nollywood producers used the direct-to-video as a primary, rather than secondary, mode for distribution and, moreoever, were not dependent upon presales like their direct-to-video Hollywood counterparts. Describing the practice as a "minor transnationalism," Moradewun Adejunmobi points out that Nollywood producers have actually claimed power over TMCs like YouTube and Netflix. She points to the example of Jason Njoku's NollywoodLove channel on YouTube, which licensed content but later left YouTube which refused to cluster advertisements that interrupted the streaming of features.[9] Njoku's Iroko Partners founded iROKOtv with both free and subscription catalog, earning it the epiteth of the "Netflix of Africa." Thinking through digital media foregrounds such structural inequalities as part of new media ecologies.

Researchers have considered how digital media usage changes the way we think and also how it may alter our neural circuitry. We are becoming digital. Hayles notes the digital interface to networked media becomes a form of embodiment "in which human agency and thought are enmeshed within larger networks that extend beyond the desktop computer into the environment."[10] Role-playing in multiplayer video games—or even single-player games against artificial intelligence (AI) opponents—becomes a way of interfacing with the world. Business, marketing, psychology, design, and, even education employ the neologism gamification. It refers to the "use of game mechanics in traditionally nongame activities."[11] Rating narrowcast videos with "likes" on YouTube or Vimeo is one such instance of gamification. Clickbait journalism is another. Nonetheless, video games are typically closed, rather than open, spaces for knowledge production. They are algorithmic machines that perform automated functions through specific, codified rule of action. They are *reactive* to user input, but they are seldom *interactive* where a player could actually modify the game. Artists have modded game technologies to produce work that rework game action rules and outcomes. In addition to "industry-sanctioned hacking," Alexander Galloway cites an important lineage of counter-gaming: JODI, Anne-Marie Schleiner, Brody Cohen, retroYou, Cory Arcangel, and Tom Betts.[12] Mary Flanagan's *[domestic]* (United States, 2003) transformed the violence of first-person shooter (FPS) games into an examination of the inner turmoil of psychological battles with childhood memories.[13]

Although electronic games have existed for nearly three quarters of a century, video games have only belatedly been considered by screen studies and have not been fully examined for ways that they change our thinking about film and television, not merely in terms of style and content, but it terms of engagement. Electronic games are conventionally traced to Edward U. Condon's design of Westinghouse's Nimatron for the 1940 World's Fair in New York. It was a computer-operated version of the mathematical strategy game *Nim* where players try to remove objects from a pile without toppling it.[14] In 1967, Ralph Baer debuted his "Brown Box," which simulated the game of tennis. It would become the prototype for Maganvox's Odyssey video game system the following year. Nolan Bushnell and Al Alcorn designed the table-tennis game *Pong*, which Atari released in an arcade version in 1972 and a home version in 1975. Steve Colley designed the first FPS game, *Maze Wars*, at the NASA Ames Research Center in 1974. FPS games would gain popularity with *Mortal Combat* and *Doom* in 1993. Taito's 1978 release of *Space Invaders* was another landmark in arcade games. Namco's released *Pac-Man* in 1980 and *Ms. Pac-Man* in 1982. Nintendo's *Donkey Kong*, featuring the Jumpman character Mario, was released in 1981. A clone of Soviet mathematician Alexey Pajitnov's puzzle game *Tetris* (Soviet Union, 1984) became part of the handheld Game Boy system in 1989. Blizzard Entertainment's *Warcraft: Orcs and Humans* (United States, 1994) would later develop in the massively multilayer role-playing game (MMORPG) *World of Warcraft* (United States, 2008). Simulation games gained wide popularity, particularly with female players, with the release of *The Sims* in 2000.

Formerly in public arcades and private consoles, video games now appear on computers, tablets, and smartphones. Arcades remain popular in places like Japan and South Korea because they serve as a public venue for the performance of gameplay skills. Media artists have written codes to design their own video games. Some can be accessed online, others are performed in gallery installations. Video games migrate from arcades and consoles to social-networking platforms like Facebook for social games like Zynga's *FarmVille* (United States, 2009) and to smartphones for mobile games like Rovio Entertainment's *Angry Birds* (Finland, 2009). PopCap's *Bejeweled* (United States, 2001) has sold well across multiple platforms. More than children's toys, video games represent one of the largest sectors of the entertainment industry. Thinking through the digital media of video games becomes a tactical means to address overlooked or controversial subjects, such as the violence of structural inequality and war under neoliberal economic and military conditions. Video games are also designed to sell a political point of view ("advergaming") to seduce us into embodying an alternative identity off-line.

Galloway defines a video game as a "cultural object, bound by history and materiality, consisting of electronic computational device and a game simulated in software." It fits broadly within the general concept of a game as "an activity defined by rules in which players try to reach some sort of goal."[15] He provides a useful critical vocabulary for analyzing and interpreting video games, distinguishing between:

1. *diegetic machine acts* or pure process, by which ambient acts are automated during nonplay moments, such as interludes and segues between levels;
2. *non-diegetic operator acts* by which the user interrupts automated machine acts in ways that the machine cannot algorithmically predict, such as pausing the game or hacking and cheating through macros, and add-ons are permitted;
3. *diegetic operator acts* by which the user plays the game by changing the position and orientation in the game environment, enacting expressive acts, or activating actionable and non-actionable objects such as buttons, doors, words, inert scenery, or non-player characters; and
4. *non-diegetic machine acts* by which enabling and disabling acts, along with machinic embodiments that are integral to game but outside its story are automated, including power-ups, goals, high-score stats, data on heads-up display (HUDs) or health-packs, deaths, as well as and "external forces" such as software crashes and freezes.[16]

He cites anthropologist Clifford Geertz's argument that a game is an "acted document." In other words, "videogames render social realities into playable form."[17] Despite their somewhat immersive qualities, players do not blur gameplay with reality. Nonetheless, video games have often taken warfare as a subject, inviting players to role-play as soldiers.

The first war game emerged during the Cold War with *Hutspiel* (United States, 1955). Red- and blue-colored characters represented Nato and Soviet forces. The theater-level game speculated on nuclear weapon deployment. The popular machinima *Red vs. Blue: The Blood Gulch Chronicles* (United States, 2003–2007; dir. Burnie Burns, Matt Hullum, and Geoff Ramsey) parodies the bifocal logic of détente. The absence of warfare leads to a quasi-philosophical questioning of war by the soldiers on both sides. Shot in the game engine of Bungie Software's FPS console game *Halo* (United States, 2001), *Red vs. Blue* also critiques contemporary US politics, then described by media in terms of polarized "red states" (Republican Party) and "blue states" (Democratic Party) during the US invasion and occupation of Iraq. The satire of *Red vs. Blue* is contingent on understanding gameplay. Experimental filmmakers have also produced machinima, such as Peggy Ahwesh's *She Puppet* (United States, 2001) shot partially in the FPS game *Tomb Raider* (United Kingdom, 1996), to question identity through the gendered and sexualized violence in commercial video games, and Jacqueline Goss's *Stranger Comes to Town* (United States, 2007), shot partially in *WoW*, to question identity through the racialized implications of biometrics used in US immigration for noncitizens.[18] In addition to machinima, digital media-makers mobilize the logic of gamification toward alternative politics, offering insights into forms of knowledge production that complicate and contradict the assumptions and expectations of mainstream media, whether European or East Asian, whether Kollywood, Nollywood, Bollywood, Hollywood, or Tollywood.

Tactical Counter-gaming

Video games also perform tactical counter-gaming. Raley argues that the "grand, sweeping revolutionary event" has "removed itself from the street and become nomadic," engaging in "a micropolitics of disruption, intervention, and education."[19] Since the Internet allows for a multitude of perspectives, video games with questionable ethics—shooting live birds, "hunting" foxes—are not uncommon. People for the Ethical Treatment of Animals (PETA) developed its own video games, including *Cage Fight* (United States, 2013; www.peta.org/

interactive/type/games/) where players "take control of real [Mixed Martial Arts] MMA fighters Jake Shields, Aaron Simpson, and Georgi Karakhanyan to see if you have the moves to foil a secret underground animal testing ring." The MMA celebrities are vegans or vegetarians; the role-playing demanded by gameplay encourages player identification with animal rights. Other organizations have modified gamplay toward alternative politics to critique forms of imperialism other than anthropocentrism. Video games speculate by simulating alternatives. They mobilize desires to win, so as to disrupt our potential complicities.

In light of the widespread misunderstandings about the Middle East and North Africa (MENA) regions, particularly Israel/ Palestine, counter-gaming becomes particularly illustrative of ways of thinking through digital media. Helga Tawil-Souri examines ways that Palestinian youth played Hezbollah's FPS game *Special Force* (Lebanon, 2003) in an Internet café in Ramallah during the Second Intifada (2000–2005).[20] Available in Arabic, English, French, and Persian, the game was enthusiastically promoted by one of the young female players as "the first game where you can shoot Israelis" and "blow up *Markava* tanks." In previous games, she explains: "I always had to shoot at my own people."[21] The young players were very aware that game engines typically enabled them only to "shoot Iran and Libya" along with "the soldiers who started the Intifada" but prevent players from shooting Israel, Europe, or the United States.[22] US media pundit Thomas Friedman predictably criticized the game.[23] Tawal-Souri's analysis of *Special Force*, however, reveals key differences between it and comparable video games designed by military organizations such as Electronic Arts' *Delta Force* (United States, 1998), Dar al-Fikr's *Taht-al-ramad/ Under Ash* (Syria, 2001) and *Taht-al-hissar/Under Siege* (Syria, 2005), and the US Army's *America's Army* (United States, 2002). *Special Force* evidences how media can be appropriated and tactically reworked toward convening critical micropublics—rather than recruiting soldiers. The use of video games by these micropublics challenges standard assumptions that video games numb thinking with mindless entertainment or incite violence through desensitization. As Galloway notes, the context in which video games are played becomes relevant: US youth playing *American's Army* typically lack experience with everyday militarization, checkpoints, and arrests without charge, which is precisely the environment in which Palestinian youth play *Special Force*.

Some psychological studies attempt to establish links between violent video games and actual violence. However, gameplay is not merely a rehearsal for life anymore than reading a violent book or screening a violent film. Video games offer a tactile, ludic imaginary storyworld for fantasy to roam. For this reason, Tawil-Souri's study offers insight to comprehend ways that video game players think *through* digital media. As one of her subjects explained, the thrill of killing an IDF soldier in the game represents an act that would never be attempted in real life. Like all Palestinians in East Jerusalem, West Bank, and Gaza, these youth were accustomed to everyday IDF violence. Moreover, gameplay re-creates Hezbollah missions during the 1980s against the IDF in southern Lebanon. The gameplay operates as a retrospective fantasy—winning a past war with Israel, which included the massacres of Sabra and Shantila refugee camps by the Lebanese Phalanges (*Al Kata'eb*) Party—rather than training for current warfare or inciting random acts of violence. Moreover, *Special Force* does not include civilians as targets or as victims of urban combat collateral damage.[24] Deployed by the IDF during Israel's 1982 invasion of Lebanon, *Markava* tanks were a familiar sight in the Jenin refugee camp. Palestinian boys threw rocks at the tanks, trying to defend their homes from being razed by bulldozers in 2002. Rocks replaced rifles in grassroots uprisings rather than the militarized strikes of the 1970s. *Special Force* was reportedly commissioned by Hezbollah to "help win the international media war with Israel."[25] It coincided with earlier radio and television news broadcasts of Hebrew-language reports on the massacres by the IDF.[26]

Another important aspect of *Special Force* is the relatively low quality of 3D graphics and gameplay, which are sometimes dismissed as poor or antiquated, incapable of sustaining an illusive immersion based on 3D photorealism. By contrast, newer editions of *America's Army* are so immersive and realist that they have been incorporated into virtual-training application in simulation centers.[27] The game focuses on detection of snipers and makers of improvised explosive devices (IEDs). David Machin and Usama Suleiman describe the extent to which US war games are designed for technical realism in terms of declassified terrain maps and the performance of aircraft.[28] The games do not simulate actual battles. Instead, they simulate clandestine operations and hypothetical missions to "kill enemies of freedom." Due to its less convincing graphics and gameplay, *Special Force* operates at the level of fantasy with little hope for actual combat application. "I know this is not real," says one young boy. "But it feels good to pretend. It feels good to…imagine that we are not victims, but we are conquerors."[29] For the young Palestinians playing the game, *Special Force* is a form of counterpropaganda to the low-grade anti-Palestinian propaganda globally disseminated through US and European news media and Hollywood films.[30] Through their comparative research on *Delta Force* and *Special Force*, Machin and Suleiman ask how the Lebanese video game counters "the view that globalization is a one-way process of Western cultural imperialism," since "Hizbollah had to both adopt and subvert an American format of representation."[31] This act of subversive adoption resonates with counter-gaming.

User-contributed games are sometimes called editorial games because gameplay integrates political interpretations of real-world events. Sometimes, major corporations have censored them. In August 2014, Google Play removed *Raid Gaza!* (United States, 2008; www.newgrounds.com/portal/view/476393) from its store after criticism mounted asserting parallels between gameplay and civilian deaths in Gaza under the IDF's Operation Protective Edge. Google Play later removed other games on the siege, including *Bomb Gaza*, *Gaza Assault: Code Red*, *Iron Dome*, *Rocket Pride*, and *Whack the Hamas* for violating its policies.[32] The games vary in style and form. In *Whack the Hamas*, players "whack" a Hamas solider as he pops out of tunnels, an animalizing trope borrowed from computerized version of the game *Whac-A-Mole* (United States, 1976). *Bomb Gaza* differentiates between black-colored Hamas militants with rifles and white-colored Palestinian civilians with children. *Gaza Defender* remains in the Google Play store since it does not name an enemy.

Initially released anonymously a few days after the IDF's 2008 Operation Cast Lead on the user-contributed animation and game platform Newground, *Raid Gaza!* positions players to "defend" the small Israeli town on Sderot against Qassam rockets at the bequest of Israeli Prime Minister Ehud Olmert. Located 800 meters from Gaza, Sderot was a transit camp for Mizrahi (Arab) Jews during the 1950s. The game opens with a citation attributed to Olmert, who led the Likud Party's so-called withdrawal from Gaza: "The parameters of a unilateral solution are to maximize the number of Jews, and to minimize the number of Palestinians." Players click on gray squares near Sderot to spend their shekels to construct missile silos, airports, barracks, and headquarters marked by both Israeli and US flags. Afterward, players fire missiles and send armed troops and *Merkava* tanks, attempting to maximize the killing of Palestinians.

When funds are depleted, players phone the United States, which offers millions in "humanity [*sic*] aid" since "the Oslo thing didn't work out." Players receive bonus points for hitting hospitals, police stations, or UN schools.

Gaza is depicted as a congested urban space with unmarked borders. Unlike the game's depiction of Israel, Palestinian military and civilian spaces are undifferentiated. No option exists to play the role of Palestine. Machine acts generate rocket launches from Gaza, crude weapons that fly in circular patterns before crashing into the vast, open fields buffering the tiny, gated Israeli city. An instrumental version of the easy-listening pop song "Close to You" (1970) by the Carpenters, a musical duo from the United States, loops during gameplay, suggesting irony. After five minutes, Olmert offers the player a ratio of Palestinians-to-Israelis killed, followed by statistics from previous conflicts. Players learn to minimize lower-cost ground attacks and maximize higher-cost missiles because the United States is always willing to finance. Some bloggers argue the game's asymmetrical violence questions unprovoked Israeli siege on Palestinian civilians. Others are less convinced, contending gameplay elicits a critical response to actual events.[33] In some ways, dialogue and debate over the video game was more nuanced than the user comments posted on commercial media outlets, particularly in the United States and Canada.

Launched in 2003, the collective Molleindustria has been called "a reaction to what games had become, the corporate power houses that now fueled them and the ideologies that the medium constantly reinforced."[34] Molleindustria games are produced in brightly colored Flash animation under a Creative Commons license. They often include a tactical element, evoking emotional responses on taboo topics such as pedophilia among Catholic priests and Islamophobia in Europe. Many games focus on the incursion of neoliberal economics into workers' lives in the tradition of Italian radical philosophy from Antonio Gramsci to Antonio Negri. Gabriele Ferri describes Molleindustria's games as effective in targeting "recognizable and well-known antagonists" and affecting players through "complex emotional engagement, frequently in the form of 'bitter' laugh, but also indignation."[35] She explains the games mobilize a nonlinear rhetoric through "schematic simulations that are simplified in some aspects but realistic and accurate in describing causal relations and ideological processes," so that ludic aspect of gameplay "serves a specific rhetoric and semiotic strategy."[36] Pedercini places the user

Figure 4.1 *Oilagarchy.*

in the position of power "to feel complicit with the 'bad guys.'" This tactic distinguishes Molleindustria's games from *3rd World Farmer* (Denmark, 2006), in which players manage an African farm, or *Darfur Is Dying* (United States, 2009), in which players experience being a political refugee.[37] Critical reflection comes in the form of being coaxed by the *lure of winning* to engage directly in questionable behaviors typically distanced from us. The game elicits empathy rather than sympathy.

Oilgarchy (Italy, 2008; www.molleindustria.org/en/oiligarchy/), for example, opens with the provocation: "Now you can be the protagonist of the petroleum era: explore and drill around the world, corrupt politicians, stop alternative energies and increase the oil addiction. Be sure to have fun before the resources begin to deplete." The game frames the green revolution as an obstacle—a "virus of environmentalism," satirizing conservative news media rhetoric. Players parachute equipment and personnel to explore lands and waters for possible oil reserves, construct wells and rigs, and demolish local housing. Players explore Alaska, Iraq, Nigeria, Texas, and Venezuela and lobby in Washington DC, attempting to influence political policy by locating "well-oiled" (i.e., easily bribed) representatives and president rather than "eco" (i.e., ecologically inclined) ones. When wells are constructed in the jungles of Venezuela, birds and monkeys flee from trees before they are felled. Jaguars and indigenous populations evacuate before their lands are appropriated. Lakes fill with the bones of dead fish. Indiscriminate oil drilling brings ecological disaster.

As in peak-oil scenarios, the need for unexplored lands in Alaska and Iraq become more apparent. When players explore Iraq, they receive a notice: "Iraq slipped away from the British grasp and is behaving like a problem child. The immense oil reserves are not available to foreign companies and the Iraqi crude tends to flow to anti-Western countries. Hopefully, sooner or later somebody will teach this nation a lesson about free markets." For Alaska, the notice complains about wildlife refuges with "noisy birds and stinky caribous." Strategies to win the game according to its rules open up questions about the ethics of the actions required to profit from oil and our complicity with a system based on fossil fuels.

Set in 2010, *Tuboflex* (Italy, 2003; www.molleindustria.org/en/tuboflex/) asks players to consider flexible-labor practices by role-playing as a worker who physically transforms to meet the needs of the "dynamic labour market" without becoming "blacklisted and expelled from the market." Although many video games involve repetitive tasks, *Tuboflex* transmutes this feature into a means of gameplay that elicits empathy for low-paid and low-skilled labor. When working at the pickup window for a fast-food restaurant, the task of clicking the desired amount of preassembled bags of hamburgers, fries, and soda for each customer requires simply holding the cursor over the bag-icon and clicking the mouse. If players succeed, they earn one-hundredth of a point, suggesting the extremely low pay for these jobs. If they do well, it does not translate into a higher salary or a better position. Instead, they are sucked by a tube into another repetitive unskilled job based on the neoliberal logic of flexible labor. Failure, however, leads to ejection onto the street, where the avatar sits on the pavement with a dog and plays an accordion for handouts from passing cars filled with laughing children. The game updates the trope of the homeless man with a pet dog from films like Raj Kapoor's *Awara/The Tramp* (India, 1951) and Vittorio de Sica's *Umberto D* (Italy, 1952) to visualize how modern progress continues to leave many behind. Constructed in five days as part of an experimental gameplay project, *Kosmosis* (Italy, 2009; www.molleindustria.org/kosmosis/kosmosis.html) presents an alternative-reality game as a socialist fantasy: a communist space shooter. The objective is to gather support: "Don't try to dominate the swarm: become the swarm." Molleindustria reroutes the acts of playing video games from competitive (following the rules to win) to contemplative (questioning the rules of winning) in the context of capitalism, which becomes an urgent question as the BRICS, MINT, and GCC states ascend to global capitalism.[38]

Edo Stern's *Waco Resurrection* (United States, 2004) asked participants to place a "specially designed voice-activated, surround-sound enabled, hard plastic 3D skin"—over their heads to play the role of a "resurrected" David Koresh. The participants relive the siege of a compound of the Christian-reformist group Branch Davidians (aka The Branch) near Waco, Texas, led by Koresh, who was accused of polygamy, statutory rape, child abuse, and stockpiling weapons. From 28 February to 19 April, 1993, US federal and Texas state officials sieged the compound with gunfire, teargas, and fire. About 76 members of The Branch died. The video game portion functions much like an FPS. Inside the "Koresh skin," however, Stern describes the experience as one of hearing sounds including "government psy-ops, internal voices and the clamor of battle, and empowered to voice messianic texts from Koresh's exegesis of the book of revelation." Players fight state authorities with "a variety of weapons from the Mount Carmel cache" and attempt to "influence the behavior of both followers and opponents by 'radiating' charisma."[39] For Stern, the siege of the Waco compound emblematized the shifting role of violent Christian fundamentalism in the United States, including Timothy McVeigh's 19 April 1995, bombing of the federal courthouse building in Oklahoma City, which killed about 168 people and injured a hundred more. The experience of *Waco Resurrection* operates in the folds between video game and documentary. Stern explains he intended to spur the experience of "a 'subjective' documentary rather than an accurate historical reenactment through game" by prompting players to think about the implications of identification *through* the acts of gameplay.[40] Stern compares the players' experience of identifying with Koresh as deliberately disconcerting—akin, he explains, to the experience of playing the role of Adolf Hitler in a video game rather than screening a documentary on Hitler. This dissonance elicits critical response.

Paolo Cirio's *The Big Plot* (Italy, 2008–2009; www.thebigplot. net/) engages the complexities of digital identities generated on social-networking and social-media platforms such as Facebook, Google, LiveJournal, MySpace, and Twitter, as well as web-based references that publish user-generated content (UGC), such as Wikipedia. The project is a "romantic spy story played into the infosphere"—an online game about piecing together identity in the Web 2.0 realm of networked and fragmented information. The game asks players to imagine being assigned to an investigation to reconstruct one's own identity from the data fragments uploaded to social-networking platforms in order to clone and counterfeit it. In *The Big Plot*, identity operates as an exercise in what Cirio calls "recombinant fiction" that migrates between alternative reality games, transmedia storytelling, and viral marketing. Participants interact with four characters with real-life presences in blogs, profiles, and tweets. Unlike most video games, users can create content that becomes part of the spy narrative in *The Big Plot*. They contribute to a story that involves a Russian oligarch, a Canadian journalist, an English psychoanalyst, and a Russian man who initiates the "Eurasian Revolution" aspiring to create a new society across Russia, Europe, and MENA regions. Players enter into the game's parallel universe of digital identities to explore love, violence, and betrayal. The project reverse-engineers storytelling with social-media reality and performance collapsing into each other.

Cirio's *P2P Gift Credit Card* (Italy, 2010; www.p2pgiftcredit.com/) offers an innovative means of wealth sharing through counterfeit money. The project presumes P2P economies provide alternatives to the limited choices of financial globalization. It appropriates the concept of virtual monies loaned by banks under the Fractional Reserve Banking system, which allows them to loan more money than they hold on deposit. People are free to distribute this wealth according to social algorithms through a gift economy. Users can activate it for their own "visionary and illicit type of VISA credit card," and begin receiving GBP 100 for each referral. The project anticipates Cirio's collaborative project with Alessandro Ludovico, *Face to Facebook*, discussed in chapter 3. By luring us with seemingly recognizable acts in gameplay, these counter-games ask us to reconsider our internalization of rules that reproduce the logic of war and violence through capitalism, which takes form in chronic malnutrition, ecological crises, and working poverty.

Narrowcasting Dissent

One of the most important media events of 2011 was the coverage of the uprisings that came to be called the Arab Spring. Inspired by the self-immolation of Mohamed Bouazizi on 17 December 2010, Tunisia's Jasmine Revolution culminated three weeks later in the deposition of President Zine El Abidine Ben Ali on 14 January 2011. Others were inspired by the Tunisian success in deposing a corrupt regime that extended structural inequalities from European colonialism where many of the leaders were close allies with the United States.

Uprisings and demonstrations ensued in Algeria, Bahrain, Egypt, Iraq, Jordan, Kuwait, Libya, Morocco, Saudi Arabia, Sudan, Syria, and Yemen.[41] Other uprisings also emerged in India over political corruption in the Congress Party and in the United States over ineffectiveness of two-party monopoly of power. Earlier uprisings include the Green Revolution in Iran from June 2009 to February 2010, following the highly contested election of Mahmoud Ahmadinejad. Despite their different histories and contexts, these various uprisings share common features of protesting corrupt bureaucracies, inadequate education, ineffectual democratic processes, and state broadcasting systems.[42] Protestors claimed political agency through performance and graffiti.[43] They bypassed state control of mobile-phone networks and the Internet by posting texts, images, and videos on social-media and narrowcasting platforms. The world belatedly noticed an Arab world, putting it under the microscope—or, alternatively, on the world stage.

Ali Kadhum's *Under the Microscope* (Iraq/Belgium, 2012) considers MENA as a region divided by geopolitical borders and cultural difference but united by blood, air, and light. *Under the Microscope* responds to the Arab Spring of pro-democracy protests throughout the Maghreb, Mashriq, Levant, and Arabian Peninsula. Defined by light, shimmering silhouettes of the MENA region contour movements across geopolitical borders to the chants of demonstrators in the streets and squares that disperse into the air as naturally as pollen. Later distributed by a bee, the region becomes united in the color of blood. From a period when all interactions seemed under the microscope of domestic surveillance to one in which all interactions seem under the microscope of international scrutiny, the video captures blaring sirens. Rigid shapes remain, filled with the blood that makes the air and light around them seem different.

The graphic representation of the MENA region simultaneously animates and deterritorializes. The territorial block looks precarious: it dangles in space, as though the rest of the world had suddenly dropped away. Geopolitical borders between the states are invisible, signifying both continuity and unity. It also looks immaterial, with the black surface of the landmass matching the background. Light varies from bright white to soft golden tones. The region hangs decontextualized; it is rendered as though under a microscope that examines detail such that the broader social context fades from view. *Under the Microscope* evokes a fragile sense of hope for the younger generation. Some uprisings fueled revolutions; others were extinguished. As elsewhere, dissent is more often narrowcast than broadcast.

As academics and critics have argued, the Arab Spring may have surprised the former colonial powers of the North Atlantic, evidenced in US Secretary of State Hillary Clinton's support for Mubarak despite police violence against protestors, but the uprisings were anticipated and rehearsed in skateboarding, graffiti, hip-hop youth culture; theater; and even popular Egyptian film and television. Popular culture allowed people to "place themselves in the center of their own narratives in profound ways," according to Tarik Ahmed Elswwei. He suggests a less narrow definition of political to recognize "new forms of political practice" that differ from the ideologically driven Arab nationalisms of past generations. These new practices use foreign technologies like Facebook and Twitter to "make ordinary people the stars of their own mediated narratives."[44] His work extends arguments from an era of broadcasting. In the context of prerevolutionary Egypt, Lila Abu-Lughod argued soap operas shaped social and political debates on modernity, particularly concerning women's roles.[45] In the case of Saudi Arabia, protest culture emerges in even less apparent forms. Saudi comedy has been described as a manifestation of the Arab Spring.[46]

Web series suggest a counterpoint to the popularity of Ramadan series or Turkish soap operas dubbed into Arabic throughout the Arabic-speaking markets.[47] Elswwei calls them "experiments with self-making," after Arjun Appadurai.[48] "Young Saudis, like others of their generation around the world, communicate in videos," explains Canadian writer and producer Jared Lorenz for the Saudi-based Arab Internet Channel. "They have grown up with cameras and software that lets them make movies and understand the basic grammar of film."[49] Short videos are the "self-expression of the generation," he adds. For Elswwei, new media platforms become "production and consumption" that "bypass both the authoritarian state and trite binaries between local and global."[50] Although state television during the 1950s could mobilize Nasser's construct of "the Arab common people" (al sha'ab al 'arab), contemporary Arab soap operas are often "produced in Cairo or Damascus with Saudi or Gulf Arab money, Egyptian writers, Syrian actors, and Lebanese cinematographers, and can ultimately be delivered through satellite, terrestrial television, DVDs, and the Internet." He points out "Turkish, Mexican, or Argentinean soap operas are dubbed into widely understood Arabic dialects and then distributed on pay satellite channels" and are more concerned with profit than censorship.[51] With growing diasporic populations, Egyptian, Syrian, Lebanese, Palestinian, and other Arab identities are diffused. The male-oriented humor of many Saudi and Egyptian web series, for example, becomes a means to rethink what it means to be part of a Saudi or Egyptian generation that might be educated in a post–9/11 United States and aware of new forms of institutional and informal racism retaining mid-1970s' "Oil Crisis" stereotypes of Saudi Arabians as "oil-rich sheikhs."[52].

Saudi television broadcasts comedy series, such as the Ramadan series *Tash Ma Tash*/*No Big Deal* (Saudi Arabia, 1993–2011), which included the controversial episode titled "Terrorist Academy," a parody of *Star Academy* franchise. "What is remarkable about *Tash Ma Tash*," writes Eric Jensen, "is that it is being broadcast with the consent of the government through national media."[53] It was not until Haifaa Al Mansour's feature film *Wadjda* (Germany/Saudi Arabia, 2012), about a young girl wanting her own bike, that international film festivals took notice of Saudi films. Viola Shafik identifies the subject of socially oppressed women as one of international film festival milieu's "hot topics," along with terrorism, poverty, religion, or other so-called tensions between tradition and modernity that foreigners often associate with MENA, particularly Saudi Arabia and Iran. This programming sensibility excludes less sensational and exoticizing subjects, which are often not legible—or even interesting—to foreigners because they contradict dominant stereotypes.[54] *Wadjda* has been criticized for its displacement of state policies onto social norms.[55] Nontheless, the film does negotiate the complexities of indirect dissent. Although public cinema has been banned in Saudi Arabia since the 1980s, the country's 12 million Internet users view about 90 million videos per day on YouTube. Narrowcast series cross geopolitical borders and places where censorship prohibits broadcast.

Popular genres include web-soaps, hidden-camera and reality shows, animations, and satirical comedies. Through advertising embedded in YouTube, the series are profitable. Mohammed Makki's original miniseries *Takki*/*Adapting* (Saudi Arabia, 2012–present), whose title is slang for "sit down," was allegedly designed for youth attention spans. In Saudi Arabia, about two-thirds of the population is below the age of 30. The series consists of a 15-minute first episode followed by 11 ten-minute episodes per season. The series focused on Malik (Moayad Al-Thagafi), who aspires to be a filmmaker despite the absence of public cinemas. For Makki, the YouTube platform allows for audience engagement through comments and discussions across differences within Saudi society. The series becomes a site for debate, serving an important social function in Saudi Arabia. It also gives global visibility to Saudi youth culture, including the practice of drifting and joy riding, appropriated by foreign media.[56]

Describing itself as "an online entertainment channel that provides edgy, local, interactive, yet professional content for Internet users" though YouTube, Facebook, and Twitter, UTurn Productions promotes the series. *Takki* is somewhat unusual because it is a drama. Most of UTurn's series are comedic satires, such as *EyshElly/What Is* (Saudi Arabia, 2010–present) with Bader Saleh and *3al6ayer* aka *Al-Tayer/On the Fly* or *As It Goes* (Saudi Arabia, 2010–present) with Omar Hussein. *EyshElly*'s channel is the most popular on YouTube for Arabic speakers, with nearly two million subscribers in 2013. *3al6ayer* discusses controversial topics such as employer preference for foreigners over Saudis, poor manners during prayer, corruption, censorship, and the ban on female drivers. It does not cross the lines into the taboo topics of religion and the monarchy. The series is also accessible through a Blackberry app. Actors use real names, suggesting a new arena for almost-public debate, ones that are considered safer than on-site venues for stand-up comedy.

The creative potential of Talfaz11.tv, the first and largest Arabic-language online video network in the MENA region, has been recognized. The 2013 Venice Biennale showcased samples from its videos. Operating under Creative Culture Catalyst (3C) in Riyadh, Talfaz11. tv celebrates "human imagination, aspiration, and creativity." The videos constitute a part of the dynamic experimental art scene in Saudi Arabia, which is perhaps most widely recognized for art galleries in Jeddah. Proposing a "reverse cultural invasion" of the United States, Saudi comedy narrowcasts through YouTube in the standup comedy and skits of *La Yekthar/Zip It* (Saudi Arabia, 2010–present), starring Fahad Albutairi. The series flips the present media flows from Hollywood to the United States: a large number of US television series and films appear on Saudi cable, such as *Desperate Housewives* (United States, 2004–2012), which US newspapers interpret as a means to counter fundamentalist messages.[57] Al-Butairi's spin on the "International Burn a Koran Day" by Terry Jones, a Christian pastor in northern Florida, was to interpret Jones's deliberate racism as a mistake. The burning of 2,998 copies of the Qur'an—allegedly one for each 9/11 victim—became an accidental burning of Arabic-language "bibles and children's books." Albutairi asked viewers to send biology textbooks to the Christian man. The skit parodies the news-media practice of translating from Arabic into English by inserting entirely different content. It also shows Saudi knowledge

Figure 4.2 "No Woman, No Drive."

of attacks by Christian religious fundamentalist groups on US public schools for teaching evolutionary science.

Other episodes of *La Yekthar* comment on the foreign appropriation of Saudi culture, such as M.I.A.'s "Bad Girls" video, widely read by non-Arab media as a commentary on Saudi Arabia's ban on female drivers. *La Yekthar*'s Hisham Fageeh's music-video spoof "No Woman, No Drive" (Saudi Arabia, 2013) reworks the 1974 Bob Marley reggae song "No Woman, No Cry" to criticize the ban in a comedic mode. Dressed in Saudi-style white *thawb*, red-checked *shemagh*, and black *egal*, Fageeh and his friends, Albutairi and Alaa Wardi, perform as a band, some characters wearing hipster glasses that update 1980s eyewear styles. The video received nine million views within days of being posted. *La Yekthar* also satirizes Saudi stereotypes of the United States: it represents thinking through narrowcast digital media to negotiate a new transnational moment beyond colonial imaginaries. As Layan Jawdat has argued in *Jadaliyya*, the politically and socially conscious web series "work in a carefully calibrated way—raising questions and awareness without explicit criticism."[58] *La Yekthar* opens with Albutairi raising social issues, often by reciting exact lines from official television media but punctuating them with irony in the form of confused facial expression. In this way, Jawdat finds that the series "succeed in making the viewer question what he/she may have heard in the news, or laugh at what he/she may have already found ridiculous, but they do not verbalize any commentary on the subject." *La Yekthar*'s producers also launched the popular *Khambalah* (Saudi Arabia, 2012–present) series. *La Yekthar*'s spin-off *Temsa7ly* (Saudi Arabia, 2013–present) stars the puppet Temsah (alligator), who interviews people in the Gulf region, thus recognizing the Gulf as a global destination for tourism and celebrity.

Inspired by the animated web series *Happy Tree Friends* (United States, 1999–2006), Thamer al-Sikhan launched the Arab Internet Channel with two series, *Why Me?* (Saudi Arabia, c. 2007) and *Big Trouble* (Saudia Arabia, c. 2007), which starred a Syrian male actor, Mohammad Al-Qass, as the matron Shawqat. More recent narrowcast series include the hidden-camera *Slamaaat Show* (Saudi Arabia, 2014). Like *Tash Ma Tash*, which nearly ignited public controversy each season, Jensen finds that comedy series on YouTube function as "platforms for satire and criticism militating against censorship by maintaining their liminal status as entertainment programmes that humorously and ironically address current affairs issues."[59] He argues, "such programmes present a critical perspective on Saudi social structure that subaltern Saudis are currently unable to express themselves for fear of government or religious reprisal."[60] Another series produced by UTurn, Ahmed Al-Ghazi's *Housa Silicon Valley/ Here Is Silicon Valley* (Saudi Arabia, 2013), takes a more interventionist approach by teaching young viewers how they can become technology innovators and entrepreneurs in the Gulf's knowledge-based economy.

Comparable series appear elsewhere in the MENA region. Two Iranian Americans, Kambiz Hosseini and Saman Arbab, hosted *Parazit* (United States, 2009–2012), broadcasting in Farsi from the Persian New Network office of the US "public diplomacy" (propaganda) Voice of America (VOA), which funded its production. *Parazit*'s VOA connection is ironic. The show's title translates to "static," a reference to the Iranian state's efforts to jam signals from foreign governments. The series' Facebook and YouTube pages transformed into sites for Iranian political discussion, particularly about then-president Ahmadinejad, who dramatically restricted dissent after 2009. "Satire here is considered truly subversive, especially because the text is beamed into Iran from outside," writes Mehdi Semati, yet the series is also "a tool for geopolitical influence in the context of the adversarial relationship between the Islamic Republic and the United States," along with other soft warfare tactics on YouTube, such as US president Barack Obama's best wishes to the Iranian people on

Persian New Year.[61] Like several of the Saudi series, *Parazit* was inspired by the US cable network Comedy Central's *The Daily Show* (United States, 1996–present), hosted by Jon Stewart since 1999, and its spinoff *The Colbert Report* (United States, 2005–2014), hosted by Stephen Colbert. During the second US invasion of Iraq in 2003, the two series were associated with political critiques of broadcast- and cable-news networks, which were highly censored, rather than with fake news. In other words, audiences turned to them for news rather than to CNN or NBC. Its "categorization as comedy grant[s] it immunity from accusations that it violates journalistic standards," writes Geoffrey Baym. He adds: "never claiming to be news, it can hardly be charged with being illegitimate journalism."[62] The series have become news sources for audiences between the ages of 18 and 29, a similar demographic to Saudi and Egyptian comedy series reception on YouTube. In all cases, comedy grants some immunity.

Based in Cairo, Qsoft Ltd. produced *Al Bernameg/The Program* (Egypt, 2012–2014), developed from a series *B+ Show* (Egypt, 2011). Host Bassem Youssef and colleagues put the show together after the revolution that catapulted Youssef to *Time* magazine's "100 Most Influential People" list of 2013.[63] "Bassem Youssef does my job in Egypt," explains Stewart in *Time*; "The only real difference between him and me is that he performs his satire in a country still testing the limits of its hard-earned freedom, where those who speak out against the powerful still have much to fear."[64] Media critics assert *The Daily Show* might "revive a journalism of critical inquiry and advance a model of deliberative democracy" in the United States beyond sound bites and talking points.[65] The series underscores structural similarities between so-called democratic regimes, modeled after the United States, and authoritarian regimes in Egypt, Iran, and Saudi Arabia— all of whom have long histories of support by the United States.[66]

The transnational dimension of narrowcasting is also evident in antiwar videos. The Cultures of Resistance (CoR) Network responded to the second US invasion and occupation of Iraq in 2003 with the *Make Films, Not War* project.[67] The network takes its name from founder Iara Lee's feature documentary *Cultures of Resistance* (United States, 2010), which shows how art, dance, and music can be mobilized as weapons for peace and justice.[68] CoR engages in projects around film, music, food, education, and urgent action. Rejecting then-US president George W. Bush's characterization of Iran as part of an "axis of evil," CoR responded with *Postcards from Iran: Towards an Axis of Understanding*, a series of short videos.[69] Kurdish Iranian filmmaker Bahman Ghobadi helped student filmmakers produce a series of Farsi-language videos subtitled in English for narrowcasting on YouTube. As postcards, the videos deploy striking graphic composition that can be screened on a mobile device or projected onto a wall. The video postcards are designed to be *shared*. The nine-minute *On That Day* (Iran, 2008; dir. Babak Amini; www.youtube.com/watch?v=rOA2Of4kYs8), for example, begins with a female voice in voiceover. Golnar Fallahian recounts the story of Saddam Hussein's destruction of her village and killing of her parents 12 years earlier during the Iran-Iraq War (1980–1988), resulting in her emigrating from Iran. The video's narrative concerns her journey back to Iraq a few months after the United States captured Hussein and asked anyone with a complaint against him to come forward. She walks along the snow-covered land with a brown suitcase in her hand. Moving from screen right, she moves under a black *chador* against the blue sky and brown ground, both dusted with the white of snow and clouds. A solitary tree, barren of leaves, occupies the left side of the screen. At the stark border checkpoint, her *chador* billows around her, as a young male border guard, Latif (Behman Amini), examines her crossing permit. The barbed wire of the militarized border cuts through the frame as he explains that Iraq is no longer safe: she must wait three hours for the Iraqi side of the border to open. As they discuss her story, giant coils of barbed wire tower above her, suggesting the precarious position of both civilians and soldiers in the geopolitics of the region. Her hope for fulfilling her fate, however, is dashed when the guard declares Hussein has been executed. The video subtly graphs how US warfare thwarts Iraqi agency and emotional closure. In *The Piggy Bank that I Found* (Iran, 2008; dir. Arsham Naghshbandi; www.youtube.com/watch?v=dKpSG1mm5FE), a young boy discovers a landmine in a spring. Mistaking it for a piggy bank full of money, he invites two friends to help him open it. Later, an explosion is heard. The six-minute video conveys the dangerous collision of childhood curiosity and imagination with the realities of post-conflict warfare. Narrowcasting, then, provides a respite from broadcast and cable media, offering alternative perspectives, though distinctions between types of media are never clearly defined.

Interacting Connections

In uneven and unequal ways, interactive documentary often visualizes connections potentially affecting everyone, such as climate change and pandemics. Part of *The Refugee Project*, Hyperakt's *An Interactive Map of Every Refugee in the World* (United States, 2014; www.therefugeeproject.org/), for example, visualizes noneconomic refugee migrations since 1975 based on UN data. Designed and conceived by Deroy Peraza, Eric Fensterheim, Josh Smith, Ambika Roos, and Ekene Ijeoma, the map organizes data on 35 million displaced people across 126 states over the past four decades. The size of the red circle over a grey map allows the user to see the number of refugees from particular sites. By placing the cursor on one, a word balloon opens with information on the number of refugees for that particular year. Red lines trace the destinations of the asylum seekers. Users access information on the percentage of a particular state's population that became refugees during a particular year, places that offer asylum, and global conditions that produce refugees. The project unsettles assumptions—and even shocks. Academic scholarship also thinks through digital media to interact connections. Published on *Vectors*, Minoo Moallem's *Nation on the Move* (United States, 2008; http://vectors.usc.edu/issues/5/nationonthemove/index.html), for example, is a digital essay with an interface designed by Erik Loyer that draws upon digital ways of thinking about Persian carpets as art, craft, and commodity in a "mingling of the old, the new, and the emergent." Users participate in the project by weaving—connecting what seems unconnected—the threads of Moallem's essay in order to understand ways that "linkages between the current global feminization of labor and questions of political oppression and the politics of value," as she explains in her artist's statement.

Other projects mobilize paranoia and conspiracy theories, jolting users from complacency, encouraging speculation about other circumstances, even rewiring their thoughts. Jason Nelson's *Pandemic Rooms* (United States/Australia, 2006; www.secrettechnology.com/pandemicrooms/) explores the social paranoia over killer flues, diseases, and other disasters. It plays on obsessions with global viral transmissions by redrawing the spread of contaminants. A cough travels the world. Pandemics emerge. This interactive web-based project confounds irrational fears and necessary precautions. Underneath a black box with gray outlines, four syndromes can be triggered: the afflicted, the emotion, the pathogen, the cleansing. In Pathogens, pictures of an empty kitchen, office, breezeway, warehouse, and church appear. As the cursor glides, glitches and lines draw contamination onto the image. Paolo Cirio's *Drowning NYC* (Italy, 2010; www.drowning-nyc.net/) investigates audience responses to rising sea levels due to climate change on urban populations. The project questions mass media through theatrical, pedagogic, and cinematic forms. The project draws upon participatory practices of recombinant fiction.

Lauren Rosenthal's *Political/Hydrological: A Watershed Remapping of the Contiguous United States* (United States, 2006; http://lauren-rosenthalstudio.com/section/122327_River_Atlas.html) presents an eco-centric vision of the United States by swapping the land-centered cartography inherited from generations, who abused freshwater systems, with river-centered cartographies. "Rivers move from margin to center," Rosenthal explains. "Water is given priority, not as a resource to be exploited, but as the defining element of the social/biological system." This perspective on freshwater systems offers the possibility for "new American" identities. Renderings these freshwater system flows redraws the contours of water. It reimagines the iconic images of familiar geopolitical spaces of individual US states such as Florida and Michigan. Large water systems refuse state borders, whereas small ones reveal what look like deflated versions of states like Massachusetts, New Mexico, and New York—or divided versions of states like Connecticut or Washington.

Productive paranoia can also take the shape of jamming commercial mapping apps. Understanding the power of Google Maps to frame our thinking about possible ways to connect, JODI's *GeoGoo* (Netherlands/Belgium, 2008; http://geogoo.net) is a web-based performance, which disrupts the useful data-visualization in web apps. As JODI, Joan Heemskerke and Dirk Paesmans captured attention in the pre-Web 2.0 era of net.art with *wwwwwwwww.jodi.org* (Netherlands/Belgium, 1995), which thwarted expectations by transforming what functioned like a typical 1990s-era website into a labyrinth of purposeful glitches. *GeoGoo* extends the same inquiry into user expectations based on limited understanding of ways that computers produced knowledge. The web iteration of the project solicits us to confront the possibility of our digital illiteracy, despite daily use of useful web apps. With more advanced graphics and automation of functions, users open *GeoGoo* to find a webpage already in motion. Placemark icons, such as airplanes or cups of coffee, which are easily understood when superimposed onto basemaps, no longer work. Instead, they dance atop the ocean like digital flotsam in a typhoon. Navigation sometimes functions according to expectations, such as the scale tool; at other times, it is incomprehensible to nonspecialists, with drop-down menus titled "geo," "goo," and "." that offer choices such as "90–90–40y," "xypl2r," "mpowcos," and "ge/rot." Selection activates a page refresh, followed by a parade of icons generating geometric designs resembling mandalas or DNA models. The screen continually refreshes itself without user input. A thick red polyline scrawls a jagged pattern across the basemap, mocking the conventional use of line to visualize direction between locations. The line often extends over the map's edge. The project simulates a so-called first-world problem of infinite magnitude. It unsettles centuries of misconceptions about space and prejudices about people drawn from them.

JODI's digital performances are aesthetically innovative and politically engaged. Audiovisual and temporal intervals (glitches, unexpected detours) disrupt the invisible, seamless interface of networked communication. JODI questions our assumptions and expectations of everyday practices like clicking on hyperlinks to access information immediately and entering street addresses to services visualizing their spatial and temporal relations. Although *GeoGoo* does not critique Google's use of a modified Mercator projection, it does ask us to reflect upon ways that the seemingly open architecture of customizable web apps is closed. Users can pin data, but they cannot alter or correct the basemap distortions, such as the much-noted flattening of the difference in the size of Africa and Greenland on the Mercator projection. JODI invites us to recognize that without a basic digital literacy to understand the underlying code that makes web apps function, we cannot control the means of knowledge production from the available data. Google's *Map Maker* app hardly makes us mapmakers. We simply tag maps someone else has made. We are out of control, quite literally, in a so-called information age. JODI's work evokes insights into digital divides we might not care to recognize, such as our illiteracy despite dependency on web and smartphone apps. These strategies share affinities with Audre Lorde's insights into the futility of opposing racism and homophobia with tools made available by racists and homophobes: "For the master's tools will never dismantle the master's house."[70] Working with the tools made available by corporations like Google does not really liberate us from their control.

Performing Existence

Invoked by indigenous groups from Chiapas to Gaza, the expression "existence is resistance" underscores that acts of resistance need to be continuously performed. More significantly, mere existence is a powerful expression of resistance. Digital media offers opportunities for artists to work across the conventionally defined media of video and performance in modes that combine documentary and experimental practice to think through digital media. If identities must be continuously performed, as philosopher Judith Butler argues, then the existence of a history of other identities also needs to be performed to overcome misrepresentation or underrepresentation.[71] Video performances become modes of constructing and contesting identities.

Digital media reinvigorates documentary as networked and performative. Nina Simões's "docu-fragmentary" *Rehearsing Reality* (Brazil, 2007; www.rehearsingreality.org/film/engine.html) examines the landless movement or MST (*Movimento dos trabalhadores rurais sem terra*) deployment of Augusto Boal's Theatre of the Oppressed as a mode of rupture and interaction to prompt social transformation and cultural formation. Users interact with the documentary project by activating short sequences of varying duration and content. Rather than linear, casual, and chronological development, the docu-fragmentary functions according to the logics of disintegration: it encourages users to forge their own networks of connection. The project questions documentary assumptions about the indexicality of visual evidence because this privileging of conventions of realism and rationalism sometimes obscures other forms of knowledge, such as performance. Activist media, by contrast, emphasizes enacting policy change. It dislodges ideologies of impartiality and balance, naturalized by commercial broadcast media, and channels anger and outrage over injustice into productive outlets.

Like Boal's spect-actors, users click on images for segments that document performances and interviews from opposing points of view, opening to multiplicities of meaning toward education and activism. Both the content and the structure of the project require self-reflection about performance. The MST is Latin America's largest social movement with an estimated 1.5 million members. In Brazil, almost half of the arable land is controlled by about 1.6 percent of the population—and two-thirds of it by 3 percent of the population. The MST enacts land reform by peacefully occupying lands to establish cooperative farms, houses, schools, and health clinics. Members camp until the government recognizes them, invoking a stipulation in the Constitution that maintains land that remains unproductive should be used for what is called "a larger social function." The MST seeks to "develop a sustainable socio-economic model that offers a concrete alternative to today's globalization that puts profits before people and humanity."[72] Boel's training in Theatre of the Oppressed methods is geared toward training members to disseminate what they have learned at the settlement camps. Intervention occurs at the micropolitical level. It spreads through layers and across nodes, doubling the structure of the Internet.

If Baghdad was once a center of arts, sciences, and education, it had been reduced to a memory of unending war, particularly after the second US invasion in 2003. Deena Al-Adeeb and Sama Alshaibi's collaborative *Baghdadi Mem/Wars* (United States/Iraq, 2010) explores how war and displacement perform memory on the body.[73] Each of the project's three suites explores a different aspect of corporally, intellectually, and emotionally embodied responses. In "Still/Chaos," the artists perform the roles of two women dressed entirely in black in a tiny white room with padded walls. The women thrash against the walls and resign themselves to imprisonment in what feels like an insane asylum. They perform a sensorium of living with memories of war. "Efface/Remain" shows a woman write a line from Nezak Al Malaika's poem "The Stranger," repeatedly, as though trying to fight against social amnesia that erases cultural memory and against self-censorship. In "Absence/Presence," the two artists stand in a vast open field, where their bodies reveal feelings of suffocation and entrapment, even more so than in the small white rooms of "Still/Chaos." Desaturated video renders the open field snowy white, a site where identities are engulfed and lost in solitude. The three-part performance graphs a collaborative exploration of the memories of two Iraqi exiles.

Similarly, Markus Keim and Beate Hecher's videos explore performance and documentation to consider how revolutions and civil wars affect everyday life, whether tourism to Egypt or European and Syrian artistic collaboration. Their power emanates from dislocation and absence. In a moment of Vine and GIFs, the videos ask us to look and listen for longer than six seconds. A reconstruction of a collaboration that never happened, *In Abwesenheit/In Absentia* (Italy/Austria, 2012) evokes Syria and its civil war through the Egyptian desert a thousand kilometers away from Damascus where the collaboration was planned to take place. Two figures dressed in black move against the light-colored sand. Later, they drop and blend into a pattern of black plastic sheets that mark the ground like graves, flashed by dates and locations of civilian massacres around the world. In *All Inclusive* (Italy/Austria, 2012), the camera pans to reveal a lone snorkeler, standing in an unfinished construction. The figure evokes images of Jean Painlevé and Chris Marker. As the camera pans, clones of the lone snorkeler are revealed. Police sirens and explosions create an eerie soundscape. Later, a German-language male hotelier assures a German-language female voice that the political situation in Egypt has not disturbed his guests' ability to "indulge in a rich buffet" since "ordinary tourist life continues normally."

Gazing at one of the new global capitals of tourism, Anne Spalter's *Sky of Dubai* (United States, 2012; http://vimeo.com/55865257) reworks footage of the city through kaleidoscope and color filters. Here, geometric patterns of traditional Islamic art infuse daily life with the colors of the Arabian Gulf and Ramadan. Rendered from original video shot from a helicopter, *Sky of Dubai* visualizes identifiable modern architectural and engineering landmarks of Dubai like the Marina and the Jumeirah Palm blending seamlessly via a blue kaleidoscope filter into abstract geometric patterns. Their fractal organization merges patterns found in traditional Islamic art with aerial views of the city itself. Eurocentric critics might dismiss Dubai as "the real capital of Second Life," but the artificial land and manufactured water bodies resemble the natural geometries of Dubai, Sharjah, and Abu Dhabi shorelines. Islands look like fountains, and fountains look like islands.[74] Blue and turquoise evoke the crystal waters of the Arabian Gulf and the glass lanterns of Ramadan celebrations, turning natural and artificial environments into microtopias for a new century. "The Dubai phenomenon is part of an upheaval in the Arab region whereby the centre of power has shifted to the Gulf states (GCC)," writes Yasser Elsheshtawy, "and of course leading this 'revolution' is the city of Dubai," which uniquely adapted neoliberal economics.[75] Spalter's video shows the reemergence of Dubai after the 2009 crash when the Dubai model of speculative cities had come into question. It looks down from above in an aspirational mode, evoking Dubai's potential as what some have dubbed "the new Adalusia" in terms of religious and cultural openness despite structural inequalities inherited from European and US systems.[76]

Shambhavi Kaul's *Scene 32* (India/United States, 2009; www.shambhavikaul.com/open/SCENE_32.html) reworks HD video and hand-processed 16mm film of barren salt fields of Gujarat into a landscape rich with color, performing a complex identity of a particular space. Reworking Central Kutch from a specific landscape in Gujarat into a nonspecific landscape that could be anywhere, *Scene 32* obliterates familiar psychological moorings to place-based size and scale, replacing them with a world where microscopic textures form precipices for wind sounds. The salt fields emerge as a site for meditation, an alternating succession of higher and lower resolution images and compressed and uncompressed spectrums of lights and color distinguishing HDV from black-and-white celluloid. Kaul's images of Kutch are remarkable beyond the textures of different formats. Located close to Ahmedabad in India and Karachi in Pakistan, the Kutch District has been the site for political tensions between the two states since Partition in 1947. The Rann of Kutch was designated a disputed area in 1960, and became a site of conflict in 1965. Some even interpret the invasion of Pakistani tanks in Kutch as part of a broader military strategy than an attack in Kashmir as a primary site for Indo-Pakistani conflict.

Indian films about the border with Pakistan tend to focus on Jammu and Kashmir, especially the Line of Control (LOC), seldom considering the border between Kutch and the province of Sind in Pakistan. Although peace was established, the precise demarcation of the border within the Sir Creek in Rann of Kutch remains unresolved, particularly following the attacks on Mumbai by Pakistani citizens in 2006. Tensions continue, with incidents such as India shooting down a Pakistani surveillance airplane in 1999.[77] Although parts of Kutch remain militarized, the Indian state has also become a popular tourist destination, promoted by Amitabh Bachchan for Gujarat Tourism. Kaul's images conjure the silence of the salt marshes, a different Rann than the one that appears in recent Bollywood films, including *Goliyon Ki Rasleela Ram-Leela* (India, 2013; dir. Sanjay Leela Bhansali), *R ... Rajkumar* (India, 2103; dir. Prabhu Deva), *Gori Tere Pyaar Mein* (India, 2013; dir. Punit Malhotra), and *The Good Road* (India, 2103; dir. Gyan Correa). One patriotic Guajarati blogger pondered whether a "Kutch era" had replaced the "Kashmir era."[78]

The performance of space also becomes a preoccupation in Donald Abad and Cyriac Allard's *Entre Deux* (France, 2006), a series of 20 video-performances between two artists. Far from "civilization," human bodies confront nature with endurance, contemplation, defeat, and cooperation.[79] Clad in white tennis clothes and armed with a piece of rope, the artists perform experimental meditations on the body's relationships with another body and the environment to hilarious or poignant ends. Their surroundings defeat the human characters when they fight each other in "Jumeaux" (*twins*) video-performance. They merge with these spaces when they cooperate with each other in "Épaule contre épaule" (*shoulder against shoulder*). In many performances, nature is ambivalent to human interactions. In "Suspendu" (*suspended*), one human anchors a rope hanging over a tree branch to suspend the other human. In "Pendus" (*hanged*), the two humans hang side by side by the arms from the branch of a tree. In "Défense" (*defence*), two humans challenge one another from opposite side of a white strap dividing a field of grass like tennis court lines. In "Liés" (*linked*), the two humans attempt to move in opposite directions in an open field, against the tension of a binding white cloth. In "Victoire" (*victory*), one of the humans stands suspended in the position of a runner crossing a finish line. Here, the broken white finish line waves in the wind from the body of the inert human and the trunks of the two trees. In front lies a deep ravine, suggesting a pregnant moment in an imaginary narrative. The video performances are staged within the Aravis range in Haute-Savoie in eastern France or on the Island of Icaria in the Aegean Sea, where Icarus and Daedalus attempted to fly on artificial wings.

Comparably, Sarah Kanouse's *Don't Mourn* (United States, 2007; http://liminalities.net/3-3/dontmourn.html) investigates the environment through performance. The project combines video recording of artist's live performances as she made pilgrimages from 2005 to 2007 to postindustrial sites left to rust and decay by the global economies of free trade. Often, they were sites for labor uprisings and strike violence. In each visit, Kanouse carries with her "a battered, vinyl-sided suitcase and HAM antenna cut to a commercial FM frequency." As a radio memorial (or counter-memorial), she broadcasts a distorted version of the Communist *International* into empty space. If no one has a radio receiver, the performance appears silent; however, if someone is listening, her performance interrupts regular radio broadcasts. Collectively, her performances map forgotten geographies, the majority of which have not been recuperated for recycling or for storage. Instead, their rust and decay bear witness to what she calls "old and not-so-old" labor struggles between unions and bosses, between striking white workers and black labor imported from elsewhere.

The project develops Kanouse's thinking about radio as a material simultaneously eternal and ephemeral and about electromagnetic radiation moving infinitely through space yet blocked or distorted by object. These tropes create "memorials to difficult, violent, yet largely forgotten moments in American [*sic*] history," so that the "material characteristics [of radio] echo the selective and hazy processes of cultural memory" that is contingent and unstable.[80] Working at the arts organization free103point9's residency program "Wave Farm" in the Hudson Valley of New York State, Kanouse explains they began "to think about 'radio art' as something *made from* rather than *received by* radio waves," settling on the term "transmission art" for projects that engage with electromagnetic spectrum spatially as well as temporally.[81] She describes transmission and radio art as exploring the electromagnetic spectrum as a site and material for art that can be combined with digital and networked forms. With *Don't Mourn*, a website functions as a digital archive for video of Kanouse's performance with notes and historical information on the histories that haunt each site.

Brannon Dorsey's *Zetamaze* (United States, 2014; http://zetamaze. com) invites users to participate in the performance. *Zetamaze* is an open-source game in which players construct a maze, decorate its walls with virtual graffiti, and fill folders with files to share with other players. Drawing upon W. H. Matthews's *Mazes and Labyrinths: Their History and Development* (1922), *Zetamaze* updates meandering by translating the "lure of the labyrinth" into 3D virtual space. Interaction with other players is entirely anonymous. The project moves away from digitally mediated reactions and toward digitally mediated interactions by allowing players to alter the structure of a maze. They express themselves by adding graffiti to the walls of the maze or dropping files into folders within the maze's corridors. The player imagines forms of anonymous communication in a space that appears free of the typical data-harvesting features in video games on social-networking platforms or in mobile apps. Participants can paint political slogans—"We Are All Khaled Said," "No Justice, No Peace," "Siamo tutti clandestini" ("We are all 'illegals'"), or "Black Lives Matter"—on the maze's walls to evoke the graffiti in Tahrir square after the death of the young Alexandrian in 2010, sentiments around Italy after the *carabiniere* assassination of Carlo Giuliani during protests against the 2001 Group of Eight (G8) talks in Genoa, protests against anti-immigration policies of Fortress Europe, and protests against racial violence by US police in 2014. If these slogans reclaim public place, then *Zetamaze* suggests a small way to take back Internet spaces. Users can also drop files for entire books into the maze's folders through a form of relatively anonymous P2P file-sharing. The game adds an element of unpredictability to the otherwise well-ordered Internet. Unlike commercial maze games, meandering aimlessly often becomes more meaningful than strategic play to solve the maze. Not thinking and acting in relation to preset goals transmutes into both a form of protest and a figuration of potential community outside dominant structures.

Animating Histories and Futures

Animation has become an important mode to explore often over-looked and under-examined stories about places in the world who hold great importance but are overshadowed by larger, more spectacular, conflictual stories. Activist films about oil spills often concentrate on the destruction of nature but ignore stories of people who work in the energy industry or make their living from these oceans or lands. Whether produced for US public television or made by Chinese independent filmmakers, films about China focus on characters or situations but ignore the processes and people that explain and complicate China's rapid modernization and position within globalization. Films and investigative news stories probing commodity production in Cambodia, China, India, and Indonesia reduce globalization to sweatshops and their immiserating labor situations, disconnecting products from the global flows, transnational processes, and contradictory subject positions across the commodity chain. The projects analyzed in this section deploy a less confrontational conceptual strategy that opens up multiple paths and voices through social and political problematics such as migrant labor, the British Petroleum (BP) oil spill, the Congo, Chinese textile manufacturing, and media saturation that can numb us to ongoing war and occupation. These projects animate histories with more polyphonic structures, opening up through multiplicity. They eschew borders, lines, and deductive arguments. They offer explanation through exploration, assembling myriad voices, positions, and viewpoints.

The driving force behind the counter-gaming collective Molleindustria, whose *Oilgarchy* and *Tuboflex* are discussed above, is Paolo Pedercini, whose short animation *Welcome to the Desert of the Real* (Italy, 2009; http://vimeo.com/4750691) is a reverse-propaganda machinima. It combines text sampled from the post-traumatic stress disorder (PTSD) checklist with 3D animated images shot in the game engine of the advergame *America's Army: Special Forces* (United States, 2003). The title functions as a mise en abyme: it borrows the title from Slavoj Žižek's 2002 book, which in turn borrows its title from a line in the Hollywood film *The Matrix* (Australia-United States, 1999; dir. Wachowski Brothers), which borrows the line from Jean Baudrillard's 1981 book *Simulacres et simulation/Simulacra and Simulation*. These embedded allusions reflect upon reality and simulations of experience, memories, feelings, patriotism, and guilt. In Žižek's critique of an "American holiday from history" that ended with 9/11, global capitalism and religious fundamentalism are both symptoms manifested in unjustified torture and terrorism. Pedercini's machinima mobilizes the psychoanalytic symptoms of PTSD: difficulties in sleeping, remembering, experiencing pleasure, or conceiving a future. After the pre-title sequence of a kill seen through a POV shot of a crosshair, the video is composed of shots of a solitary solider, who drops his machine gun to wander through a desert. A black screen interrupts with passages about PTSD symptoms. Whereas *Red Vs. Blue* prompts contemplation about the US War on Terror, *Welcome to the Desert of the Real* asks us to ponder the consequences of such delusions upon the lives of US soldiers. It also invites us to question ethics of the military's use of video games as recruitment tools.

Born in Israel and now residing in the United States, Eddo Stern is familiar with the use of religion in settler colonies to legitimize dispossession and genocide. His machinima *Sheik Attack* (United States, 2000) is a "contemporary non/fiction horror" that weaves together "pop nostalgia, computer war games, the sweat of virtual commandos, the blood of Sheiks and a mis-remembrance of a long lost Zionist Utopia."[82] Shot in the game engines of Westwood Studios' *Command and Conquer* or C&C (United States, 1995) and Raven Software's *Soldier of Fortune* or SoF (United States, 2000), *Sheik Attack* mobilizes US militarism to critique Israeli militarism. It is based on Stern's own obligatory IDF service.[83] Due to incongruities between setting and avatars rendered by the game engines and the context of audio of patriotic songs, the machinima exposes the twin colonial logics of the United States and Israel. As Stern explains, the video critiques the commercial games industry's desire to "capitalize on political tension and fantasies of war while never being held accountable for a specific point of view since everything is abstracted into fantastical versions of reality."[84] His *Vietnam Romance* (United States, 2003) advances a similar critique of what might be called the "Vietnam War Industry," a national imaginary producing a barrage of books, songs, television series, and films about the failed US colonial invasion of Southeast Asia during the 1960s and 1970s.

An aerial view of political territories from Israel to Lebanon opens *Sheik Attack*. Labeled "1966," the first scene shows C&C game-play in which armies construct bridges, towers, and rivers. Naomi Shemer's "Zeheerut Boneem" / "Careful, We're Building" (1966) plays, in a later recording by folksinger Chava Alberstein, whose post-1967 music critiqued state policies toward Palestinians. In pre-1967 Israel, Alberstein was a star of the IDF. The opening scene in *Sheik*

Attack can be read as unsettling colonial mythologies. Subsequent scenes show a never-ending pan down a cityscape of skyscrapers that undercut kibbutz communalism with neoliberal capitalism, particularly through the prison- and military-industrial complexes. Later scenes move from Israeli to Lebanese territory with additional gameplay from C&C of coordinated helicopter maneuvers. A final scene of undoing uses footage from SoF of soldiers looking through night-vision crosshairs and entering into buildings to assassinate targets. In one scene, a woman is made to kneel on the ground before she is assassinated with a shot to the neck, followed by the shooting of another man in the head. Most striking, the final two and a half minutes of the 16.5-minute video contain headlines from various online news sources about Israeli abductions and assassinations after the disappearance of IDF pilot Ron Arad during a secret air raid on Lebanon in 1986.[85] By layering the story of Israeli violence onto gameplay from US war video games, Stern's machinima renders a critique of the expansionist militarism in both settler colonies within their foundational myths of escaping religious persecution in Europe.

Xuan Chen's animated video *Out* (China/United States, 2010; www.xuanchen.net/out.html) captures the geopolitics highlighted by anti-trafficking organizations. Its textured animation conveys the harsh lives of Chinese migrant laborers, deploying symbols of women, cities, and power that facilitate dialogue about human trafficking, labor issues, and the possibility of activating changes in the migrant worker's circumstances. Rendered in black-and-white hand-drawn images of identical women living underground, the video counters the glitzy skyscrapers of China's neoliberal modernization with the handmade. Digging out, the women encounter large buildings and men in top hats, signifying the Chinese male bureaucracy. The animation is inspired by the phenomena of migrant workers who have constituted a large portion of China's workforce since the early 1990s. Income disparities, rural poverty, and rapid urban modernization propelled country dwellers to leave their hometowns to work in the big cities near Special Economic Zones (SEZs) and Free-Trade Zones (FTZs) for the economic advancement of their families, representing the largest migration in human history. These migrant workers constitute China's most valuable economic asset. *Out* genders this migration. Women populate the manufacturing industries; men constitute the majority of China's coal miners and construction workers. While their efforts built Chinese skyscrapers and presented the world with "Made in China," the lives of migrant workers have been difficult. They live precariously in the cities while their hometowns remain undeveloped, paralleling the trajectories of Latin American and Caribbean workers in the United States, along with South Asian, Southeast Asian, and African workers throughout the MENA regions, and Southeast Asian workers in Japan and South Korea.

Offshore (Canada, 2012; http://offshore-interactive.com/site/) by Brenda Longfellow, Glen Richards, and Helios Design Labs is an animated documentary that dives into offshore oil drilling. At 71 minutes, it is feature length, but can be accessed in sections in any order. A recurring motif consists of aerial shots of bayous and Gulf of México, peppered with rigs, oil tankers, and fishing boats. The slow ambient soundscape features electronic and string music without melody, mixed with sounds of water and machines, in a repetitive loop, a sonic Brechtian device communicating the threat of deep-water oil exploration. Rather than presenting a simplified linear narrative bolstered by argument and political analysis, the documentary reveals complexities to open different forking paths into this complex nexus of energy, oil, offshore drilling, people, fishing, spills, and environmental protection. Users become more like workers as they wind their way through the documentary's architecture to access its content. Users are put on helicopters flying over bayous and the gulf in aerial shots. Users also enter the offshore rig, descending stairs and entering control rooms. *Offshore* prompts reflection upon our investment in actually knowing more than corporate talking points and legal settlements. How far will you go? How deep is too deep? How dangerous is too dangerous? Organized in a mosaic structure, *Offshore* tackles offshore drilling from a series of different positions: executives, policy makers, analysts, rig workers, shrimp- and oyster-fishing-boat captains. Different sections of the project complicate and specify the vagueries of offshore drilling and the BP spill, such as "A Danger Frontier: The High Risk of Extreme Oil," "Deep to Ultra Deep: Histories of offshore in the Gulf of Mexico," "Port Fouchon: Oil Capital," and various portraits of rig workers and fishing-boat captains discussing different points of view on offshore drilling. On one side, offshore rigs moved some Louisianans into the middle class; on the other side, shrimp and oyster populations have declined.

A film about indentured labor, Paolo Unger Dvorchik's *Modern Slavery* (United States, 2010; www.highimpactart.org/slavery.html) highlights different types of trafficking and slavery via encounters with both victims and activists. Focusing on the resilience of victims, their assessments of their situations, and what lies ahead after their rescue, *Modern Slavery* extends beyond the fetishism and glamorizing of trafficked victims found in so many contemporary broadcast documentaries. The project also inverts the ideological fantasies and geopolitical imaginaries engulfing trafficking. A typical trope of US broadcast documentaries is a focus on trafficking in Guatemala, India, México, Pakistan, Southeast Asia, and the former Soviet Union—a projection of everywhere else as a space for human rights violations. *Modern Slavery* returns to the United States, resituating it as part of these flows of people. It also invokes the legacy of chattel slavery and indentured servitude in US history. Although slavery was outlawed in the United States in 1863, the US Department of Justice estimates that between 14,500 and 17,500 individuals are trafficked each year. This video explores modern slavery, the plight of trafficked persons, and the possibility of life after rescue.

Promoting awareness of our complicity with war and violence in the Congo through the conflict minerals that enable our digital devices, *All Eyes on the Congo: Films for Peace in the DRC* is a partnership between Cultures of Resistance in the United States and Friends of the Congo and Salaam Kivu International Film Festival (SKIFF), in the Democratic Republic of Congo (DRC).[86] In particular, the project focuses attention on the role of foreign powers, such as Rwanda and, indirectly, the United States, in escalating and sustaining war and violence with some of the world's most horrifying statistics of murder and rape. Friends of the Congo's *Crisis in the Congo: Uncovering the Truth* (United States, 2011; http://congojustice.org/) is a 26-minute preview of an activist documentary conceived to educate about relationships with the crisis in Congo. Available for streaming or download, the video untangles misconceptions and paradoxes, such as DRC's rich natural resources yet economic poverty and its waves of rebel factions that sustain the power of long-standing players. The activist documentary also questions silence as complicity with the deaths of more than six million people, half of whom were under the age of five. A primary argument is that DRC's borders were determined in the Berlin Conference of 1884, when it was given as personal property to King Leopold of Belgium. Leopold amassed a fortune by forcing Congolese into servitude to acquire ivory, rubber, gold, diamonds, copper, and minerals. Slavery was followed by colonialism, a dictatorship, and then war. Today, automotive, aeronautic, electronic, and jewelry industries globally continue to depend on minerals and other natural resources extracted from the DRC, often via proxy forces through DRC's neighbors in the absence of a functional national government. Under the cover of what the media often frames as so-called ethnic wars, *Crisis in the Congo* explains illegal exploits, including rape as a weapon to destroy communities.

The international community, particularly the United Nations and United States, remained silent on the genocide and the invasions by Rwanda and Uganda. In addition to economic interests, the Rwandan and Ugandan armies facilitate US interests in central Africa to sustain tyranny and dependency. Congo is also important to the global community in terms of the fight against climate change. It has the second largest rain forest. The activist video ends with "educate yourself," "educate others," and other phrases that emerge from a black screen. *All Eyes on the Congo* also contains information about Salaam Kivu International Film Festival (SKIFF). Since 2003, the festival has taken place in Goma (North Kivu), near the border with Rwanda, for film screenings, community discussions, workshops, and performances to inspire youth to "keep on building rather than destroying."[87] Guided by filmmaker and activist Petna Ndaliko Katondolo, the festival is organized by the Yolé!Africa youth center that Ndaliko founded in 2000 with Dutch anthropologist Ellen Lammers to promote peace through art, and Alkebu Film Productions, which Ndaliko founded with producer Yehudi Van de Pol to produce "challenging work by exploring the narrative possibilities of creative imagination, documentary, feature films, music videos and art based films." SKIFF carves a space for role models like rapper S3, whose 2012 song and video "Je vote" ("I Vote") won third place at Fair Play's Anti-Corruption Youth Voices Award, a global competition for musicians aged 18 to 35 on the theme of anticorruption.[88]

Ezra Wube's videos combine stop-motion animation and live-action footage. An adaptation of Hadis Alemayehu's 1968 novel *FeQir Iske MeQabir* ("Love to the Grave"), *Hidar* (Ethiopia/United States, 2011–2012; www.ezrawube.net/hidar.mov) places art in interaction with the environment, where a cutout drawing of a person opens an actual door. The video reinvents the images and stories of the classical Amharic text about the journey to peace. Moreover, it visualizes a major work in modern African literature for a global population that has only recently come to appreciate African novels. Its play of textures, light, and color animate digital video that can often seem flat. Guided by an artist's hands, *Mela* (Ethiopia/United States, 2011; www.ezrawube.net/mela.mov) shows colorful paperclips crawling like caterpillars over the edges of buildings in Johannesburg, animating lifeless cityscapes.

Figure 4.3 *Hidar.*

The colors of the paperclips evoke Rainbow Nation utopic discourses in post-Apartheid South Africa, particularly ones used on maps of the involuntary migrations (*mfecane* or *difaqane*) of Sotho, Swazi, Tswana, Xhosa, Zulu, and other nations due to environmental and political changes. Wube's other videos offer comparable transnational African perspectives on history and the present.

Cao Fei's *iMirror* (China, 2007) engages China's changing urban landscapes and increasing personal alienation through futuristic animation in the form of machinima in Second Life (SL). Based in Guangzhou, Fei creates an SL avatar named China Tracy, a curvaceous, action figure with long ponytails. The name China Tracy alludes to young Chinese adopting an "American" or "English" name to aid their interaction with foreigners. The title *iMirror*, a 28-minute, three-part documentary about China in the multiuser platform of SL, puns Apple products (iPhones are produced near Guangzhou in Shenzhen). First screened for the 2007 Venice Biennale China Pavilion, *iMirror*'s three sections are also posted on YouTube. The film counters the idea of documentary chronicling the past or the present by creating a futuristic landscape. It is part of a larger project called RMB City, consisting of a website for a fake city, events, projects, shop, and city hall. As the website explains, RMB City is about "exploring the creative relationships between real and virtual space, and is a reflection of China's urban and cultural explosion."[89] Robin Peckham has pointed out that in Mandarin, RMB City is called *Renmin Chengzhai*, translated as "walled city of the people," a twist on the historical walled cities of previous dynasties.[90]

The film is shot in SL with floating neon buildings. The images reference contemporary Chinese landmarks like the CCTV tower, pandas, and skyscrapers. However, this cityscape is empty, the camera constantly panning. China Tracy barely interacts, floating. Part One of *iMirror* begins with a spinning neon red sign that says, "Land for Sale," then a spinning large green neon dollar sign. Tall, grey buildings emit smoke; screens are inserted into buildings. The camera alternates between low-angle shots and bird's-eye views. Barrels of toxic waste pour into an ocean. Fires erupt from factories. Throughout, a slow, whispered song suggests alienation and melancholy. Part Two features a romance between China Tracy and another avatar, Hug Yue, a non-Asian (white) man of 65 who is a former activist. The avatars play piano and guitar. Empty cityscapes, subways, squares, and streets mark this landscape. Underneath the images, the online conversation between China Tracy and Hug Yue ensues, typed out like subtitles. It details alienation in real and virtual worlds. For example, Hug Yue states, "I suppose SL is a drug." China Tracy later observes, "Sometimes I don't know where I am," and Hug Yue responds, "We are all in the Panoptican." Part Three features a series of avatar portraits, couples, pole dancing and couple dancing in a nightclub. The music by the group Prague is slow, ambient, and pondering. All three parts of *iMirror* ruminate about constructed fantasy spaces where the real of China in the twenty-first century collides with the virtual China imagined as a place without people, crowds, environmental destruction, overcrowding, and polluted skies. *iMirror* invokes the documentary essay film, with its meditative tone and distancing from the subject, but inflects this mode with longing, sadness, isolation, and slowness.

Cotton Road (United States/China, 2014; www.cottonroadmovie.com) by Laura Kissel with Li Zhen is an ambitious transmedia project that animates the histories and transnational relationships imbedded in the manufacturing of cheap clothing. Inexpensive jeans, blouses, dresses, and sweatpants, spilling from racks in Target and Wal-Mart, are presented as static consumer objects, good deals for fashion updating and style enhancement in the malls of the Global North and night markets in the Global South. *Cotton Road*'s website, film, and exhibition strategies render transparent the submerged and concealed global supply chain of cotton from planting seeds in South Carolina, United States, to container shipping, ports, and manufacturing plants near Shanghai, China.[91] The project proposes the complexities of globalization can only be fully understood through the construction of a mosaic of multiple voices of labor across the entire supply chain of cotton.[92] The project rejects the character-driven, conflict structure of many broadcast documentaries about outsourced textile manufacturing, which figure women workers as victims who lack agency and install binaries between China and United States. Instead, *Cotton Road* follows the seeds as they transform into clothes that return to the United States, exploring the flows, processes, polyphonic voices, and multiple stories sewn into cotton clothing.[93] Following the path of the cotton seed, the project gestures toward confounding false binaries between East and West or North and South, farmers and factory worker, Mexican migrants, and rural Chinese migrants, local and global.

Kissell collaborated with Sourcemap (http://free.sourcemap.com) to produce an interactive map, tracing the movement of cotton from South Carolina to Shanghai. Sourcemap represents a critical cartography project to map the supply chains and carbon footprints of consumer items like Tom's Toothpaste, iPhones, apricots, Starbuck's coffee, Adidas, trainers and Ralph Lauren jeans. "Find out where things come from," the site asserts. The crowd-sourced directory includes both activist and corporate uploads of lines connecting sourcing nodes to graph supply chains. The *Cotton Road* sourcemap features maps of the southern United States and the eastern coast of China. When scrolling over a location, a description of the supply-chain process appears with a link to a short clip of that site and its people and processes from the long-form film, such as the farmers, cotton products factory, the Shanghai Farmers Market, the recycling of fabric scraps. The project released the sourcemap before the film.

Identifying itself as "a supply side journey," *Cotton Road* is also an 83-minute feature-length analogue film. Kissel, who directed, produced, shot, and edited the film, collaborated with Shanghai producer Zhen. With carefully composed tableau shots, the cinematography visually connects the various people in the supply chain of cotton whether in South Carolina's fields, Yangshuan ports, or textile city of Chongzhou. Both receive equal compositional mass as well as subtle natural lighting, deep color saturation, and variegated textures, visually restoring people to the process. Tableau shot in long takes—for example, cotton-processing plants in South Carolina, weaving plants near Shanghai—insist on a human scale. They open a space for conversation and direct address to Kissel, displacing the tradition of the interview. They generate conceptual counterpoint to the unrelenting flow of cotton, manufacturing and globalization, inviting us to think about labor and labor processes and not simply commodities. Kissel as camera operator is always positioned at eye level with her subjects, in dialogue, referencing the critical ethnography of David MacDougall advocating for documentary as marking an encounter rather than providing evidence.

Cotton Road's exhibition strategy parallels the media socials of *Lunch Love Community*. Although the film has garnered awards and screenings in various environmental film festivals, its exhibition disengages from auteurism toward a more collaborative transnational politic. Its screenings connect to Fashion Revolution Day (commemorating the collapse of Rana Plaza in Bangladesh), the Clean Clothes campaign, and the Inside Out movement of wearing one's clothes with the seams and tags showing to make visible labels with places of manufacture. For her world premiere screening at the Finger Lakes Environmental Film Festival (FLEFF) in 2014, Kissell engaged interns and Ithaca College students prior to the screening to mobilize them to come to the screening wearing their clothes "inside out."

Making "Noise" through Viral Dissonance

If one of the greatest hopes in going online is finding community, then one of the greatest fears is catching a virus, but viruses can also have productive associations. "The virus as a metaphor," argues Ravi Sundaram in the context of India's pirate modernity, "suggests parasitic attachments to larger structures, rapid replication, disruption, and transformation of official networks through nonlinear communication."[94] Brian Larkin examines the vast viral infrastructure in Nigeria that moves with the speed of globalization through postcolonial material conditions. He claims piracy's "parallel economy has migrated onto center stage, overlapping and interpenetrating with the official economy, mixing legal and illegal regimes, uniting social actors, and organizing common networks."[95] Viruses and piracies can be forms of dissonance that disrupt the status quo of silence as "civility." Viral networks of piracy and disruption transform by contamination, producing locative places for dissonance within transnational spaces. Dissonance makes visible and audible an ever-expanding multiplicity of clashes, tensions, disharmonies, and disequilibriums so integral to everyday life that they pass unmarked and seem unremarkable. Dissonance thrives on contradictions, moving restlessly toward irresolution. It intervenes through imbalance. Neither noise nor cacophony, dissonance pairs together the incompatible with results that surprise, offend, invite, disturb, and excite, spurring action and creativity.

Digital media projects make an important counterargument to corporate and state talking points about participation and flexibility. They can localize micro-publics against corporatized media through satire and postcolonial mimicry.[96] The concept of viral dissonance pairs two terms to explore ways that artists, activists, and intellectuals have mobilized dissonance as an object and method to investigate everyday life. They propose dissonant ways of thinking that can be transmitted virally toward productive ends. These projects ask us to think: they expose deep secrets on corporate and state collusions or by nudging us to imagine other ways of becoming. They ask us to open space to dissent and contestation. In everyday usage, going viral is largely equated with viral videos. It is associated with Internet memes: ideas replicate themselves and spread, jumping between social networks. With their unpredictable movement, viruses themselves often frighten. Epidemic viruses like SARS, H1N1, and MERS emerge at the intersections between human and nonhuman, casting chickens, pigs, camels, and bats as "natural" transmitters rather than addressing the possibilitiy for human-made conditions that enable to such viruses spread and mutate, such as industrial farming and GMOs. They also develop where science and superstition converge. Computer viruses spread through self-replicating malware programs, disabling proper functionality—or even shutting it down through worms like Code Red, Nimda, and ILOVEYOU. Viruses travel quickly against dominant flows. They often defy attempts at isolation and containment, making them ideal carriers for dissonant ideas. Ulises Mejias advocates for disruption through *parasitology* and *paralogy* that "disrupt the flow of information by adding noise (information outside the logic of the system) and forcing the network to adjust to its presence" and "concerns itself with everything that cannot be resolved within the (capitalist) system."[97] He identifies forms of disruption that decenter nodes. Disruption can be located "nowhere, elsewhere, and everywhere," he suggests.

Grassroots forms of dissonance have erupted to open space from Tunisia and Egypt to Syria, Spain, Greece, United States, and Brazil. People have gathered in the streets and in squares to demand to be heard and to be seen. News media have occasionally offered space for these dissonant expressions. People have also mobilized digital technologies like SMS and social networking, working around and within the control of states and corporations. Working with Electronic Disturbance Theater (EDT), the Zapatistas (EZLN) built websites and, more significantly, stages denial-of-service (DoS) attacks on state websites, as activism against the dispossession of indigenous nations by neoliberal corporations with state collusion during the early days of the WWW. Following their lead, movements like Occupy in the United States and Los Indignados in Spain, among others, have garnered middle-class momentum by using social media alongside word of mouth. Even the global campaign of Boycott, Divestment and Sanctions (BDS) to pressure Israel to end its occupation of East Jerusalem, Gaza, and the West Bank has gained unprecedented support in the United States, partly driven by blogs, posts, and tweets. Groups like Anonymous mobilize hacktivism across divisions imposed by states, such as nationality papers and passports, and corporations, such as software licenses and even DVD regional codes. Social media can help dissonant ideas become viral and open space, but it also makes dissonance easier to police. People have spoken against data mining of citizens, police corruption, and against the financialization and militarization of everyday life. They have also spoken against corporate co-option of dissonance as Twitter or Facebook revolutions.

Miyö Van Stenis's *Totally Not a Virus, Trust Me...I'm a Dolphin (or I'm a Dolphin)* (Venezuela, 2013; http://miyovanstenis.com/dolphin/) is a whimsical look at moments of paranoia over computer viruses in an era of ever-tempting clickbait. The work asks us to think about nonhuman life in the wake of recognition of the right to rights of life and liberty for cetaceans, such as bottlenose dolphins and orcas in places like India. Like other malware, computer viruses infect software, files, and drives, rendering computers less useful or utterly useless and disrupting the Internet as a platform for sharing information. An infected computer might render the Internet inert. Unlike computer worms, *I'm a Dolphin* declares its innocence graphically while a code window reveals a computer worm (ILOVEYOU.txt.vbs) in code. Since we no longer require click-here instructions to operate GUI, *I'm a Dolphin* asks us to think about the machine acts we initiate by clicking our mouse on innocent-looking images, particularly the clickbait of tantalizing images and suggestive headlines. It considers the potential hazards of clicking on impulse, such as clickbait journalism that not only hyperlinks to advertising but transmits spyware.

No Television (México, 2006) was a performance by Fabián Giles that critiqued the mass media's banal fictions and distractions that manipulate thinking and action. The blog contained submissions of graphic, photo, and audiovisual work from Europe, North America, and South Asia, including video.freegar.org, which interrogates various ideas about México and Giorgio Celon's "11–9" which takes an MTV-style look at the 9/11 attacks of the World Trade Center in New York. The project's logo reworks the MTV ones into an NTV for "No TV." While *No Television* despairs of television consumption, Giles's short video *I Hate* distils the simplicity of media icons and hatred. Memorable images such as a bottle of Coca-cola announcing, "I hate god," and an atomic explosion proclaiming, "I hate CNN." Comparably, the collective lemeh42's *Per fare un tavolo/How to Make a Table* (Italy, 2008; http://www.vimeo.com/711136) poses questions about self-assembled home furnishings, which conceal how flat boxes reduce container shipping costs by outsourcing assembly to the consumer while increasing the demand for low-skilled, low-paid, flexible labor in the shipping and packing sectors. *Per fare un tavolo* spoofs the faux environmental friendliness of the furniture industry. Taking on the style of instruction manuals for Ikea furniture, lemeh42 reflects on the globally successful trade in self-assembled home furnishing for the middle classes. A lively, upbeat, lilting song, sung by a man with the chorus sung by children, describes the environmental history backward as table, legs, seed, fruits, flower, tree, branch, mountain, and earth. The images adopt the flatness of an assembly manual, with lines drawn between the seeds and the fruit, the reduced graphic style and very minimal animation refencing the simple assembly instructions inserted into manufactured products.

Dara Greenwald, Josh MacPhee, and Steve Lambert's *The Samaras Project* (United Staates, 2006–present; www.samarasproject.net/about/) operates as an anti-advertising collaborative project that engages multiple layers of the commons: open source, free access, street teams, alternative economies. A transmedia campaign mimicking corporate product campaigns, it "sells" ideas like open source, gleaning, local currency, co-ops, and common networks. It produced five postcards with headlines such as "We Mint It," "We Own It," and "We Share It" over images of groups of people. Short explanations of each strategy are printed on the back of each postcard, available for free download. The blog includes useful information about sustainable economies as alternatives to transnational capitalist enterprise, with notices of conferences, gatherings, book publications, and initiatives for creating local economies circumventing global captial. For instance, the blog entry dated 20 February 2006, discusses worker-owned cooperatives. The project toggles between online and embodied worlds. In October 2006, the Anti-Advertising Agency assembled a street team to pass out the postcards in the San Francisco Financial District. The team wore blue Samaras Project t-shirts and blue messenger bags emblazoned with the samaras seed, a winged seed that flies and can grow almost anywhere—a counter-image to Monsanto's GMOs.

Under the leadership of Julie Ristau, Ana Micka, Jay Walljasper, Alexa Bradley, and Camille Gage, the collaborative *On The Commons* (United States, 2001–present; http://onthecommons.org/) offers reports of events and possibilities that harness the capacity of the commons. It postulates public spaces need to be at the center of thinking through how to live in the world in a sustainable, interactive way in the face of globalization, virtualization, the fracturing of community, and the decline of face-to-face interactions. The website offers strategies from green activism and common creativity that advance positive social change concerning global climate crisis and the commodification of nature. *On the Commons* connects anyone who identifies with the common movement and its principles of equitable access, democratic values, transparency, and social fairness. Through its essays and blogs, commoners exchange knowledge that escapes corporate media. The commons transforms simple stories into complex histories. *On the Commons* contends: "some forms of wealth belong to all of us, and that these community resources must be actively protected and managed for the good and all." These other forms of wealth include open air, wide oceans, deep forests, libraries, public spaces, scientific research, and creative works. *On the Commons* invites us to become "commoners."

If projects like *The Samaras Project* and *The Commons* convene micropublics, then other projects convene funders through crowd-sourcing. Amit and Naroop's *The Singh Project* (United Kingdom, 2014) is a collection of 35 images of British Sikh men celebrating their identity by emphasizing beards and turbans.[98] Beards and turbans are visible markers of Sikh men, perhaps more recognizable to non-Sikhs than the five traditional attributes—*kesh* (uncut hair), *kara* (brace-let), *kirpan* (short sword in a *gatra* strap), *kachehra* (cotton undergar-ment), and *kanga* (small wooden comb). Raised in Southall in West London, Amit and Naroop are commercial photographers, special-izing in music-industry work. To realize this noncommercial project, they turned to social networking and crowdsourcing. The inspiration for the project also arose from seeing the popularity of "big" beards on non-Sikh models in television and print advertising and on bill-boards. The subjects of their photos range from "doctors to boxers, temple volunteers to magicians and I.T professionals to fashion stylists," as Amit and Naroop mention on the project's Kickstarter and Facebook pages.[99] For the photographs, they want their subjects to be the focus, so they standardized the framing and background. The project counters the racial profiling of Sikhs, particularly in a post–7/7 United Kingdom or post–9/11 United States. In 2001 and 2002, Sikhs were frequent targets of violence. In August 2012, a white gunman attacked a gurdwara (temple), killing six people. *The Singh Project* reclaims Sikh diasporic identity from Hollywood's cliché fantasy representation of Islamic terrorists with turbans tied in a Sikh style.

An interest in exploring our relationship with media also features in Geoffrey Pugen's *Utopics* (Canada, 2004–2008; http://geoffrey-pugen.com/utopics.html), probing the notion of life in virtuality, whether in the form of avatars or at the prospect of human-machine interaction. The installation of digitally composited photographs and mocumentaries that promote a fictional online community is dedicated to helping people "super modify" their bodies in order to "transform [their] nature." The promotional video *Aerobia!* (Canada, 2005; http://vimeo.com/6922386) satirizes early theories of cyberspace that heralded the Internet as a space free from the limitations of physical bodies by considering the current moment of ubiquitous avatars and visual personas. The portal introduces users to the fictional Institute of Utopics's 16-step program for super-modification of the human body. It adopts the rhetorical and aesthetic devices of late-night infomercials. Virtual selves, composed in JPEGs and recognized by usernames, may be viewed on a web-application mashup that links a NASA satellite photograph of the earth with avatar biomes from Utopics. The program helps people overcome "intimidations, doubt, negative energies, guilt, hunger [or] weakness," which are removed through the "intense modification program."

The *Utopics Video Guide* (Canada, 2004) invites viewers to overcome their personal body issues to realize their "inner animal" through body modification. Before and after images show clients whose faces transform from human to animal. Elephant-headed figures enjoy an energizing aerobics class. The female voiceover calmly instructs listeners as a tribal beat of techno music plays in the background, its four-beat structure mimicking the human heartbeat. The program is an online community with a cultist appeal of striving for perfection by looking toward animals as a means to transcend the

Figure 4.4 *Utopics Video Guide.*

foibles of human imperfections, pandemics, and ecological crisis. The program is an inverse to the transformation in H. G. Wells's 1896 novel *The Island of Dr. Moreau* and the inverse of most interpretations of the hierarchies in Charles Darwin's theories of evolution.[100] The video also evokes the mass appeal of television workout series hosted by celebrities Richard Simmons and Jake Steinfeld during the 1980s. Intercut is a vintage interview footage of professional bodybuilder Arnold Schwarzenegger discussing the feeling of "coming" (sexual orgasm and ejaculation) as he works out, pumps up, or even goes home. Men and women discuss falling in love with people whose bodies they have never seen. In the photographs, Pugen layers the texture of animal "skins" atop human skin. *Utopics* engages with scholarship in Critical Animal Studies and the Post-humanities that examine forms of knowledge from a non-anthropocentric point of view. The project satirizes the dysfunctional and asymmetrical relationship of humans to nonhumans, particularly the everyday ways that humans project anxieties and fears to nonhuman animals as objects. The project is a tactical means to open thinking through digital media to other bases of knowledge.

5
Collaborative Remix Zones: Toward a Critical Cinephilia

Our final chapter revisits the concept of cinephilia after digital media and distributed networks.[1] We seek to identify a place for critical cinephilia that moves toward an opening of meaning from the control of transnational media corporations (TMCs). Romanticized and institutionalized as an expression for an "excessive love of cinema" that emerged in postwar France for a generation of privileged (mostly male, invariably white) audiences, cinephilia has come to be associated with nostalgia for the pleasures of flickering celluloid in a darkened cinematheque.[2] We resituate mid-twentieth-century notions of cinephilia within early twenty-first-century frameworks that recognize that universalizing North Atlantic assumptions about cinema are less capable of recognizing the complexities of global articulations of cinephilia today. Film studies scholarship has appropriated the term "cinephilia" for cultural and historical contexts comparable to postwar France, including South Asian diasporic attachment to homeland through consumption of Bollywood films and the "cine-mania" surrounding contemporary South Korean films. With the consolidation of TMCs, cinephilia reproduces itself as technophilia, a consumerist obsession with the technologies and the safe harborof the home theater against an onslaught of potential threats within public spaces.[3] As counterpoint to the TMCs' free trade zones (FTZs), we offer the theoretical construct of collaborative remix zones—zones where plural pasts, multiple temporalities, multiple artifacts, and polyvocalities join together. Here, they provisionally reclaim public spaces. They operate within neoliberal economics and transnational capital, mobilizing a critical politicized cinephilia, which adopts radical historiographic and reverse engineering strategies.

Historically, the concept of cinephilia is wedged precariously between academic and popular discourses, articulating both elitist conceptions of individual pleasures (i.e., sacred objects, high art) and communal conceptions of universal pleasures (i.e., popular art, mass entertainment). Dudley Andrew locates North Atlantic cinephilia within four historical moments: the pre-academic moment of ciné-clubs by the avant-gardists during the 1920s; the *Cahiers du cinéma* critics during the 1950s; the academic moment of post-1968 "*Screen* theory"; and the post-theory moment of the return to history.[4] Cinephilia remains closely associated with auteurs whose work appropriated conventions from classical cinema, transforming filmmaking into film criticism. The "politiques des auteurs" propelled the young critics-cum-filmmakers of the *Cahiers du cinéma* to develop cinephilia-as-criticism to produce the idealized perfect audience.[5] Across the North Atlantic, the international scope of French cinephilia, which fetishized Italian, Japanese, Danish, Hollywood, and French productions, was rerouted into nationally chauvinistic auteur theory.[6] The US film distribution-marketing-criticism circuit of Hollywood and film schools reprocessed this language into consumerist desire, fueling fantasies of access to and success in the entertainment industry. This concept of cinephilia is inseparable from selective reading strategies that prioritize marginal, inconsequential, or frivolous details to locate the rare and rarified. This apolitical, ahistorical, antitheoretical, and anti-intellectual model of cinephilia is based on the production of individuality within consumerist logics. It extends nineteenth-century notions of connoisseurship. It fetishizes markers of singularity, rarity, and quality. Work as object (art*work*) overshadows work as process (the *work* of conceiving/producing art). These conceptualizations extends to transnational forms where selected (assimilable) auteurs are produced, marketed, distributed, and exchanged, whether Ritwik Ghatak, Ozu Yasujiro, and Satjayit Ray in the 1960s or Abbas Kiarostami, Mohsen Makhmalbaf, and Zhang Yimou in the 1990s. "In its most extreme incarnations auteurism can be seen as an anthropomorphic form of 'love' for the cinema," writes Robert Stam.[7] However, it is crucial to recognize that Glauber Rocha, Fernando Solanas and Octavio Getino, and Julio Garcia Espinosa questioned auteurism's eurocentrism and colonialism.[8] Dissent has always been present, though it has often been delegitimized, particularly by the industries of Hollywood and international film festivals.

An actual theory of cinephilia also emerged in the North Atlantic from modernist concepts like structuralism, Marxism, psychoanalysis, as well as from historical approaches like post-structuralism and feminism. If the cinematic apparatus of Jean-Louis Baudry modeled itself after Louis Althusser's ideological state apparatus, then the body genres of Linda Williams appropriated psychoanalytical models of desire toward feminist politicizations.[9] Manthia Diawara, Jane Gaines, and bell hooks transform Laura Mulvey's visual pleasures into models of exchange.[10] Others have expanded cinema beyond film history and theory, arguing the practices of interactive and paracinematic media fandom are structurally indistinguishable from the practices of academics and professional film critics.[11] These theorizations of cinephilia articulate a psychoanalytic model of an eternal search for what has been lost and can never be recovered. This insatiable, fetishistic desire for an unassailable object is now rerouted by TMCs offering each generation of cinephiles new and enhanced access to lost "masterpieces" and "contemporary classics" in remastered DVD transfers and special boxed editions.

For pre-digital generations, cinephilia evokes exhilaration and depletion. Paul Willemen argues that cinephilia is laden with necrophilia.[12] Indeed, psychoanalytic film theory suggests that cinema reanimates the very subject that photography kills.[13] End-of-the-millennium debates over the "decay of cinema" and the "right movies" suggested a conservative backlash against the democratization of film culture motored by new technologies.[14] Mourning the nearly simultaneous deaths of Ingmar Bergman and Michelangelo Antonioni in 2007, Peter Matthews lamented "henceforth there are to be no more masterpieces—uniquely luminous works describing the finest vibrations of the creator's soul."[15] Jonathan Romney diagnosed Matthews as bemoaning "the loss of the hushed spiritual frisson that supposedly occurs only when a film is viewed in special, privileged circumstances"—in short, "the passing of an ineffable aura in cinemagoing."[16] Walter Benjamin's concept of the aura suggests the simultaneous distance and proximity within this conception of cinephila.[17] The nostalgia of so-called cult films and classics, Thomas Elsaesser argues, constructs relationships between the past and the present emphasizing "distance and proximity in the face of a constantly reencountered past."[18] Suburban multiplexes of the North Atlantic and urban multiplexes of everywhere else screen standardized products that are now part of elaborate commodity chains. Cinephilia as necrophilia also emerges as a theme in the global art cinema sector, in *Cinema Paradiso* (Italy/France, 1988; dir. Giuseppe Tornatore), *Bye-bye Africa* (Chad/France, 1999; dir. Mahamat-Saleh Haroun), and *Good-bye Dragon Inn* (Taiwan, 2003; dir. Ming-liang Tsai). These films express how nearly empty theaters have become objects of mourning and melancholia due to their imminent closing or renovation into venues for pleasures others than cinematic ones.[19]

Despite obsessions with singularity, originality, and rarity within cinephilia, TMCs expand these desires to encounter the sacred object of 35mm celluloid master-prints by digitizing images, reproducing them for DVD, VOD, and countless other formats and uses.[20] This repurposing and multiplatforming of cinema, to adopt the language of TMCs, actually denotes a *multiplication* of the past and the archive, a move from one pristine cinematic artifact as an essential, unified, unassailable ur-text to many different iterations, versions, explanations, juxtapositions, and platforms presentations. No longer destroyed after a film's initial theatrical run, images are reanimated as director's cuts, special editions, ancillary products, tie-ins, and spin-offs. Cinephilia in an era of DVDs was associated with ownership in the home space, rather than with spectatorship in the theatrical space. Barbara Klinger argues DVD collectors focused on acquisition and organization, often purchasing the same titles in different special editions as TMCs endlessly remake commercial films.[21] With their special behind-the-scenes and making-of features, DVDs draw this new generation of cinephiles into an illusory identification with the industry. Cinephilia, then, converges with technophilia. Restorations of classical films couple the discourses of originality and authenticity with the ideology of technological advances. Contemporary technologies improve the past by remastering its sounds and images.[22]

Beyond marketing and distribution, commercial film content incorporates cinephilia. Contemporary corporate and independent narrative filmmaking now emphasizes "producing media images saturated with memories" of evocative pastness, "condensations of clichés."[23] Marijke de Valck and Malte Hagener propose that cinephilia uses "history as a limitless warehouse that can be plundered for tropes, objects, expressions, styles, and images."[24] VOD allows users to access an archive of new and old content—blockbusters and independent films, often from around the world—via cable and satellite television or Internet or mobile download. Transnational Hollywood functions as both a content and software broker, though its TMCs still fear loss of market control since their business models continue to operate according to analogue models. Despite the adoption of Digital Cinema Packages (DCPs) in theaters, the entertainment industries do not think through digital media.[25] Pleasures once confined to theaters merely migrate to television and computer screens—and to the brand-name screens of mobile phones, laptops, tablets, game consoles, and other consumer-grade devices. Within transnational capitalism and the Web 2.0, cinephilia shape-shifts into mediaphilia—an excessive love of mediated images across analogue and digital technologies.

However, digital, non-eurocentric, orphaned, indigenous, and ambient media dislodge and deterritorialize eurocentric and celluloid-fetishized cinephilia. They acknowledge diasporic, exilic, and other bottom-up transnational practices that challenge the top-down transnational practices of TMCs. Unlike the derivative epithets for nonwestern film during the golden eras of classical cinema, such as "Hollywood on the Nile" for the Cairo industry or "Hollywood of the East" for both the Shanghai and Hong Kong industries, a global proliferation of neologisms appropriate and relocate the so-called global model of Hollywood. Although such neologisms sustain illusions that Hollywood once served a global standard, they actually refer to sustainable film industries with local, regional, and global aspirations. These systems operate according to models as radically different as Bollywood, Mumbai's glamorous and globally recognized megahit industry, and Mollywood, Malegaon's micro-budget filmmaking, such as Nashit Shaikh's *Malegaon Ka Sholay* (India, 2000) and *Malegaon Ka Superman* (India, 2009), are perhaps best known only in the Nashik Distrct of Maharashtra about 300 kilometers outside Mumbai.

Cinephilia expands into the subnational love of the Tamil films of Kollywood (Chennai) in south India, the transnational love of Egyptian musical comedies in Palestine, and the love of Hindi films during Israeli bans on Egyptian films.[26] Cinephilia includes the love of Bollywood films by non-Hindi–speaking audiences in Nigeria that merges within the rebirth of Nollywood with the success of *Living in Bondage* (Nigeria, 1992; dir. Chris Obi Rapu). The love of classical Egytpian film throughout the Arabic-speaking world prompted Founoon Film Distribution (UAE) with Digital Press Hellas (Greece), and later the Rotana Group (Saudi Arabia) with the Prasad Corporation's Digital Film Technology (India), to digitize and restore 1650 35mm film negatives and positives for DVD, Blu-Ray, streaming, and in-flight entertainment, so that films like *Ayyam wa layali/Days and Nights* (Egypt 1955; dir. Henri Barakat) and *Seraa fil Nil/Struggle on the Nile* (Egypt 1959; dir. Atef Salem) are again available in high-quality versions.

The Chiapas Media Project/Promedios, an indigenous media project based in Chiapas, Guerrero, and Chicago, appropriates digital-video technologies to combat deforestation, lack of water, and cultural annihilation. Indigenous media festivals draw upon traditions established in indigenous radio and often end with the collective writing of a manifesto. Unlike most festivals, which offer awards to "best" filmmakers, actors, and technicians, indigenous media festivals offer awards for social commitment, suggesting an alternative mode for cinephilia.[27] Scholar and programmer Amalia Córdova describes the CLACPI International Film and Video Festival of Indigenous Peoples as a "deterritorialized festival," moving from site to site and regularly changing the look and navigation of its website, thereby resisting the compulsion to brand itself like a commercially driven competitive film festival. Ambient media utilizes open-source models, utilizing preexisting images and code rather than creating anew. Thousands of users manipulate flame algorithms to generate collaborative screen savers via Scott Draves's "Electric Sheep" as alternatives to corporate presets. Nonetheless, these forms of cinephilia are often marginalized and discredited in North Atlantic media. Orphaned media restore perspectives of the past that have not been repurposed for profit by TMCs or salvaged by film archives.[28]

Cinephilia now exceeds TMC control of copyright through staggered releases or rereleases of classical cinema, international arthouse fare, and blockbusters in theaters, home video, pay-per-view (PPV), cable, commercial television, VOD, as well as product tie-ins and spin-offs. Abandoning obsessive searches for rare and forgotten images, cinephilia can engage a critical methodology of *reverse engineering* or taking things apart to see how they work and how they can be applied in other contexts, and *radical historiography*, a notion of historiography based in contiguities rather than continuities, polyphonic structures rather than unities. Within an overabundance of proliferating images, cinephilia can *politicize* rather than commodify. Moving away from passive spectatorship and insider knowledge of DVD extra features, cinephilia can mobilize active engagement and more symmetrical interactions where *practice* overshadows product. The materiality of the cinematic is no longer sacralized: it is now endlessly reworked.

Cinephilia, whether in auteurist theories or in its consumerist TMC fetishized forms, represses history and its materiality by immobilizing images and psychic imaginaries within the confines of a past that is always only a rarefied object caught within unfulfilled desires. Within cinephilia's quest for the authentic, the pristine, the uncontaminated, the insider quotation, the restoration, and the ur-text, lurks a dangerous control of borders, content, and ideas, situating cinema as a closed procedure with no trespassing. An imaginary wholeness constitutes the cinematic object. New technologies restore lost images.

Imaginary fantasies project cinemas lost, dying, or dead. The historical as that which signifies and marks changes is abandoned, replaced
with a fantasmatic, inert, monumentalized, and static historical construct. Tzvetan Todorov has cautioned that the monumental in historical discourse almost always suggests the authoritarian.[29]
A more radical historiography would remove the object from the
monumentalizing position and open it to the multiple vectors of recir-
culation for new connections and new meanings. This conception of
history rejects the idea of the historical monolith, the linear story, the
fetishized object, the causal explanation, the perfect object, and the
distancing between spectator/user and artifact/content. A radical historiography reanimates artifacts, remapping them within polyphonic
and multiple frameworks. This radical historiography disposes the
unitary object and the one-way relationship. Historiographers such
as Ranajit Guha, Dipesh Chakrabarty, Philip Rosen, and Robert F.
Berkhofer have argued for a historical practice that is fluid, multiple, polyphonic, plural to generate and create new forms of explanation, echoing the ideas of alterative modernities mentioned in our
introduction.[30] For Jacques Derrida, the archive always looks to the
future, not to the past, because the past is, to quote Hayden White,
a place of fantasy.[31] Heterogeneity is vital in this reconceptualization
of historiography, an antidote to the isolating immobilizations of
cinephilia. This historiography focuses on the creation of new forms
of knowledge production. As Berkhofer has argued, this new historiography requires moving away from unitary history toward the
construction of multicultural plural pasts. Chakrabarty and Rosen
have advanced the idea of layered multiple temporalities to combat
cinephilia's linear causality. These conceptualizations entail multiple viewpoints, contradictions, disjunctures, and the formation of
networks of meaning. Conventional notions of film production, for
example, can be reworked as digital media practice by foregrounding
critical and nonhierarchical collaboration.
Comparably, anthropologist and filmmaker David MacDougall
has proposed to move ethnographic film away from making a film
"about" toward making a film "with." Rather than considering filmmaking as a strategy of omniscient monologue, he proposes the act of
filming can be a contemplative and participatory, an act of collaboration, encounter, and dialogue between the subject and the person
filming. He argues for interconnection—rather than separation—to
produce a compound work within an elaborative, embodied knowledge. He explains culture is "a continual process of interpretation
and invention."[32] Drawing upon the praxes of radical historiography

and reverse engineering, critical cinephilia within collaborative remix zones enacts such processes.

Since many TMCs accumulate annual profits larger than the GNPs of 90 percent of the nation-states recognized by the UN, public media redefines itself within digital media ecologies. Throughout the 1970s and 1980s, independent and oppositional media were pitted against corporate media in a binary opposition based on different positions within political economics and nation-states: nonprofit versus for profit, independent versus corporate. In the present millennium, these borders and bifurcations have become increasingly blurred and fluid. Indiewood has developed, where independent feature narrative films in the United States are distributed by TMCs as boutique Hollywood. With the reorganization of the TMCs into distribution companies and the subsequent outsourcing of production, many independents now make their living as freelancers. Further, the proliferation of new distribution and exhibition technologies has contributed to a dramatic shift in an independent sector away from this bifurcation into a more complexly layered media ecology constantly in flux, interaction, and movement. This public media ecology creates spaces for subnational, supranational, transnational, minoritized, and indigenous media to emerge.

Collaborative remix zones mobilize the logics of digital media to create anew from what already exists, selecting and compositing in a conceptual space that functions in real time. They politicize what TMCs call the repurposing of classical film as content to be distributed across DVD and VOD platforms. Collaborative remix zones embrace new media's foregrounding of remediation, which rehabilitates media in "a process of reforming reality as well."[33] They also reflect the *jugadu* solutions to real-world media problems. Whether on laptops, mobile devices, or the Internet, collaborative remixing extends the active production of meaning embedded within cinephilia into the regime of radical historiography, summoning interventionist pleasures. Reverse engineering and radical historiography imagine archives as open and recombinant, active rather than static, evolving not fixed, radically deterritorialized rather than regionally encrypted.[34] Critical cinephilia within collaborative remix zones moves beyond the anonymity of private spaces for individual memory, the materiality of celluloid, and the fixed location of theaters into the accountability of public spaces for collective process, the immateriality (and new materiality) of digital code, and locative and virtual locations. Collaborative remix zones politicize notions of cinephilia subsumed by TMCs. Although the borders dividing nation-states are increasingly policed, collaborative remix zones produce spaces for transnational contestation over the control of media and its meaning, pointing to ways that cinephilia generates accountable spaces. While transnational capital reproduces depoliticized and dehistoricized differences within FTZs, collaborative remix zones open flows across and within differences.

Collaborative remix zones counter the individualism and fetishism of cinephilia with collective transgressions across borders, images, styles, and ideas. Collaboration happens between humans and nonhumans, including machines. We distinguish collaborative remix zones from plagiarism as media piracy, a discourse spanning the TMCs' international policing of copyright, mods, and mashups. The act of piracy implies an act of transgression, of imbibing and handling the distant, fixed image. Whether the non-licensed Hollywood narrative films for sale in Tepito, Kuala Lumpur, or Shanghai, or the amateur video mashups that transform Tony Blair and George W. Bush into contestants on BBC's *The Weakest Link* (United Kingdom, 2000–2012; cr. Cathy Dunning and Fintan Coyle) or unwitting lip-synchers of romantic duets, piracy remains somewhat trapped within the logics of transnational consumer capital, a cinephilia that exposes itself. Even the politicized redirection of "cine-mania" in South Korea since the election of a civil government in 1991 seems truncated. South Korea's National Security Law's enforced racially homogeneous national narrative developed according to traditional conceptions of private, collective, and unified identity.[35] In the South Korean context, cinephilia "functions to unify different groups with different positions" within a psychoanalytic structure of desire to see what cannot be seen.[36]

Instead, the collaborative process refocuses on the workings of cinema, rather than on cinema as an object of rarefied adoration and fantasy. This process redraws cinema as experience and exchange, rather than as text and author. It differs significantly from piracy, which, almost always implies a relationship to the TMCs, often within the binaries of legal/illegal, licensed/unlicensed, commercial/noncommercial, and proprietary/open source. Instead, the collaborative remix process works with many other images and cinemas circulating outside transnational networks. These amateur films, orphaned films, travelogues, abandoned commercials and narrative works, located in archives, operate in a different territory beyond piracy and fetishized cinephilia. Collaborative remix zones exhume these artifacts, reanimating them into the present and the future. Collaborative remix zones peel away their preciousness and energize them within plural pasts. Rather than cinephilia's fetishized surplus value, collaborative remix zones emancipate collective use value. The terms of engagement shift from transgression and exchange to direct collaboration with to create new explanations and new futures.

For example, the multimedia performance group Emergency Broadcast Network (EBN)'s live performances demonstrated that VJing (live performance involving the remixing of video) could be political. EBN became the spokespersons for the radical potential of disturbed authorship, data sharing, image and sound appropriation, and an entire culture based on sampling and reusage.[37] Collaborative remix zones are ubiquitous, yet often appear invisible because they eschew territorialized and corporatized cinephilia. The examples of critical cinephilia within collaborative remix zones described below suggest practices of deterritorialized, decorporatized, and politicized cinephilia. Some examples operate with the support of archives and institutions that provided digitized versions of footage for remixing; others, within the liminal spaces between corporate ownership of archives and user-generated content (UGC). All unsettle assumptions about preservation and conservation as ends into themselves. All question the systemic control of access to archives by TMCs, especially practices and protocols that monopolize media, enforce copyright, reinforce unified ("official") interpretations of film, and exploit amateurs as outsourced or freelance research and development. Critical cinephilia within collaborative remix zones moves from the voyeuristic to the interventionist, through multiple iterations of remixing.

Remix as Performative Historiography

Remixing can become a performance of radical historiography. By filtering and recombining digitized images from the past or digital images from the present, thinking through digital media facilitates a critical engagement with the production of knowledge through mediation. Jay Bolter and Richard Grusin term this process "remediation." The archive is no longer conceived exclusively as a hermetically sealed knowledge repository for knowledge accessible only to an elite few; instead, it is conceived as open, incomplete, and unresolved. Historiography sheds the shackles of official evidence and closed documents, unlocking itself to contingent meanings.

Les LeVeque's videos provide an example of ways that artists have mobilized digital paradigms to examine the political economies of classical cinema's ownership of meaning. He remixes the found footage of Hollywood's canons of classics: *The Birth of a Nation* (United States 1915; dir. D. W. Griffith), *Gone with the Wind* (United States, 1939; dir. Victor Fleming), *Spellbound* (United States, 1945; dir. Alfred Hitchcock), *The Searchers* (United States, 1956; dir. John Ford), *Forbidden Planet* (United States, 1956; dir. Frederick M. Wilcox), *Vertigo* (United States, 1958; dir. Alfred Hitchcock), *Lawrence of Arabia* (United Kingdom, 1962; dir. David Lean), and *The Sound of Music* (United States, 1965; dir. Robert Wise). He also mashes talking points, such as Bill Gates's testimony before the US Senate Committee on American Standard Code for Information Interchange (ASCII) in *A Song of the Cultural Revolution* (United States, 1998) and George W. Bush's blinking during a television speech in *Notes from the Underground* (United States, 2003). LeVeque's reworking of Hitchcock's *Spellbound* and *Vertigo* deconstructs the psychological structuring of desire in classical Hollywood through algorithms that highlight the materiality of the filmic images, which can be inverted, reversed, and superimposed.[38] *Spellbound* becomes *2 Spellbound* (United States, 1999), a 7.5-minute flickering ambient video with house music punctuated by looped dialogue. *Vertigo* becomes *4 Vertigo* (United States, 1999–2000). LeVeque's recombinant videos explore ideas of machine interface via mathematical reprocessing, remediating, and reverse-engineering mass media forms. These videos unsettle assumptions about spectatorship and copyright through mobilizing a notion of the unexpected which is exhumed and reprocessed.[39]

LeVeque takes apart classical cinema by writing algorithms: programs to sample frames at controlled intervals. He then reassembles these frames according to a modular rather than narrative structure. The results are compressed versions of the films, but they are not compressed in the ways that 35mm prints are typically digitized for DVDs, that is, he does not reproduce lossy compression.[40] LeVeque's automated mashing of the digitized version of the film decomposes the invisible style of classical Hollywood continuity editing. Instead of a relatively seamless experience of the narrative as a simulation of reality, the experience visually emphasizes random variability and disruption. An image flashes on screen for a few seconds only to be followed by an inverted version of itself for the next few seconds, followed by an upside-down version. The automated logic of the visual mashup by the algorithm deconstructs the manual construction of desire through continuity editing on a Steenbeck table. Automation refracts the Taylorist logic of commercial film production. There is no space to project psychic desires; instead, the rhythm of modular editing deposits them someplace else. Editing sometimes aligns with techno music whose beats per minute double that of the human heart. LeVeque's videos "propose that Hollywood films are not proprietary property but circulatory, etherealized phantasms, that lodge within us as a parasitic psychic fungus, occupying cells."[41] Although they appropriate copyrighted content under copyleft protection, they are not freely available. In contrast, other artists have issued comparable critiques of classical cinema on open-access narrowcasting sites like YouTube and Vimeo.

Since 2003, filmmaker Anders Weberg and ethnologist Robert Willim have collaborated on a series of *Elsewhereness Projects*, which probe imaginary geographies and nonrepresentation. It focuses on places the artists might never have visited, disturbing site-specific and ethnographic conventions. They describe their collaborative objective "to mix art and science to unveil and utilize the potential of the seemingly mundane."[42] The collaborations ponder the non-representational through digital media. Weberg's concept of an "aesthetics of ephemerality" in "peer-to-peer art" (or "p2p art") proposes artists make available a digital object, which is deleted along with all material used to create it after the file has been downloaded by another user. The art exists only when and so long as others share it.[43] This conception of art extends conceptual art during the 1960s when artists such as Yoko Ono and Sol LeWitt produced ideas for art without physically producing them as objects. They often sold instructions to museums and collectors, which commissioned other artists to produce actual objects. In the case of p2p art, computer code functions as a digital surrogate for handwritten or typed instructions. Unlike conceptual art, whose instructions often required the labor of welders and electricians, p2p art is produced automatically: the code's instructions are almost entirely realized through automated machine acts.

Also unlike Ono, LeWitt, and other conceptual artists, Weberg removes the intermediary gatekeeper of the art dealer, gallery owner, or museum curator. His concept of p2p art sidesteps these hierarchies by rendering artist and audience as more-or-less equal peers. Since artists need to make a living, live performance offers an income-earning opportunity. Thinking through digital media often involves renouncing physical objects sold to collectors in favor of a giving away of digital artifacts such as video files, while charging admission for performances, evoking an indie music economic model. Faced with the near monopoly of TMCs, Brazilian independent musicians learned that giving away MP3s actually produced audiences for concerts, as

David Bollier argues.[44] Musicians elsewhere—and even a few film-makers—have followed this digital model.

Surreal Scania (Sweden, 2006) is a web-based project that combined digital video with GPS technology to explore overlooked similarities between the disparate landscapes of industrial harbors and nature reserves, as well as the incongruous objects within them, such as artificial dinosaur heads and wrecked automobiles. Willim and Weberg examine how GPS tracks the global positioning in three dimensions (longitude, latitude, and altitude) to determine speed, distance, movement, and times of sunrise and sunset. These visual contemplations of Scania, a region in southern Sweden, differ from their Google Earth and GPS units' representations. They manipulate digital technologies with practices from anthropology to unhinge familiar habits of thinking about our place in a networked world. Rather than mobilizing GPS toward exactitude, it marshals inexactitude to produce knowledge. Alluding to Jorge Luis Borges, it also parodies faith in GPS and GIS as objective, reliable, accurate, and useful.

Being There (Sweden, 2006) is a collection of six short videos that examine the question of what constitutes an authentic experience for tourists hungry for the exotic and unique. Described as "audiovisual excursions beneath the gloss of tourism rhetoric," these videos explore popular tourist destinations in London, Madrid, Moscow, Mumbai, Paris, and Tokyo. Their global visibility in commercial news media positions them as attractive to tourists as well as terrorists. "The places we have chosen are high density, they are tourist magnets and global hotspots," they explain; "they are places associated with pleasure, but also with terror."[45] The videos comprise clips from tourist "home" movies and audio is composed from demo sounds in sample libraries. These videos critique the tourism industry tropes. The videos may be streamed or downloaded onto computers and mobile phones.

For their socially oriented, site-specific, live-performance *Sweden for Beginners* (Sweden, 2010), Weberg did video field recording entirely with a mobile phone camera, while Willim remixed sounds from Lund University's Folk Life Archives with electronically generated sonic textures. Combined into "electronically engendered phantasms," explains Weberg, "sounds and images from Swedish everyday life, from objects and landscapes are entangled with twisted stereotypes like Bergmanesque gloom, erotica and nature romanticism."[46] From his perspective as an ethnologist, Willim argues for "rendering culture," an extension of James Clifford's "writing culture" that includes visual and sound images and software that might not necessarily involve the textual and narrative organization of language.

The results yield a multimodal and sensuous ethnography.[47] He favors ethnographic creation over ethnographic representation. Their collaborations subvert site-specificity in public art. "Information about a certain urban space was gathered via absence and alienation, consisting solely of audio and video material relating to a specific place culled entirely from the Internet," explains Philip Glahn.[48] They also upend conventional visual anthropology by bringing ethnographic documents into the space of the art gallery. "Where conventional academic monographs are designed to illuminate and provide historical clarity," writes Craig Campbell, "art gallery space provides interpretive frictions that can impede and confound interpretation."[49] Their intervention is significant due to the complicated histories of ethnology and anthropology, which legitimized racist discourses of colonialism and social Darwinism. Trinh T. Minh-ha's *Reassemblage: From the Firelight to the Screen* (United States, 1982) unsettled and intervened into visual anthropology by exposing objective certainties as subjective limitations. Here, Weberg and Willim use galleries, public performance sites, and P2P networks as sites for a fluid, digital file collaborative remixing that jettisons the idea that fixed documents can represent culture.

Other remix projects examine the history of commercial media. Billed as a mashup of live-feed video with Mexican pop music from the 1970s and 1980s in remixes by DJ Güagüis, DJ Pata Pata, and DJ Papichulo, *Cinema Salvaje* was produced by Cinema Tropical and Fresa Salvaje Productions and performed on 13 July 2007, in Brooklyn. Carlos A. Gutiérrez, cofounder of Cinema Tropical, conceived the event to collapse boundaries between public and private spheres and to question the proprietary issues of public-performance rights. *Cinema Salvaje* politicizes cinephilia by repurposing the opening-credit sequences to telenovelas, including Televisa's *Los ricos también lloran/ The Rich Also Cry* (México, 1979), *Dulce desafío/Sweet Challenge* (México, 1988–1989), *Dos mujeres, un camino/Two Women, One Road* (México, 1993), the well-known comedian Capulina's satire of Hollywood's *Saturday Night Fever* (United States, 1977; dir. John Badham), and *Benito Bodoque*, a Spanish-language dub of the Hanna-Barbera cartoon *Top Cat*. Non-copyright-holders uploaded this material to YouTube. Departing from conventions of identifying and commodifying key singular moments of emotional intensity or artistic expression, these images are mixed by artist Juan Luna Avin in a counterpoint to pop music as part of a performance party. Organized by visual artist Dulce Pinzon and curator Aldo Sanchez (aka DJ Papichulo)'s Fresa Salvaje promotes an alternative to "mainstream Latino music" such as salsa and merengue. It emphasizes the transnational diversity within Mexican music—kitschy ballads, *cumbias*, punk, new wave, rock-and-roll covers, wedding songs, and telenovela theme songs.

Like Turkish and Brazilian soap operas, Mexican telenovelas are popular around the world. Produced by Televisa, *Los ricos también lloran* is considered one of the world's most popular telenovelas—becoming a media sensation in the former Soviet Union during the 1990s. Star Verónica Castro sings its popular theme song, "Aprendí a llorar" ("I Learned to Cry").[50] A media conglomerate, Televisa transforms popular culture into mass culture, so that "purity of the long-suffering lower classes and the hope of redemption in the form of social mobility" becomes soft propaganda for the repressive Partido revolucionario institucional (PRI).[51] Subsequent telenovelas such as *Dulce desafío*, directed by renowned Mexican filmmaker Arturo Ripstein, and *Dos mujeres, un camino*, starring Erik Estrada, a Latino (nuyorican) actor with so-called crossover sex appeal in US television, extend the formulas of *Los ricos también lloran*. Whether watched earnestly or satirically, the telenovelas produce national and transnational communities outside the rules of TMCs.

Cinema Salvaje deterritorializes and decorporatizes transnational cinephilia among young Mexicans, Latin Americans, Mexican Americans, Latina/o Americans, non-Latina/o Americans, and non-Americans. Its media response surpasses nostalgia to become an appropriation of mass media, whether the PRI-complicit telenovelas or the dubbed cartoons from north of the border. *Cinema Salvaje* comments upon the unfair trade agreements within the FTZ created by NAFTA in 1994. Telenovelas are one of México's global exports, with media conglomerates like Televisa selling them to television stations in more than 125 countries. Product placements change according to export destination.[52] Mexican film production, on the other hand, spiraled downwards from nearly 750 films per year to slightly more than 200 in the treaty's first decade. In some ways, *Cinema Salvaje* looks to television as a source for cinema's revival in a post-cinematic, digital media moment. The project references salvage anthropology,,the collection of artifacts to preserve memory of human civilizations destroyed by settler colonialism and neoliberalism.

By appropriating fragments of the telenovelas circulating in transnational bootlegged clip culture on YouTube before their removal, *Cinema Salvaje* illustrates Néstor García Canclini argument that capitalism expands citizenship into realms of "private consumption of commodities and media offerings," often over "participation in discredited political organizations."[53] Telenovela appropriation does not obey the linear borders of nation-states. Instead, in a less neatly defined transborder, transterritorial, and multilingual market, the meaning is open to debate and contestation. Salvaging these clips becomes a way of taking them back to recover lost meaning and invent new interpretations. By sublimating television to music and erasing dialogue, clips transmute into nonnarrative artifacts. The images activate memories imperfectly: they violate the proprietary mechanisms of transnational corporations.

Similarly, Ástor Piazzolla's music mixes European music with African forms, classical formal structures with Argentine folk music's emotional address, a remix of different styles and cultures. Performed in Austin, Texas, in 2007, the multimedia live remix performance of Piazzolla's *Cuatro Estaciones Porteñas/The Four Seasons of Buenos Aires* (1965–1970) combined two pianists, Jairo Geronymo and Jeffrey Mayer, two tango dancers (*tangueros*), and live video mixing multiscreen projections of rare archival footage from Latin America, the United States, and Europe. The project collaborated with the Human Studies Film Archives (HSFA) of the Smithsonian Institution. Alluding to Vivaldi's *Le quattro stagioni/Four Seasons* (1725), *Cuatro Estaciones Porteñas* fills this Baroque structure with dissonance, syncopation, explosive melody, and sudden sonic episodes, countering the measured, consonant polyphonies of the Baroque with rapid changes in texture, tone, and dynamics. The performance addresses two issues: first, declining audiences for classical music; second, the problems of archival films remaining invisible, sequestered from public exhibition. The combination of sophisticated, complex Argentine music with amateur film resolves these challenges of engaging publics through performance, mixing the virtuosity of the classically trained musicians with the simplicity of amateur images to create frisson.

Performances of this project were not mounted in clubs or in cinemas, but in classical music concert halls. The performances intervened into the historical silent film/live-music concept of music amplifying the emotion in the narrative. The *Cuatro Estaciones Portenas* project inverts the relationship between sound and music: the Piazzolla music is primary, with the projected mediascape framing the music, visually graphing its musical influences through images. Through the juxtapositions of different media, art forms, and sensory experiences across the sound, sight, and touch, the performance physicalized the different sonic layers and musical influences imbedded in the

Piazzolla score. The multimedia projection performance intermixed images from Latin America and Europe. The two screens juxtaposed and layered temporalities of different cultural contexts and sonic environments. The images were not cued to the music, but evoked the places inferred in Piazzolla's tonalities and rhythms. They also allude to Piazzolla's work as a composer of film scores. Drawing inspiration from the score itself, the video projections combined disparate source material to generate new musical interpretations and embodied experiences, asking the spectator not only to listen carefully but also to watch and think. The two screens of the *Cuatro Estaciones Porteñas* suggest the displacements of immigration. The visual projections function as transnational, refracted textural elements rather than as denotative evidence. Rare amateur travelogues and expedition footage shot between 1915 and 1936 from Bolivia, Brazil, Ecuador, England, Italy, Perú, Spain, and United States, unfold slowly, in their original form. These archival images suggest how tango as both a dance and a musical style mixes identities, lands, violence, and experiences. These archival films connote unofficial histories of Latin America and Europe.

Digital artists Art Jones and Simon Tarr mounted a live remix with dual-screen projection called *Dismantling Empire* (United States, 2005). While many live remixes are performed in dance clubs, this remix performance was mounted in a university screening-hall. Spectators sat in theater seats, conflicted between the embodiments of hip-hop and the immobilization of their bodies. The project challenged the idea of passively watching a film with a beginning, a middle, and an end with a nonlinear live remix approach, pushing spectators to decipher connections between images. Their project points to how remix cannot be so simply reduced to an ironic play of images amputated from meaning, but instead can spawn new meanings through superimpositions and the doubling of screens. While the remix drains away the original hobbyist intentions of the amateur films, it also resituates them in a larger matrix of empire and war.

Collaborating with the Smithsonian's HSFA, Jones and Tarr generated loops from the archival images. These amateur films were shot in zones where the US empire had infiltrated either through colonial, military, or economic power: Bolivia, Cambodia, Ecuador, France, Germany, India, Iraq, México, and Yugoslavia. Jones and Tarr loaded these loops on their hard drives, which became incomplete archives of empire and colonialism. Some loops had processed images: slowed down, distorted, abstracted, speeded up, or layered with a filter of neon color. During the performance, each artist reacted to the other's images. Each screen was engaged in dialogue and was responsive to the other, a form of digital call-and-response derived from Gospel music in the United States, as well as African-derived storytelling practices such as "krik? krak!" in the Caribbean. Created in 3D by Jones, computer animations of a digital soldier, airplanes, and bombs were superimposed over the amateur footage at various, ghostly, abstracted figures exorcising the violence the pastoral imagery camouflaged. Although travelers, missionaries, explorers, ethnographers, and lecturers originally produced the footage for an entirely different purpose, the collaborative live performance disentombed the traces of empire from these images. The double-screen projection convened contiguities between different geographic locations, remapping through the cartographies of empires rather than simply nations. Shot from the 1920s through the 1960s, during the expansion of empire and war, these amateur images begin to function as evidence and documents of a more transnational colonial imaginary, as the hip-hop track remixed live by Jones with its beats and rhythms counterposed a pleasurable soundscape to more horrifying concepts. The loops were also manipulated live on the laptops, colorized, slowed down, and repeated to emphasize minute gestures, sometimes in relation to the beats of the music, and other times in counterpoint rhythms. *Dismantling Empire* processes these artifacts into new critical engagements with history. Here, remix is synonymous with the historiographic and the political.

Other artists have remixed in the space of the art gallery and looked to media typically not framed as fictions. Exhibited at the prestigious Sharjah Biennale in 2005, Tarek Al-Ghoussein and Chris Kienke's *War Room* (United Arab Emirates, 2004) is an installation of 1500 digital photographs displayed on light boxes that remix television and cable broadcasts during the second US invasion of Iraq in 2003.[54] The gallery space is transformed into a war room—that is, a space where wars are planned with maps, charts, computer simulation. The project surrounds viewers with a seemingly chaotic array of glowing images that attempt to document a military invasion as it was produced as a media event. By digitally photographing the television screens with cameras mounted on tripods, the two artists worked independently, capturing moments within a live flow of coverage on the invasion by Al-Jazeera, BBC, CNN, Dubai TV, and others available in the United Arab Emirates (UAE). Al-Ghoussein conceived and realized a similar project during the first US invasion of Iraq in 1991, using a Polaroid camera to document media coverage from Egypt

Figure 5.1 *War Room.*

where he was then living. As with his other photographs, particularly his *Self-Portrait* series (2002–2003) in which he sometimes wears a *keffiyeh*, framing and sequencing are as significant as content.[55] With *War Room*, Al-Ghoussein disrupts associations between the project and his own subjective experiences as a Palestinian from Kuwait by collaborating with Kienke, who is a non-Arab from the United States. The project avoids the reductive media trope of presenting two sides by making it difficult, if not impossible, to determine which artist shot which photograph. Images cannot be reduced to Arab and non-Arab or American and anti-American perspectives. Through digital media, the project cogitates on the role of mediation in shaping of understanding of foreign invasions.

Foreign media reported the events of the invasion in different terms—invading forces versus coalition forces—and different focuses—Iraqis protesting against, or cheering for, the arrival of US soldiers. Yet all media, in representing war, shared common visuals. US president George W. Bush and UK prime minister Tony Blair advanced a story about saving the world from Iraqi president Saddam Hussein's weapons of mass destruction (WMD). The 2003 invasion is less polarizing today;

now, it is a testament to the power of US media to galvanize support for war. Deepa Kumar calls this subjective evidence a rhetorical strategy of "guilt-through-speculation." US vice president Dick Cheney's belief in an intelligence report that linked Iraq to al-Qaeda exemplifies guilt-through-speculation—nearly 50 percent of the US population mistakenly believed some of the 9/11 hijackers were Iraqi.[56] The first U.S. invasion of Iraq in 1991 became a media phenomenon, catapulting CNN, with its 24/7 coverage, from a minor cable-news outfit to a major force. In the United States, the second invasion was more closely associated with Rupert Murdoch's Fox News, with the "Fox effect" referring to the network's policy of garnering high rating by equating patriotism with war and ridiculing dissent.

War was also given a humanitarian gloss of saving Iraqis from a tyrant who threatened to destabilize world peace. US media reported that 90 percent of strikes were achieved by so-called precision weapons rather than more conventional carpet bombing, as the United States did in Southeast Asia during the 1970s. US and UK coverage of the invasion of Iraq heavily promoted the use of so-called smart bombs, allegedly guided by advanced computer technologies to their military targets without the collateral damage of civilian death and injury, thereby ensuring support by Iraqi civilians for US occupation as liberation. Although these technologies only really reduced deaths and injuries to military personnel, they had the effect of increasing US civilian support for the war. Reports indicated that weapons used during the invasion were smart. For media critics, US media coverage of the war shuttled between propaganda and a game. Kumar, for example, argues that coverage by CNN and other US media outlets emerged through the convergence of well-tested "government information control strategies" and a "for-profit giant conglomerate media system" that silenced and erased dissenting voices.[57] She examines ways that the US military learned to manage information, correcting what was perceived as communication mistakes during the so-called Vietnam War without engaging in the media censorship of the invasion of Grenada and Panamá in 1989 and Iraq in 1991. The military worked with Viacom, Disney, MGM, and other corporations in the media-industrial complex to support governmental efforts during the War on Terror.[58]

The 2003 invasion of Iraq, however, differed from previous televised warfare. Qatar's Al-Jazeera offered dissenting points of view to CNN and BBC journalism, particularly in relation to the humanitarian aspects of invasion and occupation. US defense secretary

Donald Rumsfield accused Al-Jazeera's coverage of civilian deaths as "vicious, inaccurate, and inexcusable" since they allegedly promoted anti-US sentiments.[59] Launched in 1996 to emulate the US and UK independent press, Al-Jazeera became the most-watched and most-trusted Arabic-language news source. Philip Seib has argued Al-Jazeera's reporting on the invasion resulted in "an end to the near monopoly in global news that American and other Western media."[60] Al-Jazeera contended the invasion was illegal under international law. "Al-Jazeera's most important contributions so far may be its establishment of Arab media as a viable alternative to Western news organizations and its role in attracting global recognition of Arab media voices," he writes.[61]

Al-Ghoussein and Kienke sampled these different perspectives on events along with broadcasts of films and animation that coincided with the invasion. Thus, they reveal the televisualities of these images of warfare. They noticed parallels between images of violence in warfare and children's cartoons broadcast at the same time on different channels.[62] The result is an interpretation of an historical event (television broadcasts available in UAE) about another historical event (US invasion of Iraq). It is an interpretation about the mediation of a media event that prods us to think about the vast array of mediated images that bear on our understanding of the world. By freezing moments in a televisual flow, *War Room* asks us to contemplate Al-Ghoussein's and Kienke's idiosyncratic filtering process as each photograph represents entirely subjective decisions.

The installation foregrounds the subjective filter of television news. If news editors select images for their visual capacities, Al-Ghoussein and Kienke perform another round of selection with different criteria. This performance operates as historiography by remixing that defies news media expectations of clarity, unambiguity, and objectivity. Selection filters information, evoking CNN corporate protocols established *before* the US invasion of requiring reporters to acquire script approval by CNN monitors as a second layer of filtering after the military.[63] Anthony Downey comments about Al-Ghoussein's work more broadly: "When we are looking at these images there is a consistent questioning of the viewer's position—a placing into an abyss of interpretation—that questions any easy assertions or understanding of what it is we are looking at."[64] Nonfictional events documented by camerapersons who accompanied reporters are juxtaposed with fictional events staged and recorded by professional cinematographers and animators. The terms document, stage, fiction, and nonfiction become less distinct. For Al-Ghoussein and Kienke, the project's interrogations into subjectivity points to limits crimping the terrains where individual opinions form.[65]

Comparably, Sama Alshaibi's *The Tethered* (United States, 2012) remixes 48 short video loops on a single screen. Each clip resides within a circle, disrupting the conventional rectangular framing for video images, including the new portrait format on smartphones. This circular format refuses the closures of linearity and causality. It opens images to reevaluation. The images themselves show everyday scenes of life in Palestine pulled from 12 years of Alshaibi's personal video documentation. Like Al-Ghoussein and Kienke's *The War Room*, Alshaibi's *The Tethered* is concerned with how so-called objective news reports mediate and transform events. She first visited Palestine only in 2004. Her mother fled during the Nakba of 1948 from Jaffa to Nablus and eventually to Baghdad, where she met Alshaibi's father. In the 1980s, the family fled Iraq due to the violence of the Ba'ath Party under Saddam Hussein. In the 48 circles of the project, Alshaibi focuses our attention on images that news media typically do not report except in conflictual moments. "My art provides the 'flip side of the coin' narrative," she explains, referring to dominant accounts of Palestinian exodus and diaspora. She muses the project is "a reclaiming of a history, as well as a voice to current struggles 'silenced' by Israel's domination tactics and subsequent demonizing of the Palestinian identity."[66] She shows the dehumanization of Israeli occupation as well as Palestinian existence as a form of resistance. She elaborates the "physical and psychological oppression of occupation: harassment, humiliation, and trauma are daily norms, yet the people are called on by the international world to be accountable for those who have succumbed to the desperation of violence."[67] Over the years, repetitive, familiar images of mothers mourning their children's deaths convey a story. Other iconic images of occupation include the peace/victory sign. Inside eight consecutive circles of one row, images of IDF tanks seem less menacing until a woman in purple walks in front of them. Her purple scarf passes in front of the olive-colored tanks, slowly and steadily moving from the first to the final circles in the row. The figure's presence underscores proximity to violence as an everyday reality, much like Alshaibi's collaborative project *Baghdadi Mem/Wars*, with Deena Al-Adeeb, discussed in chapter 4.

Alshaibi presents us with a home archive of images that refuse to be made comprehensible conventionally. The colors and design of the Palestinian flag punctuate these images: horizontal bands of black, white, and green intersected by a red triangle. Modeled after the Arab Revolt flag during the 1910s, the flag came to represent Palestine in 1964. Israel banned the flag from public display inside the occupied territories from 1967 to 1993. Scenes of protests and rallies frequently show the Palestinian flag, but the yellow flag of Fatah and the green flag of Hamas also surface. The project's title conjures a tethering of successive generations to a history of competing political voices, failed accords, and uprisings. As with many of Alshaibi's performances, photographs, and videos, *The Tethered* shows the effects of conflict on the human body, which stands in for the condition of a national body. In this project, however, she does not use her own body but focuses instead on numerous bodies of others. Holding the camera, she uses her own body to perform symbolically the Right to Return denied to most Palestinians. "My body 'returned,' along with my camera," she explains.[68] She thinks through the complexity of 48 years of occupation, signaled by the number of circles. By repeating images across several circles and looping the video, a process of ever-renewing appraisal and reappraisal is launched. The project searches for tiny details that may have been missed in the moment. It thinks through digital media on one of the most misrepresented conflicts of today, inviting us to engage more critically with images we encounter.

Remix as Collaborative Pedagogy

In this section, we examine an ongoing collaborative project with which we have both been involved as university professors and festival programmers. The Onward Project combines archival research with live performance, resulting in viscerally and intellectually stimulating events. It deploys cinephilia toward performative historiography and collaborative pedagogy.[69] In these performances, silent film—or *silenced* sound film—from archives are reactivated through live remixing of visual images from the films, live remixing of recorded sound effects and music from other sources, live music, live spoken-word oration, or a combination. Composed of scholars, curators, musicians, and filmmakers, the Onward Project embodies the collaborative, political potentials of critical cinephilia by working with archivists at the National Film Preservation Foundation and the UCLA Film and Television Archive, Northeast Historic Film, and the Smithsonian's HSFA. The venues for these free live remixes are festivals, universities, and museums, underscoring their primarily pedagogical and historiographic purpose.

The work of the Onward Project differs from revivals of silent-era film at film festivals and cinemas where accompanying live music, such as those by the Alloy Orchestra, often aspires to recreate an approximate experience of the past. As film historians have argued, live musical performances during the silent era varied widely. In his study of early cinema, David Robinson remarks that the Lumière brothers were aware of the distracting effects of their cinématographe when it functioned as a projector, so they hired pianiste-compositeur M. Emile Maraval to add musical accompaniment to their films on his Gavreau piano.[70] Audiences at Nickelodeons in the United States typically watched films in silence with live piano used during reel changes or sing-along events, as Rick Altman has argued.[71] Even when film producers and distributors commissioned film-specific musical scores, exhibitors varied the actual music according to financial resources to engage an entire orchestra or ensemble of musicians, availability of musicians, and local musical preferences.

The Onward Project recuperates some of this diversity, often flattened in commercial revivals of silent cinema and publication of silent films with piano or orchestral accompaniment on VHS or DVD. With *Within Our Gates: Revisited and Remixed* (United States, 2004), the Onward Project explored African American film history by focusing on the consolidation of Hollywood's racist stereotpyes and their contestation in the birth of African American feature filmmaking. The National Association for the Advancement of Colored People (NAACP) called for the state censorship of D.W. Griffith's racist shorts and epics, particularly *The Birth of a Nation* (United States, 1915), which represented historical events of the US Civil War from the perspective of the Klu Klux Klan (KKK), a white-supremacist vigilante group and later paramilitary organization that advocated lynching and voter intimidation, particularly of African Americans. Joseph Carl Breil's three-hour score for the film included both original music and recognizable patriotic national songs like "The Star-spangled Banner" (c. 1814) and "America, the Beautiful" (c. 1895), as well as nationalist songs like "Dixie" (c. 1861) traditionally performed in blackface.

Although the Harlem Renaissance provided models for producing racially conscious art and audiences, other models emerged through film exhibition. The project draws upon resistant and oppositional practices of exhibitors whose audiences might not have been imagined as ones intended for commercial films. African American exhibitors would often hire musicians to insert critical counterpoint to the overt and casual racism in Hollywood films in the form of an empathetic musical accompaniment. "The mixture of differing and competing media in the exhibition context of black theaters created a space for audience members to recognize each other and register their conflicting and contradictory experiences of race, class, and social position," points out Anna Siomopoulos.[72] Rather than a crescendo to celebrate racialized violence as heroic, for example, musicians might play an ominous funeral dirge to mark the scene as tragic. At many African American theaters, as Siomopoulos argues, "live jazz and blues performances did not so much accompany film screenings as compete with them for audience attention and response" with musicians like Bessie Smith, Ma Rainey, Ethel Waters, Louis Armstrong, and Fats Waller receiving top billing.[73]

At the time of Griffith's rise to public acclaim and infamy, Oscar Micheaux became the first African American to produce a feature-length film and establish a distribution and exhibition circuit. Film scholars largely overlooked Micheaux's films until the 1990s when the US National Film Registry recognized them.[74] *Within Our Gates* (United States, 1919) is a response to Griffith's *The Birth of a Nation*, all the more historically meaningful since Micheaux was the grandson of a slave. Whereas *The Birth of a Nation* portrayed the lynching of African American men as a glorious, heroic, and patriotic act, *Within Our Gates* portrayed it as cowardly, barbaric, and self-destructive. With no infrastructure for the production, distribution, and exhibition of films that portrayed African Americans in non-stereotyped ways, Micheaux created Micheaux Film and Book Company in 1918 with distribution offices in Chicago, Illinois, and Roanoke, Virginia.

Micheaux's controversial subjects and treatments of films made them ready targets for censorship at the local level until the adoption of the Production Code Administration (PCA), Hollywood's self-censoring policy during the early 1930s that contributed to African Americans largely disappearing from the silver screen.[75] Micheaux rejected some of the rules of continuity and coherent storytelling that Griffith formalized in order to disrupt the potentially passive reception of narrative film. "While Griffith's film represents black male assaults on white female purity, Micheaux's film sets the historical record straight with its depiction of the attempted rape of a black woman by a white man," explains Siomopoulos.[76]

Within Our Gates: Revisited and Remixed was conceived as both a refusal of "the arbitrary divide between the past and the present, between the analog[ue] and the digital" and a provocation of a "dialectic between the past and the present, between analog[ue] and digital, between celluloid and live performance" that combined "academic research, critical theory and history, visual and musical creation, feature-length film scoring, lighting, and performance for a film that is more than eight decades old."[77] The remix emerged from the collaborative work of film historians and musicians.[78] Rather than remixing the visual images, the film was remixed primarily through sound, particularly African American jazz that distorts and plays with tonalities and textures, marshaling improvisation as an anti-racist remix logic.

As John Hochheimer argues, the sampling of music, lyrics, and sounds in *Within Our Gates: Revisited and Remixed* falls within a longer lineage of media practices: the audio collage producers of the 1950s by artists such as Richard "Lord" Buckley, Bill Buchanan, and Dickie Goodman and Ken Nordine's "free-form combination *word jazz*."[79] Such performances mobilized "the deliberate juxtaposition of various seemingly conflicting sources." Audiences were invited into "multiple possibilities for interpretation, to be drawn from often explicitly conflicting messages"[80] The spoken-word segments in *Within Our Gates: Revisited and Remixed* add layers of historical context onto the film, detailing events like the so-called race riots of the 1910s and 1920s as well as the startling statistic of one African American lynched every three days between the 1880s and 1910s. The performance opened with Billie Holiday's voice singing lyrics in a darkened auditorium: "Southern trees bear a strange fruit. / Blood on the leaves and blood at the root." The image of strange fruit describes the disconcertingly familiar sight of lynched bodies in the US South. They hang from trees like Georgia peaches and Florida oranges. The first spoken-word oration included citations from "Reasons for a Lynching" juxtaposed with quotes from cultural-studies theorists and radical and subaltern historians, including Paul Gilroy, Stuart Hall, Wahneema Lubiano, and Gayatri Spivak.[81] The spoken-word performance in *Within Our Gates: Revisited and Remixed* transformed the film into "a series of hyperlinks to other ideas, both historical and musical, thereby allowing the film to open up."[82] A Baroque clarinet solo, African dancing, djembe drumming, spoken-word performances, and digital live mixes formed the soundscape. "Our performance evoked the improvisational, immersive experience of black theaters on the south side of Chicago in the 1920s," explain Siomopoulos and Zimmermann. "In these venues, live performance of jazz and blues drove the film and inspired audience participation, thus inverting the Hollywood film convention in which music predominantly supports the film narrative."[83] The music and spoken-word script could "destabilize the film text, reanimate film reception, and complicate film spectatorship."[84]

Performed on 28 March 2006, at Ithaca College, *Trafficking in the Archives* (United States, 2006) reconsiders early US cinema through its representations of changes to the environment affected by humans in their quest for love and money.[85] Whether the local harvesting of ice and sardines or the global trafficking of women as brides or concubines, whether selling cigarettes and refrigerators or conveying the need to sail across the "South Seas" to rescue local populations from imaginary diseases, early cinema documents the lived realities and anxious fantasies of geopolitical and physical exchange. The event places the post-rock and post-minimalist music of Piano Creeps, featuring Mary Lorson and Billy Coté, in critical dialogue with the history of film exhibition. *Trafficking in the Archives* revitalizes sound-images relationships as transnational, disjunctive critical dialogue. The feminist-inflected vocal styles and alternative rhythms of Piano Creeps create space for critical reflection upon Technicolor's feature production of *The Toll of the Sea* (United States, 1922; dir. Chester M. Franklin), a 1936 Universal Newsreel documenting a so-called bumper year for ice harvesting, a 1957 US Department of the Interior propaganda film on Maine sardines, and a love story set amid times of contagion and inoculation in the independently produced narrative film *The Tahitian* (United States, 1956; dir. James Knott).

Produced by the Technicolor Motion Pictures Corporation to showcase its new subtractive two-beam color process, *Toll of the Sea* relocates the story of Madame Butterfly from Japan to China. The story rehearses the familiar early cinema and classical Hollywood sexists and racist trope of an Asian woman who must sacrifice herself for the white man to perform her "true mission," as Gina Marchetti argues.[86] Scriptwriter Frances Marion was instructed to sacrifice complexities of narrative and characterization to highlight the technical potential of the new color film process.[87] By remixing *The Toll of the Sea*, *Trafficking in the Archives* signals a moment before the standardization of color film stock. The red, green, brown, black, and white images hardly evoke the candy-box color more typically associated with the Technicolor fantasy of MGM's *The Wizard of Oz* (United States, 1939; dir. Victor Fleming). Founded in 1916 by Herbert Kalmus, Daniel Comstock, and W. Burton Wescott, Technicolor Motion Pictures Corporation was one of the primary color technology research service firms.[88] Its two-bean splitter sent red- and green-light waves onto two negatives, which were developed, dyed, and attached back to back, which was first employed in *The Toll of the Sea*. By 1935, Technicolor stipulated only its cinematographers could film using its color stocks.[89] *Trafficking in the Archives* reconfigures Technicolor's proprietary rights to technologies. Technicolor's business practices determined the style and content of classical Hollywood cinema, particularly after 1935, when it began to supervise the entire process by sending equipment, personnel, and cinematographers to the studios. The corporation also controlled what colors would become cinematic ones, avoiding bright or saturated color for pastels. As Ella Shohat and Robert Stam point out, Technicolor, Eastmancolor, and other color-film processes had a technical preference for light complexions: the film needed to be stopped down or specially lit for "darker-complected people."[90]

No longer disappearing behind coyly averted glances and intertitles in a westernized projection of what an Asian typeface might look like for malapropisms in Pidgin English, the Chinese American actor Anna May Wong appears trapped within the racial and gendered economies of classical Hollywood as interpreted by Technicolor. She is visually trapped by Hollywood's continuity editing that imposes continuity and causality on her every action and reaction. In dialogue with the other films in the performance, race and gender extend beyond Hollywood's orientalist fantasies to newsreels, official state propaganda, and individual, cinephiliac imitations of Hollywood product. The suffering faces of Asian and Asian American women in these fiction films seem strikingly authentic when juxtaposed to the smiling faces of (differently subjugated) white women who prepare sandwiches and casseroles from sardines in the Department of Interior's *Sardines from Maine Down-East Style* (United States, 1957). The film narrates a never-ending four-season cycle of unpaid domestic labor for women. The gendered hierarchies reinscribe the post–Second World War drive to employ men in manual occupations that had been performed by women during the war. The film also reveals nationalist tropes of man over nature that appeared decades earlier in Universal Newsreels' *Harvest Bumper Ice Crop* (United States, 1936). Both position nature as endlessly bountiful—much like subjugated housewives and orientalized mistresses—so that discussion of sustainable alternatives are mixed into the archival footage through the project's remix. *Trafficking in the Archives* underscores the systemic injustices and epistemological violence subdued by consumerist cinephilia.

Inspired by MacDougall's work on transcultural film as a mode of speaking *alongside* and *with* others, rather than *about* them, the Onward Project prioritizes performative acts of engagement" in a collaborative remix zone. By enlisting faculty in film studies and in film practice, as well as in music and new media, the legacy construct of analogue film can be partially severed from "an epistemological overemphasis on the text, whether in producing a new text or analyzing old ones" when it becomes a *prompt* for critical thinking rather than a *product* for consumerist cinephiliac consumption.[91] The practice of collaboration destabilizes hierarchical structures, the "more individualistic, nineteenth-century Romantic notion of the artisanal filmmaker who expresses his or her own inner feelings in a unique way," and the marketing of individual film auteurs.[92]

Conceptual and artistic British Nigerian filmmaker John Akomfrah has mused digital technologies might contribute to a remix of our expectations of media based on the often racially prejudiced chemical processes of celluloid that idealized light-colored skins.[93] Classical cinema's entelechy, Akomfrah argues, suggests an ideal of beauty that excluded Africa; digital technologies permit an opportunity to reconsider the ethical questions of such systems. By hacking the codecs in digital cameras, we might undo these technological logics of racism. Collaborative remix zones suggest a form of critical cinephilia, performative historiography, and collaborative pedagogy that are, according to MacDougall, "always about crossing into liminal zones of difference that require participation, collaboration, and acknowledgment of an encounter."[94]

Remix as Algorithm

Whereas the projects in the previous section remixed media manually according to logics of intuition and subversion, the ones in this section remix algorithmically according to the logics of automation. Steven Levy defines an algorithm as "a specific procedure which one can apply to solve a complex computer problem [...] a sort of mathematical skeleton key."[95] The work of the artist in an era of digital automation becomes conceptual. The creative labor falls upon the design of patterns of repetition, variation, frequency, duration, and design rather than the aesthetics of composition, color, and texture. The AI of code becomes an agent in the creative process, rendering nineteenth-century romanticisms about art as the expression of singular individuals obsolete. These projects recontextualize everyday images and ones we might never otherwise encounter. These projects thrust experimental media beyond its analogue traditions. Analytic montage and counterpuntal sound-and-image matches assume more urgency than conventional experimental models, such as hand processing. Experimentation transitions to the algorithmic and speculative.

Robert Spahr's *Crufts* are several series of auto-generative images from source material scraped and harvested from websites. He appropriates the hacker term "cruft," which refers to unpleasant substances, superfluous junk, redundant or superseded code, and useless and badly designed computer programming. In his projects, found image databases are the Internet's superfluous junk—or crufts—to recycle. By using the software suite ImageMagick and scripts written in the computer language of Perl, algorithms manipulate images according to automated instructions at controlled intervals 24 hours per day and seven days per week. Each *Cruft* contains an archive of images that can be downloaded, printed, and shared. "I take apart, juxtapose, recycle, and interrupt the relentless flow of media to reveal a relationship in which we don't simply consume media, but are also consumed by it," notes Spahr.[96] Ranging from the absurd to the political, the series quietly interrupt and mimic the news cycle of outlets like CNN.

Distress Cruft (my fellow Americans) (United States, 2007–2008; www.robertspahr.com/work/cruft/distress/), for example, examines the practice of camouflaging security practices as a tourist-friendly service at the Empire State Building, where visitors are offered the opportunity to purchase their security photograph as a souvenir. The images of smiling families and loving couples are composited with the image of a US flag displayed upside down to signal severe distress. The series raises questions about the ethics of security. As a potential target for domestic or foreign terrorism, the Empire State Building is highly policed with CCTVs. The staged (i.e., smiling tourist) photo serves as a template for facial recognition software. The tourist photos are tagged and stored in a digital database, where they can be filtered as needed through large-scale systems used by agencies such as the Information Awareness Office (IAO), which uses the automated biometric identification technologies Human Identification at a Distance (HumanID). The watermark proof on the image becomes self-referential to the digital image, equally a proof of a visit and potential proof of a crime. The recycling of the security photos also points to the system's vulnerability. Spahr offers the option for users to transfer the image onto personalized US postage stamps.

Babylon Cruft (United States, 2005–present; www.robertspahr. com/work/cruft/babylon) scrapes images from the US Air Force website and images from Internet sites for adult entertainment, presumably accessed by soldiers.[97] The juxtaposition of a row of three small images—proud soldiers posing with officers or politicians, military jets on a tarmac, and frail senior citizens, likely veterans, posing with US flags—across the top of the cruft with explicitly sexual images of adult entertainment at the bottom sets into motion thoughts about tags like innocence and guilt that we often attribute to images of strangers. In a cruft composed on 21 July 2014, the upper images include a smiling, white male cadet and his female partner; a multiracial group of soldiers studying; and a frontal shot of a large drone above a nude white-male torso mounted atop a nude, white, female body. The juxtaposition of the phallic-shaped drone and the image of missionary-style (man on top of woman) heterosexual intercourse evokes the torpedo/bikini scene in Bruce Conner's landmark found-footage film *A Movie* (United States, 1958). Like Conner's film, the images in the series reveal the overwhelming whiteness of both the military-industrial and adult-entertainment industries, suggesting that nominative notions of beauty in both patriotism and pornography have changed little since the 1950s. *Data Loss Cruft (Corruption)* (United States, 2013–present; http://www.robertspahr.com/work/dataloss/) inserts the text code from a report on casualties from US covert drone attacks in Pakistan, Somalia, and Yemen into the code for a photograph from Whitehouse.gov, a public relations site designed to promote the US government. File corruption occurs at the level of the image, revealing what is silenced and erased from official accounts of the US state and its foreign policy, particularly civilian deaths. Using automated content scrapers and combining different but related sources, critical glitch art highlights the darker underbellies of the institutions they represent, questioning the sincerity of the original image. Data corruption visualized in JPEGs suggests the fragility and impermanence of digital identities. In a cruft from 25 November 2013, Michelle Obama is clearly visible beneath a layer of dark green, whereas the data corruption in an image from 04 January 2014, renders the image from the White House almost unrecognizable. Spahr's crufts point toward another extension of conceptual art, where the instructions are automated and the content is randomized.

Michael Takeo Magruder's *[transcription]* (United Kingdom/United States, 2006; www.takeo.org/nspace/ns017/) and *[FALLUJAH. IRAQ. 31/03/2004]* (United Kingdom/United States, 2004–2005;

www.takeo.org/nspace/ns011/) remix media coverage in both on-site and online iterations. In *[transcription]*, Magruder samples and processes BBC broadcast in real time. The result is a montage of stills sequenced through cross-dissolves. Rather than allowing each pixel on the digital screen to represent colors from the original BBC images, he adds a digital layer that renders colors as rows and columns of *hanzi* (Chinese ideographic characters), so that the images appear stylized and seem decontextualized from the news reports in which they were originally embedded. He adds a layer of noise, so that audio from the various broadcasts seems distant and incomprehensible over scratching and breathing effects that at times sound like "digital artifacts" (glitches in the codecs). Sharon Lin Tay has argued that the project offers the user an experience of the news that oscillates "between familiarity and strangeness" through "the use of an algorithm to disrupt the linearity and veracity of news broadcasts," thereby "rendering the meanings generated by the news broadcast confused and multiple."[98] During the US-supported Israeli attack on Gaza in summer 2014, an image of 16-year-old Mohammed Abu Khdeir in a baseball cap appears, likely scraped from a recent story by BBC on the arrest of three suspects in relation to kidnapping, beating, dousing with gasoline, and burning alive the Palestinian teenager in July 2014.[99] Other images, such as the Samsung logo, are less immediately recognizable and singular in their media meaning. Noting Samsung's dropping profits, the BBC also reported on the corporation's discovery of child labor in its Chinese plants.[100] Wavering from controversial to banal, the project becomes a perpetual transcription of media events.

More boldly, *[FALLUJAH. IRAQ. 31/03/2004]* remixes censored footage of the ambush, beating, and murder of US "civilians" by Iraqi "insurgents" in March 2004. The civilians were employees for Blackwater Security Consulting, a private military security firm to which the US military outsourced aspects of its operations during the occupation of Iraq following the 2003 invasion. In 2007, after the murder of Iraqi civilians, the company's practices were questioned. For Magruder, the 2004 event was notable because of its unabashed censorship from news media. The project becomes an occasion for thinking about news media's "ethical filtering of content and manipulative remixing of data" in the presenting purportedly factual information disseminated almost instantly, thereby writing history in real-time. The project remixes still images from censored footage from the Associated

Figure 5.2 *[transcription].*

Press, text from BBC reports, and sound effects. In version 2, color images of the event appear, instantly accumulating layers of black text of English-language news reports. Visually, documentary images are slowly submerged and nearly disappear beneath news coverage. Another variation of the project's critical filtering of images breaks the screen into 12 smaller screens, each of which shows images in a layered montage of fragments that cannot be reassembled into a coherent story. Cars burn in the streets, men protest, others look bewildered by the events. The projects remix according to algorithms. Here, automation reveals the imperfections of human manual/mental filtering and framing of information in ways that recall Al-Ghoussein and Kienke's *War Room* as critical cinephilia applied to commercial news media.

Remix as Engagement

A final group of projects conceive collaborative remix zones in terms of venturing into the world to engage with social realities and work toward productive social change. They accumulate perspectives and dissemble borders, roaming freely between animation, documentary, fiction, and experimentation. Huang Weikai's *Xianshi shi guoqu de weilai/Disorder* (China, 2009) figures remix as a form of on-the-ground engagement with China's massive globalization and urbanization. Here, remix functions as an intervention into Chinese neoliberal state propaganda. The 58-minute documentary exposes the daily dysfunctions of people as they navigate the newly constructed, chaotic cityscape of Guangzhou, a megacity in southern China that was once an entrepôt for the opium trade. Disturbing scenes graph Guangzhou as a space of dysfunction, disorganization, and horror: a broken hydrant gushes water, a pig roams a city street, a man straddles a bridge threatening suicide.

Critic Chris Chang has dubbed *Disorder*, "a nightmare" and "city symphony from hell."[101] Benny Shaffer has noted the film works as a "surrealist urban ethnography."[102] Although the film can be located within the Chinese New Documentary movement of indie films produced outside commercial and state-sponsored arenas, its collage style contrasts sharply with that movement's direct-cinema style of long takes and character-driven structures.[103] Instead, the film presents fractured images assembled in an aggressive, abrupt editing style. A vendor sells bear-paws on the street. Police brutally beat a man. *Disorder* references the city-symphony tradition of documentary in Dziga Vertov's *Chelovek s Kinoapparatom/Man with a Movie Camera* (Soviet Union, 1929) and Jean Vigo's *À propos de Nice* (France, 1930) with their emphasis on cinematic explorations of modernity, public space, mobility, daily life, and formal experimentation.[104] City-symphony films eschew characters and linear causality based on events, concentrating instead on mapping urban space through transportation, streets, architecture, and people—a conceptual tactic *Disorder* extends. The first period of city-symphony films emerged in Europe during the rise of consumer capitalism. *Disorder* resituates the city-symphony film in China, deploying its nonlinear form to unpack the contradictions and difficulties of daily life under transnational capitalism. If Vertov proposed a utopian vision of the socialist city as a place of work and leisure, Huang counters with a dystopian vision of the city as a place of hardship, violence, and chaos. While the first wave of city films not only emulated musical structures but also utilized musical soundtracks, *Disorder*'s soundtrack is composed solely of harsh ambient city noises.

Rather than experimenting with the visual possibilities of cinematic *form* like Vertov and Vigo, *Disorder* explores the possibilities of new cinematic *machines*, proposing that the diffusion of amateur technologies can counter the state propaganda of skyscrapers, manufacturing, and access to consumer goods with a more multiple representation, suggesting democracy narrated from below rather than propaganda from above. Huang collected over one thousand hours of footage shot by amateurs on DV cameras in Guangzhou. He established a structural paradigm in assembling the material: no two scenes could be derived from the same source. All the footage is black and white, quoting the first wave of city films. Critic Hua Hsu has argued that *Disorder* is organized on the idea of "Chinese absurdity," and it "is a film about every day effects of globalization and progress" and "about people who had accepted a measure of absurdity in their lives."[105]

EngageMedia is a new media portal for video file sharing and a generator of sustainable media development and networks for environmental and social justice work from the Asia Pacific.[106] EngageMedia operates between globalized development and environmental and human-rights degradation in Indonesia as an example of social-media remix as contestation. EngageMedia's website, for example, presents a remix/mix of genres, including documentary, experimental, fiction, animation, music, and news. A searchable list of topics creates connections through and across ASEAN states, East Asia, and South Asia: poverty, indigenous, migrant, health, corporations, labor, conflict, human rights, racism, religion, arts, environmental, forests, water, food security, biotech, civil liberties. Based in Indonesia and Australia, EngageMedia exemplifies transregional contestatory remix. It aggregates and contextualizes user-generated social media about environmental and social justice issues in the Asia Pacific region. Often heralded as the "YouTube for Asian activists," EngageMedia assembles genres, topics, and countries to expose the other side of the massive economic development now redefining the Asia Pacific. It showcases works from activists, NGOs, aid organizations, youth groups, health educators, and artists, mixed together.

In the ever-expanding world of social media, Indonesia boasts the second highest number of Facebook users in the world. EngageMedia developed from activists, journalists, and technologists, who identified the massive usage of social media in Indonesia in relation to the problems of distribution of emerging video works. Conglomerates with links to the energy and communication sectors control mainstream Indonesian film and television. Inaugurated in 2005, EngageMedia was formed to bridge the gap between experimental works, social activist video, and the political urgency to track the many voices opposing rapid development in Indonesia and the Asia Pacific. EngageMedia, then, as a video file-sharing portal, aggregates the diverse media, topics, regions, communities, and politics of the Asia Pacific. EngageMedia also curates projects highlighting significant issues for the Asia Pacific, such as the *Migrant Workers Stories* (Indonesia, 2012).

Indonesia is the world's largest archipelago, with 17 thousand islands. It is the third largest state in Asia with most extensive rainforest cover on the continent. The largest economy in Southeast Asia, it is also the most rapidly expanding Asian economy after China.[107] The largest Muslim country in the world, Indonesia is also a multicultural and multiethnic state. The Indonesian government has encountered a continuing global perception of political instability and economical corruption.[108] According to the World Bank, the pressures of an expanding population, rapid development, exploitation of natural resources (e.g., palm oil, rubber, fishing), and inadequate environmental management have also produced devastating environmental challenges: rapid deforestations, ocean contamination, unsafe water, and extreme air pollution.[109]

Rather than user-generated media that offers engagement with popular culture, human-rights social media figures participatory media as an expansion of public spaces for, and engagements with, civil society. This more ground-up, people-centered strategy of participatory remix suggests permeable media as a bottom-up practice of multiplicities. EngageMedia is more than an Asia-Pacific activist website: it produces networks of circulatory remix. The *Migrant Workers Stories* project demonstrates how remixing economic contexts, social issues, documentation of labor, and user-generated social media function in networked circulation. In Indonesia, large numbers of young women depart for work as maids and factory workers across Asia.[110] The International Labor Organization estimates over 4.3 million Indonesians are overseas migrants, of whom 75 percent are female domestic workers in the Middle East and East Asia.[111] One category on the EngageMedia website is called "migrant workers, refugees, and stateless people." This section features 146 short videos about migrant issues in Hong Kong, Singapore, Malaysia, Australia, Indonesia, the Netherlands, and Saudi Arabia. EngageMedia counters the trade objectives of ASEAN. *How Dare Your Say: May Day 2011 Hong Kong* (Indonesia, 2012) by V-Activist is a six-minute video chronicling a 2011 domestic and foreign workers rally in Hong Kong. In wide-angle medium shots, the video features female Nepalese, Filipina, and Indonesian workers marching in the streets with signs detailing their working conditions. Text in Cantonese and English explains the protesters' demands: standard working hours, minimum wage, and workers' rights. A slow, ethereal soundtrack counters the mood of the protest, creating a more meditative mood. Modest in execution and production values, the short nonetheless documents migrant workers as active agents of change from the ground up.

With most mainstream Indonesian stories about migrants derived from government sources, EngageMedia initiated the *Migrant Worker Stories* project. It collaborated with migrant worker advocacy organizations in Indonesia and Malaysia such as Asosiasi Tenaga Kerja, Garda BMI, Migrant Care, and Solidaritas Buruh Migran Cianjur to launch capacity-building workshops in Kuala Lumpur and West Java to train migrants to tell their own stories with inexpensive video and mobile phones.[112] They worked in two Malaysian immigrant villages, Cianjur and Indramayu. In 2012, Dhyta Caturani, from EngageMedia, trained Indonesian migrant workers in Malaysia at night after they finished working. One video interviewed an Indonesian migrant working on a construction site, another video chronicled migrant living conditions.[113] With web-interfaces for short films designed for social media, definitive answers to political and social problems are not as important as opening dialogues and encounters for making sense.[114] EngageMedia's mosaic structure suggests a way to consider portals as contestatory remix. Their site designs pathways for aggregation and curation, often pointed to particular advocacy campaigns. EngageMedia reconfigures production, distribution, exhibition, technology, microterritories, and politics as remix.

Founded by Emeka Okereke and registered as a not-for-profit in Nigeria, *Invisible Borders: The Trans-Africa Project*'s flagship project—*The Invisible Borders Trans-African Road Trip Project* (Nigeria, 2009–present; http://invisible-borders.com/)—is an ongoing "road trip" aimed at "patching of numerous gaps and misconceptions posed by frontiers within the fifty-four countries of Africa through art and photography."[115] Okereke describes his own need to get "unstuck" from his training in France, so as to become an artist capable of representing the lived realities of someone who lives in two places at *all* times. Artistic practice is remixed. He rejects the idea that a copy-and-paste approach to appropriating foreign techniques is required. Hollywood and Europe seldom facilitate African representations of Africa that are untainted by racist bias. Okereke also opposes dismissals of Africa as dysfunctional, calling attention to the organization through improvisation at work throughout the continent. The road trips become an occasion for individual and collective improvisation.

To cross borders as ordinary citizens involves patience and sometimes small bribes. The road-trip experience asks participants to travel with cameras, not only to document their experiences but also to rethink and remix their approach to art. They rethink and remix their relationship to Africa by moving from Lagos to other parts.

The project looks back to the historical imposition of another set of invisible borders: the abstract geopolitical borders formalized by the notorious Berlin Conference aka "Scramble for Africa" (1884–1885) through which European states granted themselves the right to "regulate" (to borrow a colonial euphemism) colonialism. By carving what they considered disputed territory into areas of effective occupation, European states eliminated almost all forms of local sovereignty and autonomy. These scars of colonialism continued through decolonization in the form of somewhat arbitrary groupings of people into new states. Nations and tribes were split between neighboring states or thrown together with foreign nations and tribes, sometimes aggravating earlier animosities. In addition to these geopolitical borders, European colonialism and decolonization institutionalized social borders based on class, religion, language, and assimilation to European cultural standards. Elite classes of former French colonial subjects were known as "the evolved" (*les évolués*), an overtly racist term implying Africans exist naturally in a primitive, an infantile, and an animalistic state. The corruption of many of the regimes appointed by former European colonizers ensured that colonialism would continue. When anticorruption movements began, the United States was often suspected of assassinating leaders like Congo's Patrice Lumumba.

If photography served as a tool of colonialism by documenting and categorizing different Africans into hierarchical orders and geographical distributions, then *The Trans-Africa Project* retools toward a borderless or trans-African cartography. *The Trans-Africa Project*'s manifesto summons the power of flux toward collaboration-based transformation, so as "to transcend preconceived notions of what Africa is, what African art is, and how artists can engage their audience," particularly ones that might otherwise be forgotten as laymen for art.[116] "We believe that the first border we have to cross are the limitations within our immediate localities," the manifesto outlines. Since 2009, *The Invisible Borders Trans-African Road Trip Project* invites ten artists from different media—photography, film, literature, performance art—to facilitate a "trans-Africa exchange" by "sharing real-time photographs, factual and reflective blogposts, as well as video diaries."[117]

The first group of artists from Lagos traveled to Bamako in a black Volkswagen minibus they named "Maria," suggesting an appropriation of the Edison Company's "Black Maria," which historians consider as the world's first commercial movie studio. To experience the distance between the two cities and the borders between states, they drove rather than flew. In his blogpost, Nike Ojeikere, one of the participating artists, notices physical and psychological differences between the traffic jams of urban Lagos and the palm trees, unspoiled territory, and vast beaches of rural countryside. At the border between Benin and Togo, photography is prohibited. They record surreptitiously the sounds of the transaction.[118] Borders are experienced as distance is experienced: in increments of time rather than space. Borders signify delays, negotiating with agents over passports and identification cards; distance by delays of minibus repairs, unanticipated accidents, or food poisoning. Ultimately, the group overcomes its own international invisible borders to produce a video of their trip, a collaborative remixing of their experiences and expectations. *Invisible Borders 2009: The Film* (Nigeria, 2009; dir. Emeka Okereke) and *Invisible Borders 2011: The Film* (Nigeria, 2011; dir. Emeka Okereke) stream on the project's website. The project has been also recognized in a short documentary for Al-Jazeera English, *Africascape: The New African Photography: Invisible Borders* (Qatar, 2013; dir. May Abdalla). *Invisible Borders* employs a strategy of remixing to unthink colonial divisions that have disempowered African artists. *Invisible Borders* recognizes them as powerful agents of their own futures.

Based in Mumbai, CAMP is a group comprising Shaina Anand, Sanjay Bhangar, and Ashok Sukumaran. With media artists, programmers, and other collaborators, CAMP operates as both a research and practice studio, producing projects migrating between emerging technologies, experimental video, networked modalities, and databases. CAMP is an acronym for nearly 100 thousand possible names, such as "Culture According to My Peers," "Critical Art and Metaphorical Publics," "Cooperation as Per Materialist Practice," and "Camp Around More Peripheries." Each time a user goes to its website (www. camputer.org), a different acronym appears, suggesting the inscription of remix and an aesthetic and politics of fluidity. As the website notes, 100 thousand names represents less than one-tenth the number of NGOs in India.

Originally a commission of the Sharjah Biennial in the UAE to probe the relationships between trade and transport, *From Gulf to*

Gulf to Gulf/Kutchi Vahan Pani Wala (United Arab Emirates/India/ Yemen/Somalia/Qatar/Pakistan/Oman/Kuwait/Kenya/Iraq/Iran, 2009–2013; dir. Shaina Anand and Ashok Sukumaran) is a CAMP-produced, feature-length documentary comprising high-definition video, standard video, and mobile-phone video shot by CAMP and sailors. It chronicles the merchant sailors from the Kutch district of western India who labor on the wooden dhows transporting bath-tubs, batteries, pipes, beauty products, cars, goats, and pasta from the Persian/Arabian Gulf to the Gulf of Aden to Somalia. Although CAMP shot many scenes in the shipyards where the boats are con-structed, the project provides a compelling example of remix as a collaborative engagement. It also highlights cinephilia, opening with a music video shot by one of the sailors of two other sailors lip-synching to a song by popular playback singers from the film indus-try. They sailors perform the lyrics, interpreting their meaning in both the contexts of their lives and their love for film. In one scene, the sailors hold before the camera lens sheets of paper with names and credits for their video, recalling those for amateur filmmaker Tom D'Aguiar's 8mm spoofs of a British spy films, which he shot in Bangalore during the 1940s.[119] The music videos also reveal a long tradition of musical entertainment on the long voyages at sea. The important function of the music vidoes today evokes that of live musicians who used to travel with sailors in the past.

These images captured by the sailors show life on the boats and in ports: the sailors work, dance, joke, fish, cook, eat, sleep, play cards, groom, pray, and fashion dhow miniatures. The film's cred-its highlight the names of the "Mechanised Sailing Vessels (MSV) in order of appearance," suggesting the role of the vessels, rather than the sailors, as the primary subject of the sailors' videos later compiled by CAMP into *From Gulf to Gulf to Gulf*. The sailors are the film's co-producers with CAMP. Rather than anthropocentric view of the world, *From Gulf to Gulf to Gulf* reveals one about relationships between humans and nonhumans, including MSVs. The sailors pro-duce images of dolphins, sunsets, waves, the decks of their own boats or of distant boats, producing their own music videos. The speed and joy of the popular songs, qawwalis, and other musical forms con-trast with the sometimes precarious working and living conditions on the boats. Videos show the distance of the sailors from the new year's fireworks from the newly opened Burj Khalifa in 2010 and their uncomfortable proximity to tragedies like a fire aboard MSV Bhakti Sagar and MSV Zulelal in Dubai Creek or MSV Al Barakat at sea. Images are captured by different makers and set to different

Figure 5.3 *From Gulf to Gulf to Gulf.*

music, becoming documentaries in the sense of the term's etymological origins in travelogues. The videos show the world that is often visible only to the sailors. The end-credits acknowledge the "anonymous creators of music videos across many boats and many years," which points to the longevity of the videos, some of which were lost after they were shared with Anand and Sukumaran, who in turn shared them again with the sailors. The sailors are not the film's subjects but its makers.

The film features a predominance of ocean images, suggesting an epic scale of water and movement dislocated from land coordinates. The mobile-phone videos counter this large scale with close-ups of the sailors, who often perform for the cameras. The film has no voiceover explaining who these sailors are, or how this trade and transport functions; instead, the viewer experiences life on the boats, the constant drone of the motors, and the long empty vistas of the sea. Sequences feature titles establishing locations and naming the MSVs. The videos play as the sailors originally shot them, without editing. The end credits establish the collaborative structure of *From Gulf to Gulf to Gulf*, listing the 13 people who shot footage and acknowledging the anonymous mobile-phone music video creators. Doubling the cosmopolitan histories recuperated in Amitav Ghosh's anthropological work, *In An Antique Land* (1992), *From Gulf to Gulf to Gulf*, compiles the nautical crossroads between South Asia, the Arabian Peninsula, and East Africa that predate European colonialism's violent disruption of the region.[120]

From Gulf to Gulf to Gulf presents a very different notion of cinephilia than the ones produced by media corporations and industry organizations, such as Bollywood's Filmfare Awards or Hollywood's Academy Awards. The sailors produced almost all of film's footage, and they also selected all of the music that scores the images. The short videos are similar to amateur music videos (AMVs), yet they move further away from the sort of fan cultures described by media theorists such as Henry Jenkins and Matt Hill.[121] Rather than personalizing the found audio of popular music, the videos in CAMP's film enter into an ongoing dialogue between sailors, transcending different languages according to a history of navigation in the Indian Ocean that predates the lascars during the sixteenth century. *From Gulf to Gulf to Gulf* opens with an inverted and reversed map of the three gulfs—Kutch, Persian/Arabian, and Aden—that places water as the legible bearer of meaning for fluid identities. Like Paul Gilroy's Black Atlantic, territorial identities are insufficient to the task, as is the territoriality of intellectual property. Much like the sailors move from gulf to gulf to gulf without passports, their music videos flow without the restrictions of corporate copyright.

Anand and Sukumaran compiled the footage over a period of four years of working with the sailors, edited it together into the project, and added subtitles. As CAMP makes clear, its members did not give cameras to the sailors and ask them to document themselves. Anand describes her discomfort early in her career with conventional documentary practice, namely "finding a subject, interviewing, zooming in, [and] asking questions until the subject ends up crying."[122] The subject's performance of what is framed and documented as truth reveals the asymmetries of documentary practice. *From Gulf to Gulf to Gulf* moves around the typical concerns of participatory documentary, which often still maintains a particular power imbalance. Some of original material was circulated among the sailors, either by Bluetooth or bumping mobile phones, suggesting alternative circuits of media circulation. The project developed from an earlier one called *Wharfage* for which CAMP installed speakers around the Sharjah Creek that transmitted Hindi-Urdu broadcasts by Gujarati sailors, Pakistani loaders, Iranian shopkeepers, and Somali traders, along with music. As Anand and Sukumaran explain, the project examines Sharjah as a site for "free trade" in ways that do not conform to WTO definitions. Relaxed or absent customs regimes allow for goods to travel the same routes that they traveled for centuries on boats constructed in Slaya, Gujarat, that sail to Somalia though what is now the UAE, Oman, and Yemen.

Earlier projects by CAMP include ones in which residents inter-act with surveillance cameras in highly controlled places like the United Kingdom and occupied Palestine. Working with Nida Ghouse, Mahmoud Jiddah, Shereen Barakat, and Mahasen Nasser Eldin in 2009, CAMP's *Al Jaar qabla al Daar/The Neighbour Before the House* (2011) challenges discourses of victimhood by engaging dis-possessed Palestinians in (East) Jerusalem/Al Quds by placing CCTV cameras at their service to witness the daily activities of Israeli fami-lies who now occupy their homes. From eight locations, participants operated pan-tilt-zoom (PTZ) cameras with manual joystick control. As Florian Schneider argues, the project "sets out to reverse engineer the neighbourhood as a machine for self-monitoring and surveillance, one that normally turns contingency into consistency and the visible into the sensible."[123] Becoming "neither subjective nor objective," the videos reveal the visual and physical inaccessibility of the neighbor-hood "since one would not be allowed to go there, or know how to understand what is going on."[124] By inviting people to participate in surveillance, CAMP unsettles documentary's typical imbalance of power. Rather than zooming into the subject's performance of "truth"—something performed most explicitly and most controver-sially in French formulations of *cinéma vérité* when the documentar-ian provokes the subject to move outside an everyday performance of self—CAMP facilitates the subject's activation as a participant in the construction of the encounter and its cinephiliac presentation.

Speculations

Remixing returns to the question that opened this book: how to assess the political and aesthetic implications imbedded in the hacker ethic of taking things apart. Digital technologies and networks alter some of the integers of animation, documentary, experimental, inter-active, and narrative media foregrounding not the work of art and media as an object but instead augmenting a process of continual openings, questionings, reconfigurations, blurrings, invitations, and speculations. The projects examined throughout this book take apart assumptions or open up speculations rather than offer fixed conclusions. They convene micropublics, where dissent is produc-tive. Collaborative models collapse production, distribution, exhibi-tion, and participation, offering new possibilities and potentialities for critical cinephilia and thinking in new ways about interactions between social movements and arts/media practice. The performative functions of digital media exorcise technologies, rendering them visible and comprehensible as embodied power relations.

How can we think through digital media? Collaborative remix zones reactivate an aspect of cinephilia from cinema's earliest years. Tom Gunning describes early audiences as incredulous, marveling at discrepancies between reality and its representation in Lumières films of the 1890s, pointing to a moment in cinema's history when, as Sean Cubitt argues, "it was able to activate rather than absorb its audience."[125] Critical cinephilia within collaborative remix zones activate a multiplicity of histories that cannot be fixed, that remain forever transient and contradictory. Collaborative remix zones combat the commodified nostalgia embedded in the TMCs repurposing of cinema. Collaborative remix zones politicize cinephilia via a deterritorialization and decorporatization of content—and meaning. They become encounters with the co-presence of other perspectives.

Critical cinephilia within collaborative remix zones transition from immobilized and apolitical fetishistic image- or author-worship into the construction of collaborative communities where new knowledges and new connections can be actualized through a radical historiographic and cartographic practice. Collaborative remix zones radically rethink cinephilia, infusing it with political and ethical urgency as the entertainment industries repurpose cinephilia into intellectual property industries. We speculate the following shifts in critical cinephilia that constitute thinking through digital media:

(1) from a fixation on the past, including the past as reactivated through memory, to a recognition of the present;

(2) from psychic nostalgia to material artifacts, including digital code, that are suspended between history, the real, and the future;

(3) from closed circuits of connoisseurs, cultural elites, and idiosyncratic auteurs to open circuits of collaboration and networked distribution;

(4) from a fetishistic relationship to what has been created and lost (object) to an engaged relationship with what can be created (practice);

(5) from an empirical realm of "it was" toward aspirational and hypothetical realms of "what if";

(6) from a logic of individual, private, or unconscious desire to the multiple logics of collaborative, shared, and politicized exchange; and

(7) from the production of state and corporate imaginaries to the activation of repressed and suppressed discourses and practices that foreground transpolitical connections and vectors of movement.

Notes

Introduction

1. Thomas Shevory and Patricia Zimmermann, "Festival Codirectors' Welcome," *Finger Lakes Environmental Film Festival* catalogue (Ithaca, New York: Ithaca College, 2007): n.p.
2. Nicholas Mirzoeff, *An Introduction to Visual Culture* (London and New York: Routledge, 1999); W. J. T. Mitchell, *Picture Theory: Essays on Verbal and Visual Representation* (Chicago and London: University of Chicago Press, 1994). For an analysis, see Keith Moxey, "Visual Studies and the Iconic Turn," *Journal of Visual Studies* 7.2 (2008): 131–146.
3. Lev Manovich, "Cinema and Digital Media," in *Technology and Culture: The Film Reader*, ed. Andrew Utterson (London and New York: Routledge, 2005): 29.
4. Holly Willis, *New Digital Cinema: Reinventing the Moving Image* (London and New York: Wallflower, 2005): 35, 56.
5. Ibid., 33.
6. Lev Manovich, *The Language of New Media* (Cambridge and London: MIT Press, 2001): 187–223.
7. See Dan Harries, "Watching the Internet," in *The New Media Book*, ed. Harries (London: British Film Institute, 2002): 171–182.
8. Tara McPherson, "Self, Other, and Electronic Media," in *The New Media Book*, ed. Dan Harries (London: British Film Institute, 2002): 192.
9. Beth Kolko, Lisa Nakamura, and Gilbert Rodman Rodman, eds., *Race in Cyberspace* (New York and London: Routledge, 2000); Lisa Nakamura, *Digitizing Race: Visual Cultures of the Internet* (Minneapolis and London: University of Minnesota Press, 2008); Lisa Nakamura, Peter Chow-White, and Alondra Nelson, eds., *Race After the Internet* (London and New York: Routledge, 2011).
10. Faye Ginsburg, "The Parallax Effect: The Impact of Indigenous Media on Ethnographical Film," in *Collecting Visible Evidence*, ed. Jane M. Gaines and Michael Renov (Minneapolis and London: University of Minnesota Press, 1999): 156–175.
11. Mark Tribe and Reena Jana, *New Media Art* (Köln: Taschen, 2007): 10.
12. See, for example, Enrique Dussel, *Philosophy of Liberation* (1980), trans. Aquilina Martinez and Christine Morkovsky (Eugene: Wipf and Stock,

2003); Dilip Parameshwar Gaonkar, "On Alternative Modernities," in *Alternative Modernities*, ed. D. P. Gaonkar (Durham: Duke University Press, 2001): 1–23; Renato Ortiz, "From Incomplete Modernity to World Modernity," *Daedalus* 129.1 (Winter 2000): 249–260; Ravi Sundaram, *Pirate Modernity: Delhi's Media Urbanism* (London and New York: Routledge, 2010); Awam Amkpa, "Africa: Colonial Photography and Outlaws of History," in *African Photography from the Walther Collection: Distance and Desire: Encounters with the African Archive*, ed. Tamar Garb (Göttingen: Steidl Verlag, 2013): 241–252.

13. *Japan's Competing Modernities: Issues in Culture and Democracy, 1900–1930*, ed. Sharon A. Minichiello (Honolulu: University of Hawai'i Press, 1998); and Collaborative Research Project "Competing Modernities" at the German Historical Institute in Washington DC in the United States.
14. Laura U. Marks, *Enfoldment and Infinity: An Islamic Genealogy of New Media Art* (Cambridge and London: MIT Press, 2010): 37–70.
15. For a thorough discussion, see Ania Loomba, *Colonialism/Postcolonialism*, 2nd ed. (New York and London: Routledge, 2005).
16. See Robert J. C. Young, "Postcolonial Remains," *New Literary History* 43.1 (Winter 2012): 19–42.
17. Nicholas Negroponte, *Being Digital* (New York: Vintage, 1995/1996): 4.
18. Henry Jenkins, Sam Ford, and Joshua Green, *Spreadable Media: Creating Value and Meaning in a Networked Culture* (New York: New York University Press, 2013).
19. Negroponte, *Being Digital*, 6.
20. See, for example, Jonathan Sterne, "The Computer Race Goes to Class: How Computers in Schools Helped Shape the Racial Topography of the Internet," in *Race in Cyberspace*, ed. Beth Kolko, Lisa Nakamura, and Gilbert Rodman (New York and London: Routledge, 2000): 191–212; Pippa Norris, *Digital Divide: Civic Engagement, Information Poverty, and the Internet Worldwide* (Cambridge: Cambridge University Press, 2001).
21. Ulises Ali Mejias, *Off the Network: Disrupting the Digital World* (Minneapolis and London: University of Minnesota Press, 2013): 9.
22. Manual Castels, *The Rise of the Network Society* (1996), 2nd ed. (Malden: Wiley-Blackwell, 2010).
23. Mejias, *Off the Network*, 10.
24. He suggests that control by protocol is more democratic than control by panopticon, but it is "layered, stratified, and sometime hierarchical." Alexander R. Galloway, *Protocol: How Control Exists after Decentralization* (Cambridge and London: MIT Press, 2004): xvi.
25. Galloway, *Protocol*,12, xvi.
26. Ibid., xvi.
27. Mejias, *Off the Network*, 12–13, 16.
28. Timothy Murray, *Digital Baroque: New Media and Cinematic Folds* (Minneapolis and London: University of Minnesota, 2008): 5, 20.
29. Gerard Goggin, *Global Mobile Media* (New York and London: Routledge, 2011): 33–34.

30. See Mark Andrejevic, *iSpy: Surveillance and Power in the Interactive Era* (Lawrence: University of Kansas, 2007).

31. Christiane Paul, "Contextual Networks: Data, Identity, and Collective Production," in *Context Providers: Conditions of Meaning in Media Arts*, ed. Margot Lovejoy, Christiane Paul, and Victoria Vesna (Bristol and Chicago: Intellect, 2011): 107.

32. Ibid., 113.

33. Robert Scoble and Shel Israel, *Age of Context: Mobile, Sensor, Data and the Future of Privacy* (Lexington: Patrick Brewster, 2014): xiv, 1.

34. Paul, "Contextual Networks," in *Context Providers: Conditions of Meaning in Media Arts*, 103.

35. Henri Lefebvre, *La production de l'espace* (Paris: Anthropos, 1974); Yi-Fu Tuan, *Space and Place: The Perspective of Experience* (Minneapolis and London: University of Minnesota Press, 1977).

36. Tim Cresswell, *Place: A Short Introduction* (Malden, Oxford, and Victoria: Blackwell, 2004): 12, 11.

37. Ibid., 13.

38. Doreen Massey, *For Space* (London: Sage, 2005).

39. Doreen Massey, "A Global Sense of Place," *Marxism Today* (June 1991): 25.

40. Cresswell, *Place*, 84.

41. Marc Augé, *Non-Places: Introduction Supermodernity* (1995), trans. John Howe (London: Verso, 2009).

42. Étienne Balibar, "What Is a Border?" in *Politics and the Other Scene* (1997–1998), trans. Christine Jones, James Swenson, and Chris Turner (London and New York: Verso, 2002/2011): 81, 83.

43. Marc Garrett, "Revisiting the Curious World of Art and Hacktivism," *FurtherField* (03 February 2012), http://www.furtherfield.org/features/articles/revisiting-curious-world-art-hacktivism.

44. Ravi Sundaram, *Pirate Modernity: Delhi's Media Urbanism* (London and New York: Routledge, 2010): 13.

45. Brian Larkin, "Degraded Images, Distorted Sounds: Nigerian Video and the Infrastructure of Piracy," *Public Culture* 16.2 (Spring 2004): 297.

46. Tilman Baumgärtel, "The Culture of Piracy in the Philippines," *Pilipinas: A Journal of Philippine Studies* 45 (September 2005): 29–45.

47. Moradewun Adejunmobi, "Evolving Nollywood Templates for Minor Transnational Film," *Black Camera* 5.2 (Spring 2014): 85.

48. N. Katherine Hayles, *How We Think: Digital Media and Contemporary Technogenesis* (Chicago and London: University of Chicago Press, 2012): 11.

49. Ibid., 9–10.

50. Ibid., 10.

51. Ibid., 11.

52. In *Remediation: Understanding New Media* (Cambridge and London: MIT Press, 2000), Jay David Bolter and Richard Grusin describe remediation in three different ways: (1) "remediation as the mediation of mediation," (2) "remediation as the inseparability of mediation and reality," and (3) "remediation as reform" (55–56).

53. Alexander R. Galloway, *The Interface Effect* (Cambridge and Malden: Polity, 2012); Lev Manovich, *Software Takes Command* (New York, London, New Delhi, and Sydney: Bloomsbury, 2013).

54. Mary Louise Pratt, *Imperial Eyes: Travel Writing and Transculturation* (1992), 2nd ed. (New York and London: Routledge, 2008): 7–8.

55. Laura Mulvey, "Visual Pleasure and Narrative Cinema," *Screen* 16.3 (Autumn 1975): 6–18; Manthia Diawara, "Black Spectatorship: Problems of Identification and Resistance," *Screen* 29.4 (Autumn 1988): 66–76; Jean-Louis Baudry, "The Ideological Effects of the Basic Cinematographic Apparatus," trans. Alan Williams, *Film Quarterly* 28.2 (Winter 1974–1975): 39–47; Jean-Louis Baudry, "The Apparatus: Metaphysical Approaches to the Impression of Reality in Cinema," trans. Jean Andrew and Bernard Augst, *Camera Obscura* 1 (Fall 1976): 104–126; Noël Carroll, *Mystifying Movies* (New York: Columbia University Press, 1988).

56. Rachel Greene, *Internet Art* (London: Thames and Hudson, 2004): 32–33.

57. Henry K. Miller, "Home Cinema: Introduction," *Sight and Sound* 23.9 (September 2013): 221.

58. Anne Friedberg, *The Virtual Window: From Alberti to Microsoft* (Cambridge and London: MIT Press, 2006).

59. Marsha Kinder, "Hot Spots, Avatars, and Narrative Fields Forever: Buñuel's Legacy for New Digital Media and Interactive Database Narrative," *Film Quarterly* 55 (June 2002): 6.

60. David Hogarth, *Realer than Reel: Global Dimensions in Documentary* (Austin: University of Texas Press, 2006): 127–129.

61. Hayles, *How We Think*, 5.

62. Jussi Parikka, *Insect Media: An Archaeology of Animals and Technology* (Minneapolis and London: University of Minnesota Press, 2010): xi.

63. Ibid., vii.

64. Jane Bennett, *Vibrant Matter: A Political Ecology of Things* (Durham and London: Duke University Press, 2010): viii.

65. Ibid., xvii–xviii. For Bennett, "the ethical turn encourages political theorists to pay more attention to films, religious practices, news media rituals, neuroscientific experiments, and other noncanonical means of ethical will formation," so that affect is "not specific to human bodies" and "power is not transpersonal or intersubjective but impersonal" (vii).

66. Ian Bogost, *Alien Phenomenology, or What It's Like to Be a Thing* (Minneapolis and London: University of Minnesota Press, 2012): 31.

67. Ibid, 21. He prefers "units" to "objects" or "things" due to their possible confusion with digital objects, as well as the conventions by which objects imply subjects, materiality, and concreteness (23–24).

68. Timothy Morton, *The Ecological Thought* (Cambridge and London: Harvard University Press, 2010): 28.

69. Parikka, *Insect Media*, xv.

70. Flame is an acronym for "Fuzzy clustering by Local Approximation of Memberships."

71. In *Literary Theory: An Introduction* (1983), 2nd ed. (Minneapolis and London: University of Minnesota Press, 1996), Terry Eagleton explains:

"The difference between a 'political' and 'non-political' criticism is just the difference between the prime minister and the monarch: the latter furthers certain political ends by pretending not to, while the former makes no bones about it. It is always better to be honest in such matters" (182).

I Taking Things Apart to Convene Micropublics

1. Walter Benjamin, "The Work of Art in the Age of Mechanical Reproduction" (1935), trans. Harry Zohn, in *Illuminations* (New York: Schocken Books, 1968), 217–251; Siegfried Kracauer, *Theory of Film: The Redemption of Physical Reality* (1960; rpt. Princeton and London: Princeton University Press, 1997).
2. Steven Levy, *Hackers: Heroes of the Computer Revolution* (1984), 25th anniversary ed. (Sebastopol: O Reilly, 2010): 27–38.
3. For the larger context of interventionist art, see Nato Thompson and Gregory Sholette, with Josepth Thompson, Nicholas Mirzoeff, and Ondine C. Chavoya, *The Interventionists: Users' Manual for the Creative Disruption of Everyday Life* (North Adams: MASS MoCA, 2004).
4. We thank Michael Chanan for his insightful queries about political economy and political exigencies in relations to our theorizations of locative media, especially his cautionary arguments about overinvesting in the utopianism of digitality in the context of how digital networks inscribe power differently and more insidiously. For a clear exposition of how digital networks organize themselves around code, which facilitates control and power, see Alexander Galloway, *Protocol: How Control Exists after Decentralization* (Cambridge and London: MIT Press, 2004).
5. Bill Nichols has advanced the important idea that documentaries engage what he terms discourse of sobriety that is located within epistetophilia, in his *Representing Reality: Issues and Concepts in Documentary* (Bloomington: Indiana University Press, 1991). For an exposition of postcolonial historiography that is less interested in what constitutes the past than in how the past can be rethreaded through different imagined registers and vectors, see Dipesh Chakrabarty, *Provincilaizing Europe: Postcolonial Thought and Historical Difference* (Princeton and London: Princeton University Press, 2000).
6. For a discussion of locative media, see Jason Nolan, Steve Mann, and Barry Wellman, "Sousveillance: Wearable and Digital Tools in Surveilled Environments," *Small Tech: The Culture of Digital Tools*, ed. Byron Hawk, David M. Rieder, and Ollie Oviedo (Minneapolis and London: University of Minnesota Press, 2008): 179–196.
7. See Patricia R. Zimmermann, "From the Image to the Interface: Preemptive Media Collective" (January 2005), www.mediachannel.org.
8. See Thomas Kellein, *Fluxus* (London: Thames and Hudson, 1995) for examples of the Fluxus movement, linking the everyday, the performative, and the audience. For examples of how audience participation and relational

aesthetics evolved in subsequent decades internationally, see Claire Bishop, ed., *Participation* (Cambridge and London: MIT Press, 2006).

9. A variety of digital theorists have questioned how to consider the issues of digital networks and political actions. For example, see Geert Lovink, *Zero Comments: Blogging and Critical Internet Culture* (London and New York: Routledge, 2008); Mark Poster, *Information Please: Culture and Politics in the Age of Digital Machines* (Durham and London: Duke University Press, 2006); Don Tapscott and Anthony D. Williams, *Wikinomics: How Mass Collaboration Changes Everything* (New York: Penguin, 2006).

10. Many writers and organizations have observed what has been dubbed the "newly emerging transnational media ecology" as a shift away from conceptions of mainstream and alternative media, and profit/nonprofit. See Richard Kahn and Douglas Kellner, "Technopolitics, Blogs, and Emergent Media Ecologies: A Critical/Reconstructive Approach," in *Small Tech: The Culture of Digital Tools*, ed. Byron Hawk, David M. Rieder, and Ollie Oviedo (Minneapolis and London: University of Minnesota Press, 2008), 22–37; Michel Feher, ed., with Gaelle Krikorian and Yates McKee *Nongovernmental Politics* (New York: Zone, 2007); National Alliance for Media Arts and Culture, *Deep Focus: A Report on the Future of Independent Media* (San Francisco: NAMAC, 2004).

11. For a cogent discussion of collaborative media practices, see Helen De Michiel, "A Mosaic of Practices: Public Media and participatory Culture," *Afterimage* 35.6 (May–June 2008): 7–14.

12. The developing literature on critical cartography has explored the relationship between navigation, networks, digitality, rendering invisible patterns visible through visualizations and graphics, and alternative design. For an excellent overview of this field, see Janet Abrams and Peter Hall, eds., *Else/Where: Mapping New Cartographies of Networks and Territories* (Minneapolis and London: University of Minnesota Press, 2006).

13. Wendy Hui Kyong Chong, *Control and Freedom: Power and Paranoia in the Age of Fiber Optics* (Cambridge and London: MIT Press, 2008).

14. Lev Manovich, "Cinema and Digital Media," in *Technology and Culture: The Film Reader*, ed. Andrew Utterson (London and New York: Routledge, 2005): 27.

15. Analysis of *Lossless* is adapted from Dale Hudson, "Digital Performances," review of *Lossless: Rebecca Baron and Doug Goodwin* at the Carpenter Center for the Visual Arts, Harvard University, *Afterimage* 36.5 (March/April 2009): 22–23.

16. Douglas Goodwin and Rebecca Baron, "Overview of Lossless, Presskit," *Lossless* (no date), http://cairn.com/lossless/doku.php?id=start.

17. Mac McClelland, "I Was a Warehouse Wage Slave," *Mother Jones* (March/April 2012), http://www.motherjones.com/politics/2012/02/mac-mcclelland-free-online-shipping-warehouses-labor?page=1.

18. See Ayhan Aytes, "Return of the Crowds: Mechanical Turk and Neoliberal States of Exception," in *Digital Labor: The Internet, the Playground, and Factory*, ed. Trebor Scholtz (New York and London: Routledge, 2013): 79–97. MTurk is available at https://www.mturk.com/mturk/welcome.

19. Christiane Paul, "Contextual Networks: Data, Identity, and Collective Production," in *Context Providers: Conditions of Meaning in Media Arts*, ed. Margot Lovejoy, Christiane Paul, and Victoria Vesna (Bristol and Chicago: Intellect, 2011): 116–117.

20. Nick Dyer-Witheford and Greig de Peuter, *Games of Empire: Global Capitalism and Video Games* (Minneapolis and London: University of Minnesota Press, 2009): xiv.

21. Molleindustria as "Ronald McDonald," "Why This Game," *McDonald's Video Game* (2006), http://www.mcvideogame.com/why-eng.html.

22. Announcement for *Tekken Torture Tournament*, C-level (n.d), http://www.c-level.org/tekken/index.html.

23. Ravi Sundaram, *Pirate Modernity: Delhi's Media Urbanism* (London and New York: Routledge, 2010): 4.

24. Sundaram, *Pirate Modernity*, 123; Brian Larkin, "Degraded Images, Distorted Sounds: Nigerian Video and the Infrastructure of Piracy," *Public Culture* 16.2 (spring 2004): 290.

25. Sundaram, *Pirate Modernity*, 12.

26. Ibid., 112.

27. Ibid., 13.

28. Ibid., 16, 19.

29. Ibid., 106.

30. Ibid., 137.

31. Monica Narula, "Sarai: One Year in the Public Domain," *Television New Media* 3 (November 2002): 338.

32. Shuddhabrata Sengupta, "A Profile of Sarai: A Communicative Intersection," *I4D Magazine* (November 2004): 28.

33. Narula, "Sarai," 338.

34. Subsequent readers include *Sarai Reader 02: The Cities of Everyday Life* (2002); *Sarai Reader 03: Shaping Technologies* (2003); *Sarai Reader 04: Crisis/Media* (2004); *Sarai Reader 05: Bare Acts* (2005); *Sarai Reader 06: Turbulence* (2006); *Sarai Reader 07: Frontiers* (2007); *Sarai Reader 08: Fear* (2008); *Sarai Reader 09: Projections* (2009).

35. See Geert Lovink, "A Visit to the Sarai New Media Initiative Delhi," *make-worlds* (23 September 2003), http://makeworlds.net/node/39.

36. Shuddhabrata Sengupta and Monica Narula, "Mediated Cultures," *Isis International* (c.2004), http://www.isiswomen.org/index.php?option=com_content&view=article&id=276:from-horse-mail-to-intimations-of-e-culture&catid=67.

37. "The Network of No_Des," *Raqs Media Collective* (n.d.), http://www.raqsmediacollective.net/works.aspx#.

38. Ibid.

39. This description is from "Prix Ars Electronica 2005: Interactive Art, Honorary Mention," *Ars Electronica* (2005), http://90.146.8.18/en/archives/prix_archive/prix_projekt.asp?iProjectID=13382.

40. Sengupta and Narula, "Mediated Cultures."

41. Sundaram, *Pirate Modernity*, 108.

42. Pramod K. Nayar, "New Media, Digitextuality and Public Space: Reading 'Cybermohalla,'" *Postcolonial Text* 4.1 (2008): n. p.

43. As cited in Lovink, "A Visit to the Sarai." She describes Cybermohalla as creating "a context for researchers, media practitioners, web designers, programmers—from different contexts, with our specificities, pursuits, subjectivities—to interact, to collaboratively, dialogically create and transform our own and one another's practices through an awareness of and a critical engagement with one another."

44. Nayar, "New Media, Digitextuality and Public Space."

45. See Jason Mick, "China Threatens 'Severe' Punishments for Google, Apple Over NSA Spying," *Daily Tech* (04 June 2014), http://www.dailytech.com/China+Threatens+Severe+Punishments+for+Google+Apple+Over+NSA+Spying/article35008.htm#sthash.YaBaXw6V.dpuf.

46. For additional information of Fluid Nexus, visit www.inclusiva-net.es/fluidnexus/#about.

47. For additional information of TXTMOB, visit www.appliedautonomy.com/txtmob.html.

48. See Mark Tribe and Reena Jana, *New Media Art* (Köln: Taschen, 2007): 32–33.

49. Nick Knouf, telephone interview with authors, 18 June 2008.

50. For more information, visit http://www.monsantra.com/Welcome.html.

51. Anasuya Balamurugan, "First Speak Good English Campaign," *National Library Board Singapore* (2004), http://eresources.nlb.gov.sg/infopedia/articles/SIP_575_2004-12-23.html.

52. Also, see Lucy Bateman and Etienne Oliff's *Flip Flotsam* (Kenya/United Kingdom, 2003) on the "life recycle" of flip-flops in Mumbasa.

53. For more information, visit http://o-matic.com/play/paradox/index.html.

54. Mark Andrejevic, *iSpy: Surveillance and Power in the Interactive Era* (Lawrence: University of Kansas, 2007): 23–24.

55. See Rachel Greene, *Internet Art* (London: Thames and Hudson, 2004): 64–65.

56. "10 Simple Steps to You Own Virtual Sweatshop" can be streamed on blip.tv at http://blip.tv/.file/779038.

57. Workers in SL are paid 200 Lindens per hour. Due to the costs in mounting the project, prices were raised from USD 35 to about USD 50.

58. Stephanie Rothenberg, telephone interview with authors, 23 May 2008.

59. For additional information on Double Happiness Jeans, visit www.double-happinessjeans.com.

60. Steven Henry Madoff, "Service Aesthetics," *Artforum* (September 2008): 1–4.

2   Mapping Open Space to Visualize Other Knowledges

1. See Christiane Paul, "Contextual Networks: Data, Identity, and Collective Production," in *Context Providers: Conditions of Meaning in Media Arts*, ed. Margot Lovejoy, Christiane Paul, and Victoria Vesna (Bristol and Chicago: Intellect, 2011): 113–115.

2. See Martin W. Lewis and Kären E. Wigen, *The Myth of Continents: A Critique of Metageography* (Berkeley, Los Angeles, and London: University of California, 1997).

3. Jai Sen, "Other Worlds, Other Maps: Mapping the Unintended City," in *An Atlas of Radical Cartography*, ed. Lize Mogel and Alexis Bhagat (New York and Los Angeles: D. A. P./Distributed Art, 2008): 13.

4. See Bernard Rieder, "Entre marché et communauté: Une discussion de la culture participative à l'exemple de Google Maps," *Ludovia* (October 2008): 4.

5. Ismail Farouk, telephone interview with authors, 15 July 2008.

6. Michael Hardt and Antonio Negri, *Multitude: War and Democracy in the Age of Empire* (New York: Penguin Press, 2004): 82–83.

7. *UNESSO World Report: Towards Knowledge Societies* (Paris: United Nations Educational, Scientific, and Cultural Organization, 2005), 30.

8. Ibid., 29.

9. Andrew Utterson, "Destination Digital: Documentary Representation and the Virtual Travelogue, *Quarterly Review of Film and Video* 20.3 (2003): 199.

10. Sylvia Grace Borda, "Digital Image Archives as Public Artwork and Community Engagement," *Proceedings of the 2010 International Conference on Electronic Visualisation and the Arts*, ed. Alan Seal, Jonathan P. Bowen, and Kia Ng (Swinton: British Computer Society, 2010): 206–211.

11. For more information, visit http://heuristscholar.org/cocoon/heurist-test/browser/item-exp/69994/.

12. For an analysis of this project, see Hart Cohen, "The Visual Mediation of a Complex Narrative: TGH Strehlow's *Journey to Horseshoe Bend*," *Media International Australia* 116 (August 2005): 36–51.

13. Matt Cohen, "New App Warns You Of 'Sketchy' Areas in D.C., Immediately Draws Heavy Criticism," *DCist* (08 August 2014), http://dcist.com/2014/08/new_app_warns_you_of_sketchy_areas.php.

14. Svati Kirsten Narula, "The Real Problem with a Service Called 'Ghetto Tracker,'" *Atlantic* (06 September 2013), http://www.theatlantic.com/technology/archive/2013/09/the-real-problem-with-a-service-called-ghetto-tracker/279403/.

15. Teresa Iturrioz and Monica Wachowicz, "An Artistic Perspective for Affective Cartography," in ed. Karel Kriz, William Cartwright, and Lorenz Hurni, *Mapping Different Geographies* (Heidelberg and London: Springer, 2010): 75, 74.

16. Babak Fakhamzadeh and Eduardo Cachucho, "What Is Dérive App?," Dériveapp.com (n.d.), http://deriveapp.com/s/v2/about/.

17. Leila Nadir, "Poetry, Immigration and the FBI: *The Transborder Immigrant Tool*," *HyperAllergic* (23 July 2012), http://hyperallergic.com/54678/poetry-immigration-and-the-fbi-the-transborder-immigrant-tool/.

18. See Mark Tribe and Reena Jana, *New Media Art* (Köln: Taschen, 2007): 34–35, 92–93.

19. b.a.n.g. lab and Electronic Disturbance Theater 2.0, "A Mexico/U.S Border Disturbance Art Project," *Transborder Immigrant Tool* (n.d), http://bang.transreal.org/transborder-immigrant-tool/.

20. Nadir, "Poetry, Immigration and the FBI."

21. Ibid.

22. Fernando Solanas and Octavio Getino, "Towards a Third Cinema: Notes and Experiences from the Development of a Cinema of Liberation in the Third World," trans. Julianne Burton and Michael Chanan, in *25 Years of the New Latin American Cinema*, ed. Chanan (London: British Film Institute, 1983): 17–28. For an analysis of the effect of the manifesto on film theory and criticism, see Robert Stam, *Film Theory: An Introduction* (Malden: Blackwell, 2000).

23. Farah Wardani, "ruru.zip: The Ten Years of Raungrupa Exhibition," *Decompression* 10 "Expanding the Space and the Public: Ruangrupa's 10th Anniversary" (2010): 188.

24. Doreen Lee, "Images of Youth: On the Iconography of History and Protest in Indonesia," *History and Anthropology* 22.3 (September 2011): 310.

25. Like the Groupe Dziga-Vertov film of the roughly same title, *Tout va bien/ Everything's O. K.* (France/Italy, 1972; dir. Jean-Luc Godard and Jean-Pierre Gorin), Wulia's *Everything's OK* makes clear that everything is clearly not okay, particularly around notions of "free" space and "scalable" urbanization.

26. For an extended discussion of Ushahidi, see "Ushahidi: From Crisis Mapping Kenya To Mapping the Globe," Tavaana.org (n.d), https://tavaana.org/en/content/ushahidi-crisis-mapping-kenya-mapping-globe.

27. For more information, visit http://yatayat.monsooncollective.org/.

28. Saree Makdisi, "The Architecture of Erasure," *Critical Inquiry* 36.3 (spring 2010): 519–559.

29. TEDxRamallah took place in 2011 across three sites: Bethlehem (due to renovations at the Ramallah venue), Beirut, and Amman. "About," TEDxRamallah, (n.d), http://www.tedxramallah.com/en/about/.

30. For more information, see http://www.tumblr.com/tagged/tel-aviv-pride.

31. Sarah Schulman, "A Documentary Guide to 'Brand Israel' and the Art of Pinkwashing," *Mondoweiss* (30 November 2011), http://mondoweiss.net/2011/11/a-documentary-guide-to-brand-israel-and-the-art-of-pinkwashing.html. Schulman extends this analysis in *Israel/Palestine and the Queer International* (Durham and London: Duke University Press, 2012).

32. Robert Stam and Richard Porton, with a "digital afterward" by Leo Goldsmith, *Keywords in Subversive Film/Media Aesthetics* (Malden: Blackwell, in press).

33. Graham Huggan and Helen Tiffin, *Postcolonial Ecocriticism: Literature, Animals, Environment* (London and New York: Routledge, 2010): 17.

34. Paul Gipe, "Breakdown: Penetration of Renewable Energy in Selected Markets," Renewable Energy World (17 May 2013), http://www.renewableenergyworld.com/rea/news/article/2013/05/penetration-of-renewable-energy-in-selected-markets.

35. Analysis of *Permanent Transit: net.remix* is adapted from Dale Hudson, "Undisclosed Recipients: Database Documentaries and the Internet," an essay in dialogue with Sharon Lin Tay, "Undisclosed Recipients: Documentary in an Era of Digital Convergence," *Studies in Documentary Film* 2.1 (February 2008): 79–98.

36. The "ask a question" page is archived at http://web-archive-net.com/page/3858245/2014-03-19/http://www.kabul-reconstructions.net/ask/.
37. Mariam Ghani, artist statement on "Permanent Transit: net.remix," *artwurl*, republished on *Rhizome* (2004), http://rhizome.org/discuss/view/14265/2004.
38. Sharon Lin Tay, "Undisclosed Recipients: Documentary in an Era of Digital Convergence," an essay in dialogue with Dale Hudson, "Undisclosed Recipients: Database Documentaries and the Internet," *Studies in Documentary Film* 2.1 (February 2008): 79–98.
39. Vivian Sobchack, "The Scene of the Screen: Envisioning Cinematic and Electronic 'Presence'" (1994), *Technology and Culture*, ed. Andrew Utterson (New York and London: Routledge, 2005): 140.
40. Randy Malamud, *An Introduction to Animals and Visual Culture* (Houndmills and New York: Palgrave Macmillan, 2012): 87.

3 Documenting Databases and Mobilizing Cameras

1. Christiane Paul, "Contextual Networks: Data, Identity, and Collective Production," in *Context Providers: Conditions of Meaning in Media Arts*, ed. Margot Lovejoy, Christiane Paul, and Victoria Vesna (Bristol and Chicago: Intellect, 2011): 110.
2. Ursula Biemann, "Performing Borders: The Transnational Video," *Stuff It! The Video Essay in the Digital Age*, ed. Ursula Biemann (Zürich: Edition Voldemeer/Institute for Theory of Art and Design, 2003): 86, 89.
3. Ursula Biemann, "The Video Essay in the Digital Age," 10.
4. Kinder, Marsha, "Hot Spots, Avatars, and Narrative Fields Forever: Buñuel's Legacy for New Digital Media and Interactive Database Narrative," *Film Quarterly* 55.4 (Summer 2002): 6.
5. Paul, "Contextual Networks," 112.
6. N. Katherine Hayles, *How We Think: Digital Media and Contemporary Technogenesis* (Chicago and London: University of Chicago Press, 2012): 4.
7. Leo Enticknap, *Moving Image Technology: From Zoetrope to Digital* (London: Wallflower, 2005): 203.
8. Ibid.
9. Vivian Sobchack, "The Scene of the Screen: Envisioning Cinematic and Electronic 'Presence'" (1994), in *Technology and Culture*, ed. Andrew Utterson (New York and London: Routledge, 2005): 132.
10. Ibid., 136.
11. Lev Manovich, *The Language of New Media* (Cambridge and London: MIT Press, 2001): 20–22, 77.
12. Wendy Hui Kyong Chun, "Introduction: Did Somebody Say New Media?" *New Media, Old Media: A History and Theory Reader*, ed. Chun and Thomas Keenan (New York and London: Routledge, 2006): 1–2.
13. Michel Foucault, *The Archaeology of Knowledge and the Discourse on Language* (1969), trans. A. M. Sheridan Smith (New York: Pantheon, 1972): 129.

14. Jacques Derrida, *Archive Fever: A Freudian Impression* (1995), trans. Eric Prenowitz (Chicago and London: University of Chicago, 1996): 19.

15. Mary Flanagan, "Play, Participation, and Art: Blurring the Edges," in *Context Providers*, ed. Margot Lovejoy, Christiane Paul, and Victoria Vesna, 97.

16. Ibid.

17. Mark Tribe and Reena Jana, *New Media Art* (Köln: Taschen, 2007): 64–65.

18. Rachel Greene, *Internet Art* (London: Thames and Hudson, 2004): 99–100.

19. Analysis of *Goobalization* is adapted from Dale Hudson, "Undisclosed Recipients: Database Documentaries and the Internet," an essay in dialogue with Sharon Lin Tay, "Undisclosed Recipients: Documentary in an Era of Digital Convergence," *Studies in Documentary Film* 2.1 (February 2008): 79–98.

20. Jack Goldsmith and Tim Wu, *Who Controls the Internet?: Illusions of a Borderless World* (Oxford and New York: Oxford University Press 2006): 61.

21. Eduardo Navas, "Regressive and Reflexive Mashups in Sampling Culture," *vague terrain* 07: sample culture (2007), www.vagueterrain.net/content/archives/journal07/navas01.html: 3.

22. Bill Nichols, *Representing Reality: Issues and Concepts in Documentary* (Bloomington and Indianapolis: Indiana University Press, 1991): 35

23. See artists' statement: Nadine Hillbert and Gast Bouschet, "The Trustfiles," *Leonardo Electronic Almanac* 14. 5–6 (25 September 2006), http://leoalmanac.org/gallery/newmediap/trust.htm.

24. Javier Martinez Luque and Izaskun Etxebarria Madinabeitia, "UrbanWorld, Hyperreality Laboratory," in *Inédios 2006: Traducciones/Translations*, trans. Tom Skipp (Madrid: Mundo Urbano/Laboratorio de Hiperrealidad, 2007): 173.

25. Helmut Draxler, "How Can We Perceive Sound as Art," *Sound*, ed. Caleb Kelly (London: Whitechapel Gallery, 2011): 141.

26. R. Murray Shafer, "The Soundscape," *Sound*, ed. Caleb Kelly, 111.

27. Greene, *Internet Art*, 65.

28. See "The Toywar-story," *eToy* (n.d), http://toywar.etoy.com/; and Adam Wishart and Regula Bochsler, *Leaving Reality Behind: etoy Vs. eToys.com and Other Battles to Control Cyberspace* (New York: Eddo, 2003).

29. Ulises Ali Mejias, *Off the Network: Disrupting the Digital World* (Minneapolis and London: University of Minnesota Press, 2013): 7.

30. Trebor Scholz, ed., *Digital Labor: The Internet as Playground and Factory* (London and New York: Routledge, 2013).

31. Mejias, *Off the Network*, 124.

32. David Hogarth, *Realer than Reel: Global Dimensions in Documentary* (Austin: University of Texas Press, 2006): 127–129.

33. Trinh T. Minh-ha, "The Totalizing Quest for Meaning," *Theorizing Documentary*, ed. Michael Renov (New York and London: Routledge, 1993): 90.

34. Trinh T. Minh-ha, *The Digital Film Event* (London and New York: Routledge, 2005): 107.

35. For a discussion of policy's effect on shifting migration from California to Arizona, see Bill Ong Hing, *Defining America through Immigration Policy* (Philadelphia: Temple University Press, 2004): 189.

36. "iSee," *Institute for Applied Autonomy* (n.d.), http://www.appliedautonomy.com/isee.html.

37. For more information, visit http://www.appliedautonomy.com/isee/info.html.

38. Institute for Applied Autonomy, "Tactical Cartographies," in *An Atlas of Radical Cartography*, ed. Lize Mogel and Alexis Bhagat (Los Angeles, CA: *Journal of Aesthetics and Protest Press*): 29.

39. Ibid.,30.

40. Erich W. Schienke and IAA, "On the Outside Looking Out: An Interview with the Institute for Applied Autonomy (IAA)," *Surveillance and Society* 1.1 (2002): 104.

41. Institute for Applied Autonomy, "Tactical Cartographies," 31–32. For a discussion of Unnayan, see Jai Sen, "Other Worlds, Other Maps: Mapping the Unintended City" in the same volume (13–28).

42. Schienke and IAA, "On the Outside Looking Out," 109.

43. Institute for Applied Autonomy, "Tactical Cartographies," 35.

44. Schienke and IAA, "On the Outside Looking Out," 110.

45. Hing, *Defining America*, 184–185. The dramatic short-term results contributed to implementation of comparable policies, Operation Gatekeeper in San Diego, California (October 1994), Operation Safeguard in Arizona (October 1994), and Operation Rio Grande in Brownsville, Texas (August 1997).

46. Arthur H. Rotstein, "'TechnoPatriots' Use Internet to Watch Border for Migrants," *Tucson Citizen* (19 April 2008), http://tucsoncitizen.com/morgue/2008/04/19/82968-technopatriots-use-internet-to-watch-border-for-migrants/.

47. Homepage, *Minuteman Project* (2014), http://minutemanproject.com/.

48. Robert Spahr, "Cliff Dwellers," (n.d.), http://www.robertspahr.com/work/cliffdwellers/.

49. Ibid.

50. Ibid.

51. Henry Jenkins, *Convergence Culture: Where Old and New Media Collide* (New York and London: New York University Press, 2006): 4.

52. A description of the course appears at http://globalhub.eu/.

53. "AUP's First Sustainable Development Practicum: Tamil Nadu, India," *AUP Magazine* 10 (Spring 2009): 24.

54. Subrat Patnaik, "Now, Pondywood," *The Hindu* (03 March 2012), http://www.thehindu.com/todays-paper/tp-features/tp-metroplus/now-pondywood/article2955734.ece.

55. "International Film and Television Club Launches First Festival of Cell Phone Cinema," CellPhoneCinema.Org (n.d.), http://www.cellphonecinema.org/cellphonecinema.org/1st_Indian_Cell_Phone_Film

_Festival,_January,_2008.html. The festival website is located at http:// ifcpc.com/index.html.

56. Bidisha Mahanta, "The Screen Just Shrunk: FILM FEST Exploring a winnable alliance of the very small screen and the big," *The Hindu* (28 January 2013), http://www.thehindu.com/todays-paper/tp-features/tp-metroplus /the-screen-just-shrunk/article4351942.ece.

57. B[idisha] M[ahanta], "Well Connected: CINEMA Filmmaker Karl Bardosh is Constantly Striving to Adapt to New Technology," *The Hindu* (05 February 2013) http://www.thehindu.com/todays-paper/tp-features/tp-metroplus/ well-connected/article4380359.ece. Mahanta writes, "Being tech-savvy and adaptable to the changing years of cinema, Karl dismisses the opinion that such instant cinema would eventually lead to the decay of the magnificent cinematic experience. With an upcoming project with Single Shot Cinema pioneer Leonard Retel Helmrich, Karl is visibly excited about its screening in the Cannes fest." The 3D film, *Tagore's Natir Puja: The Court Dancer* (USA, 2014), is a remake of *Natir Puja* (India, 1932), a lost film by Rabindranath Tagore. Bardosh is presently working on a "narrative spiritual fantasy feature called *Burnt Offerings*, about Tagore's receipt of the Nobel Prize in 1913 and the destruction by fire of New Theatres at Tollygunge in 1933.

58. See Helga Tawil-Souri, "Cinema as the Space to Transgress Palestine's Territorial Trap," *Middle East Journal of Culture and Communication* 7 (2014): 169–189.

59. See Eva Scharrer's description of *ex libris* in *dOCUMENTA (13) Guidebook* (Ostfildern: Hatje Cantz Verlag, 2012).

60. See Jasmine Garsd and Encarni Pindado, "Crossing the Border in the Age of the Selfie," Fusion.net (28 May 2014), http://fusion.net/justice/story /crossing-border-age-selfie-724338.

61. Home page for Digital Thought Facility (2014), http://digitalthoughtfacil-ity.com/.

62. Kelly A. Gates, *Our Biometric Future: Facial Recognition Technology and the Culture of Surveillance* (New York and London: New York University Press, 2011): 22.

63. Awam Amkpa, "Africa: Colonial Photography and Outlaws of History," *African Photography from the Walther Collection: Distance and Desire: Encounters with the African Archive*, ed. Tamar Garb (Göttingen: Steidl Verlag, 2013): 241–252.

64. Elizabeth Losh, "Beyond Biometrics: Feminist Media Theory Looks at *Selfiecity*," Selfiecity (n.d.), http://selfiecity.net/#dataset.

65. Gates, *Our Biometric Future*.

66. Jacques Derrida, *Archive Fever: A Freudian Impression* (1995), trans. Eric Prenowitz (Chicago and London: University of Chicago, 1996): 19.

67. Gerard Goggin, *Global Mobile Media* (New York and London: Routledge, 2011): 40.

68. Triska Hamid, "Smartphone Obsession Drives UAE Household Electronic Spending to Dh4,875 A Year," *National* (21 April 2014), http://www .thenational.ae/business/industry-insights/technology/smartphone-obsession-drives-uae-household-electronic-spending-to-dh4-875-a-year.

69. Based on 2003 Polish study cited in GSM Association, *Mobile Phone Lifecycles Use, Take-back, Reuse and Recycle* (October 2006): 4.
70. Vodafone study in 2005 cited in GSM Association, *Mobile Phone Lifecycles Use*, 15.
71. GSM Association, *Mobile Phone Lifecycles Use*, 10–11.
72. See *StEP E-waste WorldMap* (http://www.step-initiative.org/index.php/WorldMap.html) for "interactive" information on e-waste.
73. Charles W. Schmidt, "Unfair Trade e-Waste in Africa," *Environmental Health Perspectives* 114.4 (April 2006): A232–A235.
74. Ibid.
75. Hong-Gang Ni and Eddy Y. Zeng, "Law Enforcement and Global Collaboration are the Keys to Containing E-Waste Tsunami in China," *Environmental Science Technology* 43.11 (2009): 3991–3994.
76. Basel Convention, "Overview" (n.d.), http://www.basel.int/TheConvention/Overview/tabid/1271/Default.aspx.
77. Mark Brown, "Apple Bans *Phone Story* Game That Exposes Seedy Side of Smartphone Creation," *Wired* (14 September 2011), http://www.wired.com/2011/09/phone-story/.
78. Siegfried Kracauer, *Theory of Film: The Redemption of Physical Reality* (1960; rpt. Princeton and London: Princeton University Press, 1997).
79. Ibid.; Tom Gunning, "An Aesthetic of Astonishment," *Viewing Positions: Ways of Seeing Film*, ed. Linda Williams (New Brunswick: Rutgers University Press, 1995): 114–133.
80. For information on Orbit, see http://www.comodorigs.com/comodo-orbit/. For a demo, see http://vimeo.com/63542041.
81. The *Up* series include: *Seven Up!* (1964), *7 Plus Seven* (1971), *21 Up* (1977), *28 Up* (1984), *35 Up* (1991), *42 Up* (1998), *49 Up* (2005), and *58 Up* (2012).
82. For an analysis of ways that social changes affect the family's dynamics, see Daniel Miller, "Transnational Collaborations for Art and Impact in New Documentary Cinema," *Jump Cut: A Review of Contemporary Media* 54 (Fall 2012).
83. See "Walking over the Bridge" from *Shape of the Moon* on YouTube: http://www.youtube.com/watch?v=vGkD8YFleyU&NR=1. Also see "Bamboo Camera Crane," which shows the scene being shot: http://www.youtube.com/watch?v=AqXudVX7mQk.
84. See Scott MacDonald, "Indonesia in Motion: An Interview With Leonard Retel Helmrich," *Film Quarterly* 63.3 (spring 2010): 35–41. For an analysis of the trilogy according to conventional expectations from visual anthropology, see James B. Hoesterey, "Single-Shot Cinema and Ethnographic Sympathy in Contemporary Indonesia: A Review Essay on *The Eye of the Day* (2001), *The Shape of the Moon* (2004), and *Position among the Stars* (2011) by Leonard Retel Helmrich," *Visual Anthropology Review* 30.1 (spring 2014): 85–88.
85. See Tamara Aberle, "Constructing the Future: An Interview with PM Toh," *Asian Theatre Journal* 31. 1 (Spring 2014): 290–309.

86. John Anderson, "A Master of Impossible Camera Angles," *New York Times* (09 September 2011), http://www.nytimes.com/2011/09/11/movies/leonard-retel-helmrichs-documentaries-capture-closed-spaces.html?pagewanted=all&_r=0.

4 Tactical Engagement through Gaming and Narrowcasting

1. Lev Manovich, *The Language of New Media* (Cambridge, MA, and London: MIT Press, 2001): 55–56.
2. Rita Raley, *Tactical Media* (Minneapolis and London: University of Minnesota Press, 2009).
3. Henry Jenkins, Sam Ford, and Joshua Green, *Spreadable Media: Creating Value and Meaning in a Networked Culture* (New York: New York University Press, 2013).
4. N. Katherine Hayles, *How We Think: Digital Media and Contemporary Technogenesis* (Chicago and London: University of Chicago Press, 2012): 3.
5. Ulises Ali Mejias, *Off the Network: Disrupting the Digital World* (Minneapolis and London: University of Minnesota Press, 2013): 3.
6. Ibid., 127, 129.
7. Ibid., 128. He cites Matteo Pasquinelli, *Animal Spirits: A Bestiary of the Commons* (Rotterdam: NAi, 2009): 72–73.
8. Louisa Stein, "Online Roundtable on Spreadable Media by Henry Jenkins, Sam Ford, and Joshua Green with participants Paul Booth, Kristina Busse, Melissa Click, Sam Ford, Henry Jenkins, Xiaochang Li, and Sharon Ross," *Cinema Journal* 53.3 (Spring 2014): 153.
9. See Moradewun Adejunmobi, "Evolving Nollywood Templates for Minor Transnational Film," *Black Camera* 5.2 (Spring 2014): 74–94.
10. Hayles, *How We Think*, 3.
11. Patrick Jagoda, "Gamification and Other Forms of Play," *boundary 2* 40.2 (2013): 114.
12. Alexander R. Galloway, *Gaming: Essays on Algorithmic Culture* (Minneapolis and London: University of Minnesota Press, 2006): 107.
13. See Mark Tribe and Reena Jana, *New Media Art* (Köln: Taschen, 2007): 44–45.
14. For a concise slide presentation of this history, see International Center for the History of Electronic Games, "Video Game History Timeline," *American Journal of Play* (2014), http://www.museumofplay.org/icheg-game-history/timeline/.
15. Galloway, *Gaming*, 1.
16. Ibid., 10–32.
17. Ibid., 17.
18. See Dale Hudson, "Biometrics and Machinima, Reanimated: Jacqueline Goss's *Stranger Comes to Town*," *Flow* 15.07 lead story (27 February 2012), http://flowtv.org/2012/02/biometrics-and-machinima/.
19. Raley, *Tactical Media*: 1.

20. Helga Tawil-Souri, "The Political Battlefield of Pro-Arab Video Games on Palestinian Screens," *Comparative Studies of South Asia, Africa, and the Middle East* 27.3 (2007): 535.

21. Ibid., 545.

22. Ibid., 536.

23. "The fears and accusations assume games lead to anti-Americanism (often equated with anti-Western, anti-Israeli, or anti-Semitic sentiments), which leads to violence (ironically, little is mentioned in the Israeli press about these games; the majority of fears emanate from the United States, the United Kingdom, and other Western nations)," explains Tawil-Souri, "The Political Battlefield," 542.

24. Tawil-Souri, "The Political Battlefield," 544. She continues: "Moreover, in terms of their in-humanity, terror, racism, and bloodthirstiness, *Under Siege* and *Special Force* pale in comparison to the games coming out of the United States and Israel, such as *America's Army* and *Israeli Air Force*, the latter an American-made game based on the Israeli invasion of Lebanon in which players can choose to 'carpet bomb all of Beirut'" (544).

25. "Trouble in the Holy Land: Hezbollah's New Computer Game," *WND* (03 March 2003), http://www.wnd.com/2003/03/17550/.

26. David Machin and Usama Suleiman, "Arab and American Computer War Games: The Influence of a Global Technology on Discourse," *Critical Discourse Studies* 3.1 (April 2006): 2.

27. Grace Jean, "Game Branches Out into Real Combat Training," *National Defense Magazine* (February 2006), http://www.wnd.com/2003/03/17550/.

28. Machin and Suleiman, "Arab and American Computer War Games," 1–2.

29. Souri, "The Political Battlefield," 540.

30. Jack Shaheen, *Reel Bad Arabs: How Hollywood Vilifies a People*, updated edition (Northampton: Olive Branch, 2009).

31. Machin and Suleiman, "Arab and American Computer War Games," 1–2.

32. "Google Pulls More Gaza-Israel Games from Android Store" *BBC News* (05 August 2014), http://www.bbc.com/news/technology-28668325; Matt Peckham, "Google Removes 'Bomb Gaza' Game From Play Store," *Time* (05 August 2014), http://time.com/3082253/google-bomb-gaza-game/.

33. See Ian Bogost, "Raid Gaza! Editorial Games and Timeliness," *Newsgames* (06 January 2009), http://newsgames.gatech.edu/blog/2009/01/raid-gaza-editorial-games-and-timeliness.html. Also see Gideon Resnick, "'Bomb Gaza' Game Maker: 'F**k Them All,'" *Daily Beast* (05 August 2014), http://www.thedailybeast.com/articles/2014/08/05/bomb-gaza-game-maker-f-k-them-all.html, which identified the game maker as Roman Shapiro.

34. "Molleindustria: 10 Years of Radical Socio-Political Video Games," *Indie Statik* (31 July 2013), http://indiestatik.com/2013/07/31/molleindustria/. Other other games can be accessed at http://www.3rdworldfarmer.com/ and http://www.darfurisdying.com/.

35. Gabriele Ferri. "Satire, Propaganda, Play, Storytelling. Notes on Critical Interactive Digital Narratives," *Interactive Storytelling* 8230 (2013): 175.

36. Gabriele Ferri, "Rhetorics, Simulations and Games: The Ludic and Satirical Discourse of Molleindustria," *International Journal of Gaming and Computer-Mediated Simulations* 5.1 (2013): 32–49.

37. As cited in "Molleindustria: 10 Years of Radical Socio-Political Video Games," *Indie Statik* (31 July 2013), http://indiestatik.com/2013/07/31/molleindustria/.

38. BRICS refers to Brazil, Russia, India, China, and South Africa; MINT, to Mexico, Indonesia, Nigeria, and Turkey; now officially the Cooperation Council for the Arab States of the Gulf, the GCC (Gulf Cooperation Council) includes Bahrain, Kuwait, Oman, Qatar, Saudi Arabia, and the United Arab Emirates.

39. Eddo Stern, "Waco Resurrection," (n. d.), http://eddostern.com/works/waco-resurrection/.

40. As cited in Mathias Jansson, "Interview: Eddo Stern, Pioneer of Game Art," *Gamescenes* (12 June 2010), http://www.gamescenes.org/2010/06/interview-eddo-stern.html.

41. In Egypt, a revolution against President Hosni Mubarak began on 25 January 2011, with massive demonstrations in Tahrir Square concluding a little more than two weeks later on 11 February 2011. Many Egyptians were overjoyed since they had never imagined Mubarak stepping down. Open elections brought Mohamed Morsi and the Muslim Brotherhood to the presidential office on 30 June 2012, only to see the military depose and arrest him on 03 July 2013. In Libya, a civil war against colonel Muammar Gaddafi began around 15 February 2011, and concluded eight months later on 23 October 2011, with Gaddafi's death. In Syria, a civil war against Bashar al-Assad that began on 15 March 2011, continues even today with an estimated five million internal and external refugees.

42. In Iraq, the Islamic Sates of Iran and the Levant (ISIS or ISIL) began an effort to overthrow the US-appointed government in June 2014.

43. See Lina Khatib, "The Visual Rush of the Arab Spring," *Images Politics in the Middle East: The Role of the Visual in Political Struggle* (London: I. B. Tauris, 2012): 117–167.

44. Tarik Ahmed Elswwei, "A Revolution of the Imagination," *International Journal of Communication* 5 (2011): 1197, 1198.

45. Lila Abu-Lughod, *Dramas of Nationhood: The Politics of Television in Egypt* (Chicago: University of Chicago Press, 2005).

46. Neil MacFarquhar, "In Saudi Arabia, Comedy Cautiously Pushes Limits," *New York Times* (11 June 2011), http://www.nytimes.com/2011/06/12/world/middleeast/12saudi.html?pagewanted=all&_r=0.

47. Alexandra Buccianti, "Dubbed Turkish Soap Operas Conquering the Arab World: Social Liberation or Cultural Alienation?" *Arab Media and Society* 10 (Spring 2010); also, see the documentary *Kismet: How Turkish Soap Operas Changed the World* (Greece-Cyprus 2013; dir. Nina Maria Paschalidou).

48. Tarik Ahmed Elswwei, "A Revolution of the Imagination," *International Journal of Communication* 5 (2011): 1200.

49. Faiza Salah Ambah (*Washington Post*), Saudi Comedy Writer Launches Web Site," *St. Albans Messenger* (20 July 2007): 15.

50. Elswwei, "A Revolution of the Imagination," 1198.

51. Ibid., 1199.

52. Shaheen, *Reel Bad Arabs*, 27.

53. Eric Jensen, "Mediating Social Change in Authoritarian and Democratic States: Irony, Hybridity, and Corporate Censorship," in *Culture and Social Change: Transforming Society Through the Power of Ideas*, ed. Brady Wagoner, Eric Jensen, Julian A. Oldmeadow (Charlotte: Information Age Publishing, 2012): 219.

54. Saudi features such as *Dhilal al sammt/Shadow of Silence* (Saudi Arabia, 2004; dir. Abdullah al-Moheissin); *Cinema 500 km* (Saudi Arabia, 2006; dir. Abdullah Al-Eyaf); and *Keif al-Hal?/How's It Going?* (Saudi Arabia, 2006; dir. Izidore Musallam) received much less attention.

55. See, for example, Tariq al Haydar, "Haifaa Al Mansour's *Wadjda*: Revolutionary Art or Pro-State Propaganda?" *Jadaliyya* (13 January 2014), http://www.jadaliyya.com/pages/index/15996/haifaa-al-mansours -wadjda_revolutionary-art-or-pro.

56. For an analysis of drifting and other youth-culture practices, see Pascal Menoret, *Joyriding in Riyadh: Oil, Urbanism, and Road Revolt* (Cambridge: Cambridge University Press, 2014).

57. See Max Fisher, "Video: Saudi Comedian Attempts a 'Reverse Cultural Invasion' of America," *Washington Post* (28 March 2013), http://www .washingtonpost.com/blogs/worldviews/wp/2013/03/28/video-saudi -comedian-attempts-a-reverse-cultural-invasion-of-america/. For a story that interprets US media as providing a counterpart to fundamentalist media, see Meris Lutz, "SAUDI ARABIA: Despite 'Desperate Housewives,' Media Still Not Free, According to WikiLeaks Cable," *Los Angeles Times* (10 December 2010), http://latimesblogs.latimes.com/babylonbeyond/2010/12/ saudi-arabia-media-censorship-wikileaks.html.

58. Layan Jawdat, "Laughing in the Kingdom: On Saudi YouTube Comedy," *Jadaliyya* (11 November 2014), http://reviews.jadaliyya.com/pages /index/17256/laughing-in-the-kingdom_on-saudi-youtube-comedy.

59. Jensen, "Mediating Social," in *Culture and Social Change*, ed. Wagoner et al., 219.

60. Ibid., 219.

61. Mehdi Semati, "The Geopolitics of *Parazit*, the Iranian Televisual Sphere, and the Global Infrastructure of Political Humor," *Popular Communication* 10.1–2 (January 2012): 120, 121.

62. Geoffrey Baym, "*The Daily Show*: Discursive Integration and the Reinvention of Political Journalism," *Political Communication* 22 (2005): 273.

63. Qsoft's latest venture is *Tube Star Network* (Egypt, 2013–present), which funds a pilot for series discovered on the web. Elsewhere in the MENA regions, Kharabeesh produces animated content in Jordan. Mohamed and Peyman Parham Al Awadhi's "social travel" series *Peeta Planet* (UAE,

2013–present) began on YouTube and has subsequently been broadcast on Dubai One. Each season consists of 24 5-minute episodes. Followers of the Al Awadhi brothers determine their travel through social media.

64. Jon Stewart, "Bassem Youssef," *Time* (18 April 2013), http://time100.time.com/2013/04/18/time-100/slide/bassem-youssef/.

65. Baym, *"The Daily Show,"* 259.

66. See Robert Vitalis, *America's Kingdom: Mythmaking on the Saudi Oil Frontier* (London and New York: Verso, 2009): 88–120.

67. Other CoR projects include ones on US detention center in Guantanamo Bay and civil war in the Democratic Republic of Congo, as discussed in chapter 1.

68. A citizen of both Brazil and the United States of Korean descent, Lee participated in the Gaza Freedom Flotilla that sought to bypass the Israeli blockage of Gaza and much needed humanitarian aid in May 2010. With a digital camera, she documented the siege by the IDF, which arrested and detained the passengers, confiscated their electronics, and later used footage from the high-definition cameras for state propaganda.

69. For more information, visit http://www.culturesofresistance.org/postcards-from-iran-main.

70. Audre Lorde, "The Master's Tools Will Never Dismantle the Master's House, in *Sister Outsider: Essays and Speeches* (Freedom: Crossing Press, 1984): 110–114.

71. Judith Butler, *Gender Trouble: Feminism and the Subversion of Identity* (New York and London: Routledge, 1990).

72. "About," *MST* website (no date; accessed 14 March 2010), <http://www.mstbrazil.org/?q=about>.

73. For a clip, see http://denaaladeeb.com/memvideo.html.

74. Fulvio Irace, "Dubai: Second Life City," *Abitare* 473 (June 2007): 93–103.

75. Yasser Elsheshtawy, *Dubai: Behind an Urban Spectacle* (London and New York: Routledge, 2010): 249. GCC states represent 12 percent of the Arab population but 55 percent of its economy (29).

76. In "Postcolonial Remains," *New Literary History* 43.1 (Winter 2012), Robert J. C. Young argues that al-Andalus was hardly equalitarian, but it was tolerant and remains "Europe's most sustained and successful experiment in communal living in a pluralistic society; yet, because it occurred under Muslim rule, it merits little discussion among analysts of multiculturalism or toleration today" (33). Special thanks to Sheetal Majithia for bringing this article to our attention and making a connection to our arguments.

77. See "Rann of Kutch 1965," GlobalSecurity.Org (2000–2014, http://www.globalsecurity.org/military/world/war/rann-of-kutch.htm.

78. "Remember Kashmir Era of Bollywood? It's Kutch Era Now," *DeshGujarat* (23 November 2013), http://deshgujarat.com/2013/11/23/remember-that-kashmir-era-of-bollywood-its-kutch-era-now/.

79. http://www.donaldabad.com/Entre-deux.

80. Sarah Kanouse,"Transmissions between Memory and Amnesia: The Radio Memorial in a New Media Age," *Leonardo* 44.3 (2011): 202.

81. Ibid., 201.
82. Eddo Stern, "Sheik Attach," (n.d.), http://eddostern.com/works/sheik-attack/.
83. The credits include the following video games: Blue Byte Software's *Settlers III Amazons* (1999), Maxis's *SimCity3000* (1999), Electronic Arts' *Nuclear Strike* (1997), Novalogic's *Delta Force* (1998) and *Delta Force 2* (1999), Westwood Studios' *Command and Conquer: Tiberiun Sun* (1998), Blizzard Entertainment's *StarCraft* (1997), and Red Storm Entertainment's *Tom Clancey's Rainbow Six* (1998).
84. As cited in Robert Nashak, "Eddo Stern and the Art of Games," KCET (10 September 2013), http://www.kcet.org/arts/artbound/counties/los-angeles/eddo-stern-ucla-games.html.
85. The headlines are as follows: "July 1989 Israeli commandos abducted Sheik Abdul Karim Obeid from his home in south Lebanon"—CIA World Factbook; "May 1991 Israeli commandos abducted the senior leader of an Islamic resistance organization, Mustafa Dirani, from his home in the central region of the Biqua' Valley"—The US State Department gopher; "February 1992 Israeli helicopter gunships rocketed the car of Hizbollah leader Sheik Abbas Musawi, killing him, his wife and son"—Al Mashriq "the Levant"; "April 1996 Israeli gunships fired on a civilian ambulance in the southern port city of Tyre. The vehicle carried a senior Hebbollah leader"—The New Standard Web Edition; "September 1997 A Team of Israeli commandos attempted to snatch Sheik Abdul-Amir Kabaian from his home in Insariyeh"—INTELLIGENCE N. 67 New series, 22 September 1997; and "Feb 2000 Israeli Air Force helicopter gunships rocketed a car carrying a senior Hizbullah commander in the Lebanese village of Barish east of Tyre, Israel Radio reported. The Hizbullah commander and seven civilians were reported wounded in the raid"— *Jerusalem Post Internet Edition*.
86. For a trailer, see http://www.culturesofresistance.org/congo-films.
87. *Salaam Kivu International Film Festival* (n.d.), http://www.salaamkivu.org/.
88. Thomas Gesthuizen, "Congo's Hidden Cultural Hub," *The Guardian* (13 March 2013), http://www.theguardian.com/world/2013/mar/13/congo-cultural-hub-goma.
89. *RMB City* (n.d.), www.rmbcity.com.
90. Robin Peckham, "Cao Fei: Demolishing the Virtual, RMB City and the Crisis of Art Reality," *Digicult: Digital Art, Design, Culture* (n.d.), http://www.digicult.it/digimag/issue-059/cao-fei-demolishing-the-virtual-rmb-city-and-the-crisis-of-art-reality/.
91. Supply-chain studies includes books tracking commodities such as Robert J. Foster, *Coca-globalization: Following Soft Drinks from New York to New Guinea* (New York: Palgrave Macmillan, 2008) and *Orla Ryan, Chocolate Nations: Living and Dying for Cocoa in West Africa* (London: Zed Books, 2012).
92. For a more nuanced analysis of Chinese migrant women in textiles, see Leslie T. Chang, *Factory Girls: From Village to City in a Changing China* (New York: Spiegel and Grau, 2009).
93. *Cotton Road* can be located within an emerging transnational genre of what environmental justice scholar and programmer Tom Shevory calls

"the commodity documentary," which includes films such as *Darwin's Nightmare* (Austria, 2005; dir. Hubert Sauper), *Black Gold* (United Kingdom/United States, 2007; dir. Nick and Marc Francis) and *Mardi Gras: Made in China* (United States, 2005; dir. David Redmon).

94. Ravi Sundaram, *Pirate Modernity: Delhi's Media Urbanism* (London and New York: Routledge, 2010): 112.

95. Brian Larkin, "Degraded Images, Distorted Sounds: Nigerian Video and the Infrastructure of Piracy," *Public Culture* 16.2 (spring 2004): 309.

96. Homi Bhabha, "Of Mimicry and Man: The Ambivalence of Colonial Discourse," *Location of Culture* (London and New York: Routledge, 1995): 85–92.

97. Mejias, *Off the Network*, 90–91; Jussi Parikka, *Digital Contagions: A Media Archaeology of Computer Viruses*, (New York: Peter Lang, 2007): 5.

98. For more information, visit http://www.amitandnaroop.com/singh.

99. https://www.kickstarter.com/projects/205078810/the-singh-projecthttps://www.facebook.com/singhproject?fref=photo.

100. See Dale Hudson, "Horrors of Anthropocentrism: 'Improved Animals' on the Islands of Dr. Moreau," in *Transnational Horror across Visual Media: Fragmented Bodies*, ed. Dana Och and Kirsten Strayer (London and New York: Routledge, 2013): 209–227.

5 Collaborative Remix Zones: Toward a Critical Cinephilia

1. Parts of this chapter are adapted from Dale Hudson and Patricia R. Zimmermann, "Cinephilia, Technophilia, and Collaborative Remix Zones," *Screen* 50.1 "Screen Theorizing Today: A Celebration of Screen's Fiftieth Anniversary," ed. Annette Kuhn (Spring 2009): 135–146.

2. See, for example, Antoine de Baecque, *La Cinéphilie: Invention d'un regard, histoire d'une culture, 1944–1968* (Paris: Librarie Arthème Fayard, 2003).

3. Barbara Klinger, *Beyond the Multiplex: Cinema, New Technologies, and the Home* (Berkeley, Los Angeles, and London: University of California Press, 2006): 50.

4. Dudley Andrew, "The 'Three Ages' of Cinema Studies and the Age to Come," *PMLA* 115.3 (May 2000): 341–351, as cited in Christian Keathley, *Cinephilia and History, or The Wind in the Trees* (Bloomington: Indiana University Press, 2006): 5.

5. Colin McCabe, *The Eloquence of the Vulgar* (London: British Film Institute, 1999): 152.

6. See, for example, Andrew Sarris, *The American Cinema: Directors and Directions 1929–1968* (New York: Dutton, 1968).

7. Robert Stam, *Film Theory: An Introduction* (Malden: Blackwell Press, 2000): 88.

8. Glauber Rocha, "Cinema of Hunger," trans. Burnes Hollyman and Randal Johnson; Fernando Solanas and Octavio Getino, "Towards a Third Cinema: Notes and Experiences from the Development of a Cinema of Liberation in

the Third World," trans. Julianne Burton and Michael Chanan; and Julio García Espinosa's "For an Imperfect Cinema," trans. Julianne Burton, *25 Years of the New Latin American Cinema*, ed. Michael Chanan (London: British Film Institute, 1983): 13–33. For responses to these manifestos, see Catherine Grant and Annette Kuhn, eds., *Screening World Cinema: A Screen Reader* (London: Routledge, 2006), particularly Julianne Burton-Carvajal's "Marginal Cinemas and Mainstream Critical Theory" and Teshome H. Gabriel's "Colonialism and 'Law and Order' Criticism" (17–47).

9. Jean-Louis Baudry, "The Ideological Effects of the Basic Cinematographic Apparatus," trans. Alan Williams, *Film Quarterly* 28.2 (Winter 1974–1975): 39–47; Jean-Louis Baudry, "The Apparatus: Metaphysical Approaches to the Impression of Reality in Cinema," trans. Jean Andrew and Bernard Augst, *Camera Obscura* 1 (Fall 1976): 104–126; Linda Williams, "Film Bodies: Gender, Genre, and Excess," *Film Quarterly* 44.4 (Summer 1991): 2–12.

10. Laura Mulvey, "Visual Pleasure and Narrative Cinema," *Screen* 16.3 (Autumn 1975): 6–18; Jane Gaines, "White Privilege and Looking Relations: Race and Gender in Feminist Theory," *Cultural Critique* 4 (fall 1985): 59–79, revised in *Screen* 29.4 (Autumn 1988): 12–27; Manthia Diawara, "Black Spectatorship: Problems of Identification and Resistance," *Screen* 29.4 (autumn 1988): 66–76; bell hooks, "The Oppositional Gaze: Black Female Spectatorship" in *Black Looks: Race and Representation* (Boston, MA: South End Press, 1992): 115–131.

11. Henry Jenkins, *Textual Poachers: Television Fans and Participation Culture* (London and New York: Routledge, 1992); Jeffrey Sconce, "'Trashing' the Academy: Taste, Excess, and an Emerging Politics of Cinematic Style," *Screen* 36.4 (Winter 1995): 371–393; Matt Hills, *Fan Cultures* (London and New York: Routledge, 2002); and Kate Egan, "The Celebration of a 'Proper Product': Exploring the Residual Collectible through the "'Video Nasty,'" in *Residual Media*, ed. Charles R. Acland (Minneapolis and London: University of Minnesota Press, 2007): 200–221.

12. Paul Willemen, *Looks and Frictions: Essays on Cultural Studies and Film Theory* (Bloomington: Indiana University Press, 1994): 231, as cited in Marijke de Valck and Malte Hagener, "Down with Cinephilia? Long Live Cinephilia? And Other Videosyncratic Pleasures," in *Cinephilia: Movies, Love and Memory*, ed. Marijke de Valck and Malte Hagener (Amsterdam: Amsterdam University Press, 2005): 14.

13. Christian Metz, "Photography as Fetish" (1984), *October* 34 (1985): 81–90.

14. See, for example, Susan Sontag, "The Decay of Cinema," *New York Times Magazine* (25 February 1996), Stanley Kauffmann, "A Lost Love," *New Republic* (08 and 15 September 1997), and David Denby, "The Moviegoers: Why Don't People Like the Right Movies Anymore?" *New Yorker* (06 April 1998). More recently, see André Gaudrealt and Philippe Marion, *La fin du cinéma: Un media en crise à l'ère du numérique* (Paris: Armand Colin, 2013).

15. Peter Matthews, "The End of an Era: A Cinephile"s Lament," *Sight & Sound* 17.10 (October 2007): 17.

16. Jonathan Romney, "Back to the Future: A Cinephile"s Response," *Sight & Sound* 17.11 (November 2007): 24.

17. Walter Benjamin, "The Work of Art in the Age of Mechanical Reproduction" (1935), trans. Harry Zohn, in *Illuminations* (New York: Schocken Books, 1968), 217–251. Under neoliberalism, capitalism also won as is evident in looking back to Perry Barlow"s "Declaration of Independence," which argued that cyberspace would eschew the laws of industrial capitalism.

18. Thomas Elsasser, "Cinephilia, or the Uses of Disenchantment," in *Cinephilia: Movies, Love and Memory*, ed. Marijke de Valck and Malte Hagener (Amsterdam: Amsterdam University Press, 2005): 38.

19. Robert E. Davis, "The Instantaneous Worldwide Release: Coming Soon to Everyone Everywhere," in *Transnational Cinema: The Film Reader*, ed. Elizabeth Ezra and Terry Rowden (London and New York: Routledge, 2006): 77.

20. Cinephilia's desire for singularity, originality, and rarity would seem entangled with the modernist myths that Rosalind Krauss describes in *The Originality of the Avant-Garde and Other Modernist Myths* (Cambridge: MIT Press, 1989).

21. Klinger, *Beyond the Multiplex*, 58–73.

22. Ibid., 121.

23. Marijke de Valck and Malte Hagener, "Down with Cinephilia? Long Live Cinephilia? And Other Videosyncratic Pleasures," in *Cinephilia: Movies, Love and Memory*, eds. Marijke de Valck and Malte Hagener (Amsterdam: Amsterdam University Press, 2005): 16–17.

24. Ibid., 15.

25. Davis, "The Instantaneous Worldwide Release," 77–78.

26. For an analysis of the transnational cinephilia of Hindi films among Palestinians and Israelis, see Monika Mehta, "Reading Cinephilia in *Kikar ha-Halomot/Desperado Square*: Viewing the Local and Transnational in *Sangam/Confluence*," *South Asian Popular Culture* 4.2 (October 2006): 147–162.

27. See Juan Francisco Salazar and Amalia Córdova, "Imperfect Media and the Politics of Indulgence Video in Latin America," *Global Indigenous Media: Cultures, Poetics, and Politics*, eds. Pamela Wilson and Michelle Stewart (Durham and London: Duke University Press, 2008): 39–57.

28. Dan Streible, "The Role of Orphan Films in the 21st Century Archive," *Cinema Journal* 46.3 (Spring 2007): 124–128.

29. Tzvetan Todorov, "The Uses and Abuses of Memory," in *What Happens to History: The Renewal of Ethics in Contemporary Thought*, ed. Howard Marchitello (London and New York: Routledge, 2001): 11.

30. See Ranajit Guha, *History at the Limit of World-History* (New York: Columbia University Press, 2002); Dipesh Chakrabarty, *Provincializing Europe: Postcolonial Thought and Historical Difference* (Princeton and London: Princeton University Press, 2000): 180–213; Philip Rosen, *Change Mummified: Cinema, Historicity, Theory* (Minneapolis and London: University of Minnesota Press, 2001): 20–87; and Robert F. Berkhofer Jr.,

Beyond the Great Story: History as Text and Discourse (Cambridge and London: Harvard University Press, 1995): 53–75.

31. Jacques Derrida, *Archive Fever: A Freudian Impression*, trans. Eric Prenowitz (Chicago and London: University of Chicago Press, 1995), 68; "Interview with Hayden White," in *Encounters: Philosophy of History after Postmodernism*, ed. Eve Domanska (Charlottesville: University of Virginia, 1998): 34.

32. See David MacDougall, *Transcultural Cinema* (Princeton and London: Princeton University Press, 1998): 95.

33. Jay David Bolter and Richard Grusin, *Remediation: Understanding New Media* (Cambridge: MIT Press, 2000): 56.

34. Patricia R. Zimmermann, "A Manifesto for Reverse Engineering: Algorithms for Recombinant Histories," *Afterimage* 34.1–2 (fall 2006): 66–72.

35. Kim Soyoung, "From Cine-mania to Blockbusters and Trans-cinema: Reflections on Recent South Korean Cinema," in *Theorising National Cinema*, ed. Valentina Vitali and Paul Willemen (London: British Film Institute, 2006): 189–191.

36. Soyoung Kim, "'Cine-mania' or Cinephilia: Film Festivals and the Question of Identity," in *New Korean Cinema*, ed. Chi-Yun Shin and Julian Stringer (New York and London: New York University Press, 2005): 82.

37. Holly Willis, *New Digital Cinema: Reinventing the Moving Image* (London: Wallflower, 2005), 70. Formed in 1991 by a group of graduates from the Rhode Island School of Design (USA), EBN is a multimedia performance group of DJs, video artists, performers, and other artists. EBN makes artistic and political statements on events covered in the news media by remixing video and music, such as its work on the 1991 US invasion of Iraq. For a sense of EBN"s work, visit its homepage at http://emn-usa.com/ebn.

38. Sharon Lin Tay and Patricia R. Zimmermann, "Throbs and Pulsations: Les Leveque and the Digitization of Desire," *Afterimage* 34.4 (January/February 2006): 13.

39. Ibid., 12.

40. "Lossy" formats that translate celluloid images into digital code for storage on DVD and playback on computers and DVD players, such as JPEG and MPEG formats, involve compression by a deletion of some of the information, so that the infinite reproduction of the object without loss is possible theoretically but not actually. Lev Manovich, *The Language of New Media* (Cambridge: MIT Press, 2001): 54.

41. Tay and Zimmermann, "Throbs and Pulsations," 16.

42. Anders Weberg and Robert Willim, "*Being There* by Anders Weberg and Robert Willim (2008)," *Rhizome* (02 December 2008), http://rhizome .org/portfolios/artwork/50944/.

43. Anders Weberg, profile on Rhizome (no date), http://rhizome.org/profile /andersweberg/?page=2.

44. See David Bollier, *Viral Spiral: How the Commoners Built a Digital Republic of Their Own* (New York and London: Basic Books, 2008). This book can be downloaded at http://www.viralspiral.cc/download-book.

45. "About" (no date), http://www.recycled.se/willim-weberg/.
46. Anders Weberg, "Performing 'Sweden for Beginners' Live March 22 at the 28th Ed. of Videoformes in France," Artist's blog (23 February 2013), http://www.recycled.se/blog/2013/02/23/performing-sweden-for-beginners-live-march-22-at-the-28th-ed-of-videoformes-in-france/.
47. Tom T. O'Dell and Robert Willim, "Composing Ethnography," *Ethnologia Europaea* 41.1 (2011): 26–39. Cf. Robert Willim, "Rendering Culture : Elsewhereness, The Ethnographic, The Surreal," unpublished conference paper (2012), https://lup.lub.lu.se/search/publication/2856201.
48. Philip Glahn, "Digital Productivism: New Participatory Mass Culture," *Public* 23.45 (June 2012): 172.
49. Craig Campbell, "Terminus: Ethnographic Terminalia," *Visual Anthropology Review* 27.1 (2011): 54.
50. "Produced by a Jewish émigré from Chile, adapted from a Cuban radio script," the telenovela is "an episodic melodrama designed for commercially-based television, bore the generic ancestry of a format developed for Mexican broadcast by Procter and Gamble in 1958." Andrew Paxman, "Hybridized, Glocalized and hecho en México: Foreign Influences on Mexican TV Programming Since the 1950s," *Global Media Journal* 2.2 (spring 2003), article no. 4.
51. Andrés Martínez, "'La Vida' loca", salon.com (28 February 2000), http://archive.salon.com/ent/feature/2000/02/28/telenovelas/index.html.
52. Toby Miller, Nitin Govil, John McMurria, Richard Maxwell, and Ting Wang, *Global Hollywood 2* (London: British Film Institute, 2005): 274, 166.
53. Néstor García Canclini, *Consumers as Citizens: Globalization and Multicultural Conflicts*, trans. George Yúdice (Minneapolis and London: University of Minnesota Press, 2001): 5.
54. For more information, visit http://www.kienke.com/gallerymain.asp?galleryid=58510&akey=j5adjn8b.
55. A *keffiyeh* is a black-and-white checkered headscarf that became a symbol of Palestinian nationalism during the 1960s in iconic images of Yasser Arafat. In later series, Al-Ghoussein dispenses with the *keffiyeh* because of its often overdetermined meaning.
56. Deepa Kumar, "Media, War, and Propaganda: Strategies of Information Management during the 2003 Iraq War," *Communication and Critical/Cultural Studies* 3.1 (March 2006): 54–55.
57. Ibid., 48–69.
58. Ibid., 50, 51.
59. As cited in Shahira S. Fahmy and Mohammed Al Emad, "Al-Jazeera Vs Al-Jazeera: A Comparison of the Network's English and Arabic Online Coverage of the US/Al Qaeda Conflict," *International Communication Gazette* 73.3 (2011): 218.
60. Philip Seib, "Hegemonic No More: Western Media, the Rise of Al-Jazeera, and the Influence of Diverse Voices," *International Studies Review* 7 (2005): 601.
61. Ibid., 604.

62. Gerhard Haupt and Pat Binder, "Tarek Al-Ghoussein," *Nafas* (July 2004), http://universes-in-universe.org/eng/nafas/articles/2004/al_ghoussein.

63. Kumar, "Media, War, and Propaganda," 51.

64. Anthony Downey, "Stereotyping the Stereotypes" (interview with Tarek Al-Ghoussein), *Ibraaz* (November 2012): 4.

65. Tarek Al-Ghoussein and Chris Kienke, "The War Room" (unpublished artists' statement).

66. Sama Alshaibi, "Memory Work of the Palestinian Diaspora," *Frontiers: A Journal of Women Studies* 27.2 (2006): 31.

67. Ibid., 33.

68. Ibid., 39.

69. Anna Siomopoulos and Patricia R. Zimmermann, "Silent Film Exhibition and Performative Historiography," *The Moving Image: The Journal of the Association of Moving Image Archivists* 6.2 (Fall 2006): 109–111.

70. David Robinson, *From Peepshow to Palace: The Birth of American Film* (New York: Columbia University Press, 1997): 171.

71. Rick Altman, *Silent Film Sound* (New York: Columbia University Press, 2007).

72. In "Race, Reception, and Oscar Micheaux's *Within Our Gates*," *The Moving Image: The Journal of the Association of Moving Image Archivists* 6.2 (fall 2006), Anna Siomopoulos writes: "As film historian Mary Carbine has shown, the music of these performers did not punctuate action, heighten emotion, or support character development; in fact, the music accompanying white films often ignored the story altogether, to the horror of some black film critics who wanted black spectatorship to resemble white spectatorship in white theaters. One such critic bemoaned a performance of the song 'Clap Hands, Here Comes Charlie' that brought down the house in the middle of a death scene" (114). She cites Mary Carbine, "'The Finest outside the Loop': Motion Picture Exhibition in Chicago's Black Metropolis, 1905–1928," in *Silent Film*, ed. Richard Abel (New Brunswick: Rutgers University Press, 1996): 234–262.

73. Siomopoulos, "Race, Reception, and Oscar Micheaux's *Within Our Gates*," 112.

74. Lost for 70 years, *Within Our Gates* was rediscovered at the Filmoteca Española in Madrid and was restored by the Library of Congress in 1993.

75. Ella Shohat and Robert Stam, *Unthinking Eurocentrism: Multiculturalism and the Media* (New York and London: Routledge, 1994).

76. Siomopoulos, "Race, Reception, and Oscar Micheaux's *Within Our Gates*," 111.

77. Patricia R. Zimmermann, "Revisiting and Remixing Black Cinema," *The Moving Image: The Journal of the Association of Moving Image Archivists* 6.2 (Fall 2006): 119.

78. Launched as an event in Black History Month at Ithaca College and later performed at the Orphans of the Storm Symposium at the University of South Carolina in the United States, *Within Our Gates: Revisited and Remixed* included a commission jazz score by pianist Fe Nunn, which was performed by a jazz quartet, along with spoken-word by the Body and

Soul Ensemble and the Ida B. Wells Spoken Word Ensemble. The primary collaborators on *Within Our Gates: Revisited and Remixed* were Grace An, Chang Chun, John Hochheimer, Meg Jamieson, Fe Nunn, Olivia, Anna Siomopoulos, Simon Tarr, Elisa White, Baruch Whitehead, Zachery Williams, and Patricia R. Zimmermann.

79. John Hochheimer, "Media Antecedents to *Within Our Gates*: Weaving Disparate Threads," *The Moving Image: The Journal of the Association of Moving Image Archivists* 6.2 (Fall 2006): 125.

80. Ibid., 126.

81. For a transcript and analysis of the spoken-word text, see Grace An, "Spoken Word in *Within Our Gates: Revisited and Remixed*," *The Moving Image: The Journal of the Association of Moving Image Archivists* 6.2 (Fall 2006): 128–132.

82. Zimmermann, "Revisiting and Remixing Black Cinema," 123.

83. Siomopoulos and Zimmermann, "Silent Film Exhibition and Performative Historiography," 110.

84. Ibid., 111.

85. The primary collaborators on *Trafficking in the Archives* were Chang Chun, Dale Hudson, Lisa Patti, Simon Tarr, and Patricia R. Zimmermann.

86. Gina Marchetti, *Romance and the "Yellow Peril": Race, Sex, and Discursive Strategies in Hollywood Fiction* (Berkeley, Los Angeles, and London: University of California Press, 1993): 79.

87. Scott Simon, program notes to *Treasures from the American Archives* (Washington, DC: National Film Archives, 2000): 45.

88. David Bordwell, "Technicolor," in *The Classical Hollywood Cinema: Film Style and Mode of Production to 1960*, ed. David Bordwell, Janet Staiger, and Kristen Thompson (New York: Columbia University Press, 1985): 353.

89. Ibid.

90. Shohat and Stam, *Unthinking Eurocentrism*, 186.

91. Zimmermann, "Revisiting and Remixing Black Cinema," 119.

92. Ibid.

93. See *Afro@Digital* (Congo/France, 2003; dir. Balufu Bakupa-Kanyinda).

94. Zimmermann, "Revisiting and Remixing Black Cinema," 121.

95. Steven Levy, *Hackers: Heroes of the Computer Revolution* (1984), 25th anniversary ed. (Sebastopol: O Reilly, 2010): 32.

96. Robert Spahr, "CRUFT: Art from Digital Leftovers," Artist website (no date), http://www.robertspahr.com/work/c1/#babylon.

97. The project scrapes images from www.af.mil and www.pornstardevil.com.

98. Sharon Lin Tay, "Undisclosed Recipients: Documentary in an Era of Digital Convergence," an essay in dialogue with Dale Hudson, "Undisclosed Recipients: Database Documentaries and the Internet," *Studies in Documentary Film* 2.1 (February 2008): 84.

99. "Three Charged over Palestinian Mohammad Abu Khdair Murder," *BBC News: Middle East* (17 July 2014), http://www.bbc.com/news/28347001. The murder of Abu Khdeir follows the kidnapping and murder of three

Israeli teenagers from an illegal settlement in the West Bank. The Israeli government allegedly censored the story of the discovery of the bodies of the teenagers until the IDF could search for Hamas supporters in the West Bank. Later, Israel launched Operation Protective Edge, a massive offensive against Hamas in Gaza. The attack began to receive media attention in the United states after the Israeli police beat Abu Khdeir's US cousin, Tariq. According to Nir Hassen, "Chief Suspect Named in Abu Khdeir Murder," *Haaretz* (20 July 2014), http://www.haaretz.com/mobile/.premium-1.606266?v=D2826EF8D2B02202E55FF660B9CB07F5, the primary suspect for his murder, Yosef Chaim Ben David, pleaded temporary insanity.

100. "Samsung Finds China Child Labour 'Evidence,'" *BBC News: Business* (14 July 2014), http://www.bbc.com/news/business-28289652.

101. Chris Chang, "Hot Property: *Disorder*," *Film Comment* (n.d.), http://www.filmcomment.com/article/hot-property-huang-weikais-disorder.

102. Benny Shaffer, "The Films of Huang Weikai: Towards an Urban Documentary Surreal," *Leap: International Art Magazine of Contemporary China* (01 December 2010), http://leapleapleap.com/2010/12/huangweikai/.

103. Chris Berry, ed., *The New Chinese Documentary Film Movement: For the Public Record* (Hong Kong: Hong Kong University Press, 2011).

104. Michael Chanan, *The Politics of Documentary,* (London: British Film Institute, 2008): 108–143.

105. Hua Hsu, "Huang Weikai's Absurd New Film," *The Atlantic* (19 October 2010), http://www.theatlantic.com/entertainment/archive/2010/10/huang-weikais-absurd-new-film/64480/.

106. For more information, visit www.engagemedia.org.

107. See Steve Crabtree, "Opinion Briefing: Indonesia's Economic Emergence," *Gallup World* (31 May 2013), www.gallup.com/poll/162848/opinion-briefing-indonesia-economic-emergence.aspx; *Indonesian Economic Quarterly: Adjusting to Pressures* (Jakarta: World Bank, July 2013).

108. See Greg Felker, "The Political Economy of Southeast Asia," in *Contemporary Southeast Asia*, ed. Mark Beeson (New York: Palgrave Macmillan, 2009): 46–73.

109. "Indonesia Overview," *The World Bank* (n.d.), http://www.worldbank.org/en/country/indonesia/overview.

110. Palmira Permata Bachtiar, "Chaotic Statistics of Indonesian Migrant Workers," *Jakarta Post* (26 January 2012), www.thejakartapost.com/news/2012/01/26/chaotic-statistics-indonesian-migrant-workers.html. Also see Anne Loveband,"Positioning the Product: Indonesian Migrant Workers in Taiwan," *Journal of Contemporary Asia* 34.3 (2004): 336–348; Nicole Constable, *Maid to Order in Hong Kong: Stories of Migrant Workers*, 2nd ed. (Ithaca, New York: Cornell University Press, 2007).

111. International Labour Organization, "Combating Forced Labour and Trafficking of Indonesian Migrant Workers," (01 January 2008–31 December 2011), www.ilo.org/jakarta/whatwedo/projects/WCMS_116048/lang--en/index.htm.

112. See EngageMedia, *Cerita Buruh Migran/Migrant Worker Stories* (2012), http://www.engagemedia.org/Projects/migrant-workers.

262   Notes

113. Dhyta Caturani, "Video Production and Distribution Training for Indonesia Migrant Workers in Malaysia" (24 August 2012), EngageMedia, www.engagemedia.org/blog/video-production-and-distribution-training-for-indonesian-migrant-workers-in-malaysia.

114. Helen De Michiel, "Open Space Documentary Workshop," National Alliance for Media Arts and Culture Conference, Minneapolis, Minnesota (09 September 2012).

115. We are grateful to Awam Amkpa for bringing this project to our attention.

116. "Manifesto," *Invisible Borders: The Trans-Africa Project* (2014), http://invisible-borders.com/manifesto/.

117. "Road Trip Project," *Invisible Borders: The Trans-Africa Project* (2014), http://invisible-borders.com/road-trip-project/.

118. Nike Ojeikere, "Writing The Journey: From Lagos to Lomé," *Invisible Borders: The Trans-Africa Project* (03 November 2009), http://invisible-borders.com/2009/11/writing-the-journey-from-lagos-to-lome-by-nike-ojeikere/.

119. See Ayisha Abraham, "Deteriorating Memories: Blurring Fact and Fiction, in Home Movies in India," *Mining the Home Movie*, ed. Karen L. Ishizuka and Patricia R. Zimmermann (University of California, 2008): 168–184.

120. Amitav Ghosh, *In an Antique Land: History in the Guise of a Traveler's Tale* (New York: Vintage, 1992).

121. See Henry Jenkins, *Textual Poachers: Television Fans and Participation Culture* (New York and London: Routledge, 1992) and Matt Hills, *Fan Cultures* (London: Routledge, 2002).

122. Emma Davie, "Staying with the Trouble: The Radical Work of CAMP," *DOX European Documentary Magazine* 103 (September 2014): 18–20.

123. Florian Schneider, description of *Al Jaar qabla al Daar/The Neighbour Before the House*, CAMP (n.d.) http://studio.camp/event.php?id=98.

124. Ibid.

125. Tom Gunning, "An Aesthetic of Astonishment: Early Film and the (In)credulous Spectator," *Art and Text* 34 (1989): 31–45; Sean Cubitt, *The Cinema Effect* (Cambridge and London: MIT Press, 2004): 16.

Index